# THE
# ETERNAL WORD
# IN THE
# MODERN WORLD

# THE ETERNAL WORD
## IN THE
# MODERN WORLD

*Expository Preaching on the Gospels
and Epistles for the Church Year*

BY

BURTON SCOTT EASTON

AND

HOWARD CHANDLER ROBBINS

CHARLES SCRIBNER'S SONS · NEW YORK
CHARLES SCRIBNER'S SONS · LTD · LONDON
1937

COPYRIGHT, 1937, BY

CHARLES SCRIBNER'S SONS

Printed in the United States of America

A

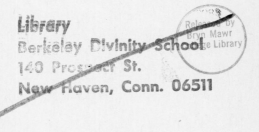

TO

HUGHELL EDGAR WOODALL FOSBROKE

# INTRODUCTION

Whatever value these liturgical, expository and homiletical notes may possess is due to the fact that they come from the laboratory of the classroom. For several years the authors have given a course in expository preaching, open to graduate students and seniors in the General Theological Seminary. In this class the professor of Literature and Interpretation of the New Testament has provided the exegesis of the Gospel or Epistle selected for study, the students have made sermon outlines on the basis of this critical exegesis, and the professor of Pastoral Theology has then criticised the proposed sermon, having in view especially the application of the theme to the needs and problems of the present time. After this preparation the students have often written out their sermons in full and preached them in the churches to which they minister. It is their belief that sermons constructed in this way have enabled them to exercise a teaching ministry, and have helped to bridge the wide and perilous gulf which today separates clergymen trained in modern knowledge of the literature and intrepretation of the Christian Scriptures from laymen who have not received this training.

The advantages of preaching from the Gospels and Epistles of the Christian Year are evident. The Word of God is contained within the Scriptures as a river is contained within its banks. Expository preaching means that the preacher is giving his congregation the Word of God and not his own; liturgical preaching means that he is selecting from the Scriptures those sections which the church through centuries of experience has come to regard as of especial value. This judgment of the church is by no means infallible. For example, the Easter Gospels are unfortunate in finding their center in the empty sepulchre instead of in the Risen Lord. But the reason for this is made plain by study of liturgical backgrounds, and the preacher is free to select a more vital theme for his Easter sermons. With this qualification, faithful following of the Christian Year is of inestimable value to the preacher, giving him a variety of themes, and a co-ordination of them, which will save him from narrowness and idiosyncrasy. The strong liturgical trends at present evident in the non-liturgical churches, culminating in the consideration by the Committee on Worship of the Federal Council of Churches of Christ in America of a proposed calendar closely resembling the traditional Church Year, embolden the authors to hope that this book will be of use not only to Episcopalians and Lutherans, but also to ministers of the non-liturgical churches in the English-speaking world.

The expository notes which follow are not designed to take the place of commentaries. In the classes at the General Theological Seminary the students are expected to study the assigned sections in the Greek original, to familiarize themselves with parallel passages, if there are such, in a Harmony of the Gospels, and to make full use of approved modern commentaries, such as that of G. H. C. Macgregor on *The Gospel of John,* C. H. Dodd on *The Epistle of Paul to the Romans,* and James Moffatt on *The Epistle to the Hebrews,* to cite three illustrious examples of present-day New Testament criticism. It is hoped that preachers who use this book will use it with similar auxiliaries. Sermon themes are provided for all the Sunday Gospels and Epistles, but are expanded only from Advent through Whitsunday, with the expectation that the reader will apply for himself the general idea and method during the long Trinity Season.

The point of view of the authors is that which today is shared by Liberal Catholics and Liberal Evangelicals within the Anglican Communion. They accept the positive and constructive results of New Testament criticism as a gift of the Holy Spirit who, according to Christ's promise, is guiding His people into all truth; they also accept without reservation the Nicene theology as a revelation to the church by the same Spirit of the mystery of the Person of Christ, true God and true Man. In other words, the authors are neither fundamentalists nor modernists in any proper understanding of these often misused terms.

Fundamentalism is a word with a specific and definite meaning. It denotes the belief of those whose religious convictions are based upon the dogma of the verbal infallibility of the Bible. It carries with it the cosmogony of the opening chapters of Genesis, and thereby flings defiance at the whole vast and noble fabric of modern scientific knowledge. In an English writer's phrase, it "insists upon the credibility of the whole of Judges and the edibility of the whole of Jonah." It wars upon science in the name of religion, and that is a suicidal war. God is the God of the ultimate values, truth, beauty and goodness, and the truths of science are to be attributed to His inspiration as fully as are the truths of religion. The authors believe that the alienation of many truth-loving young people from organized religion is due to the influence of the fundamentalism of their home churches more than to any other single cause, and that only the most frank, courageous and truth-loving acceptance of modern Biblical criticism will recover them to the church and to that Lord of the church who proclaimed Himself not only the Way and the Life but also the Truth.

Modernism is also a word with a specific and definite meaning. Modernism denotes the attempt made toward the close of the nineteenth century by a group of Roman Catholic thinkers to combine an affirmation of the spiritual and religious truth of the dogmas of their church with the claim of freedom to deny any or all of the alleged facts of history upon which the dogmas rest. The modernist contention is that what it terms the Christian myth will survive and be beneficial even if its underpinning of history is removed. If this is an accurate account of modernism, the authors cannot but be sympathetic with the papal condemnation of it. They base their life and fellowship in the church upon the foundation of historic fact. They believe that the gospel is a "given" thing, an historic revelation of the eternal God, divinely reasonable and divinely real, and that the birth and life and death and resurrection of the Lord Jesus Christ belong to the world of fact, not to the world of myth; that indeed in this world of fact these constitute the one Fact of central and commanding significance, interpreting all history and determining its ultimate destinies.

In conclusion, the authors wish to remind the preachers who may use this book that exposition of the Word of God is the beginning of the preacher's task, not the end. The end is a presentation of it in such a manner that by metaphor and illustration which excite the imagination and by persuasion which affects the will, men and women will be moved to accept the engrafted Word which is able to save their souls. It is not enough that they should give intellectual assent to the doctrine presented. Being a Christian is more vital, more intimate, more personal than that. It is necessary to appropriate Him for whom the sermon is the introduction; the unseen, present, spiritual Christ, Lord of nature, Lord also of history; the one Mediator who brings the life of God to be new life for man. Never was there greater need than now. The challenge of the times is the challenge of trumpets. Only those who are "in Christ" can minister His salvation, and to a world now lying in desolation give beauty for ashes, and the garment of praise for the spirit of heaviness.

BURTON SCOTT EASTON
HOWARD CHANDLER ROBBINS

General Theological Seminary,
New York,
Saint Mark's Day, 1937.

# CONTENTS

xi

# CONTENTS

# CONTENTS

## PART III

## EPISTLES AND GOSPELS FOR HOLY DAYS

## PART IV

# APPENDIX

# PART ONE
# THE CHURCH YEAR

# THE CHURCH YEAR

A T THE beginning of the third century a conception of a "church year" was as yet foreign to Christianity. Easter was everywhere a festival and was preceded by a fast on Saturday and, for those physically able to fast two days, on Friday also. Whitsunday was likewise generally observed, except perhaps in Spain, and the period between Easter and Whitsunday—known as "the pentecost"—was increasingly regarded as a joyous season within which fasting and penitence were inappropriate. Otherwise, except for the regular routine of Sundays, individuals were free to feast or fast as they wished.

The feasting usually took the form of holding agapes, which might be held for any cause or without special reason at the giver's pleasure. But of particular significance were the anniversaries of local martyrs, regarded as the "birthdays" of the saints into the higher life and so as festal occasions. On such an anniversary the friends and admirers of a particular martyr would meet at his tomb (at Rome usually in the catacombs) for an agape, with or without a eucharist.

Fasting was generally practised as "keeping stations." *Statio* is the military term for "sentry-duty," and the word describes the custom: the "stationer" remained awake—either all night long or from midnight—abstained from food and gave himself to prayer. No one was obliged to keep such stations, but their practice was considered meritorious, and they were often kept by groups as well as by individuals. Wednesday and Friday had long been considered

3

the approved days, but corresponding vigils were often kept on Saturday night as well, the fast being broken at the Sunday eucharist. On Easter Eve the vigil was obligatory on all and two all-night services were held simultaneously; one for the catechumens who were to be baptized at dawn and the other for the rest of the congregation. After the baptisms were completed both groups joined in a common eucharist.

Individuals also held less formal and taxing fasts, limiting themselves to bread and water; these later became distinguished from fasts as "abstinences." And on special occasions general fasts for all the members of any local church might be prescribed, particularly in times of persecution.

During the third century, especially during its second half, the cult paid to martyrs increased rapidly and took on a more and more official character; in the case of the more important saints the bishop usually officiated at the service—now invariably eucharistic —and the faithful attended in numbers. In this way the anniversaries became festivals observed by the whole local congregation, and churches were built over the shrines to accommodate the crowds. But the occasion was not at first commemorated in the other churches of the locality; such observance belongs to a later period after 537.

At Rome the greatest feast was that of Saints Peter and Paul on June 29; this can be traced back to *ca.* 256. The other martyrs honoured in the third century Roman calendar are not all certainly known but, with the exception of a few who had suffered in the sister church of Carthage, they were saints whose passion took place in or near Rome, no attention being paid even to apostles whose deaths had occurred elsewhere. "Martyrs" was construed widely enough to include some who had only been tortured or imprisoned by the authorities, but the "confessors" of a later day were not yet canonized.

Fasting rules grew stricter. The fast before Easter was by the end of the century extended to include all of Holy Week, while on the weekly station days (Wednesday and Friday) some sort of abstinence was expected of all believers. And in Rome three new fasting periods were added, whose origin is obscure. Apparently, however, they were meant as a protest against pagan nature festivals: one came shortly after Pentecost at the time of the wheat harvest, when the Romans kept the *feriæ messis,* one around the September equinox, the time of the vintage (*feriæ vindemiales*) and the third in late November or early December at the occurrence of the *feriæ sementinæ,* when the latest fruits were gathered. When the non-Christians feasted, the Christians fasted. These fasts were kept on the station days of the respective weeks and on Saturday as well, with an all-night vigil as on Easter Eve. On these nights the eucharist was celebrated at dawn on Sunday and no further eucharist was held that day, so that such a Sunday was termed "vacant."

At the opening of the fourth century a growing desire for a festival in honour of Christ's birth finally found official favour in Egypt and the date selected was January 6; why is not known. The observance of this day spread throughout the East and then into Gaul and Spain, where Eastern influence was strong. The Greeks named the day either Ἐπιφάνεια—transliterated into Latin as *Epiphania* or translated as *Adventus*—or Θεοφάνεια —transliterated as *Theophania.* But the Roman church decided to observe it—the earliest evidence is *ca.* 335 or a little later—on December 25, the very ancient festival of the winter solstice. (Desire to establish a Christian counterpart to the heathen Saturnalia was certainly influential.) The conflict between the two dates in East and West lead to a compromise, the earlier day being observed in honour of the actual Nativity and the latter in honour of Christ's manifestation of Himself to the world; for this day the Greek name was retained. (For a long time *Theophania* was more popular in Rome than *Epiphania.*)

During the fourth century the calendar of martyrs continued to grow and the observance of the feasts grew correspondingly more elaborate. And in Rome the bishop's custom of officiating in certain churches of the martyrs was elaborated and systematized by Damasus (366–384). He named certain Roman churches "station churches" (the title has little connection with the old fasting "stations") for certain of the Sundays and greater feasts. On each such day he went to the appointed church, accompanied by his clergy in solemn procession, and preceded or followed by the laity in great numbers. (The names of these station churches are still printed in the Roman missal, although the custom has been obsolete since the Avignon exile.) In particular special stations were provided every day in Easter week for the newly baptized, who were taken in succession to the most important churches in Rome; this extension of the Easter services throughout the week created the first "octave."

Otherwise in the fourth century the Roman fast before Easter was lengthened to two and then to three weeks, so that *ca.* 400 what is now the Fourth Sunday in Lent was observed (apparently) as a quasi-carnival like the later Shrove Tuesday. With the enormous increase of membership that came after Constantine the night vigils grew to be a source of scandal and were transferred to the preceding afternoons. And the pressure of candidates for baptism necessitated making Whitsunday a secondary baptismal season (in Gaul and Spain Christmas also was added).

The fifth century saw a further elaboration of the results reached in the fourth. As the Nestorian controversy caused the orthodox to stress the completeness of Christ's divinity from the moment of the Incarnation, Christmas was correspondingly magnified. Like Easter it was given a vigil and an octave, although the date of these is uncertain. And when the first Epistolaries and Evangelaries appear, they open with Christmas, distinguishing thus between the "civil" and the "church" year. A corresponding elaboration of Whitsunday appears to have been more gradual, its octave being often interfered with by the *feriæ messis* fast, whose position, in fact, became finally fixed in Whit-week after much (later) experimenting.

Fasting rules continued to grow more stringent and by the end of the fifth century Lent was extended to include forty days. These were counted from Lent 1 to Maundy Thursday afternoon, including the Sundays, on which the fast was only slightly relaxed; Good Friday and Easter Eve being reckoned separately. And early in Lent—although not yet always in the first week—the fast was intensified by adding yet another of the "seasons" fasts, possibly through the influence of Zechariah 8:19. These "four seasons" ("quattuor tempora," corrupted in English into "ember" days) were appointed by Gelasius (492–496) as the regular times for ordination. On the other hand the rigour of the vigils was modified by pushing them back from the afternoon to the morning.

At the opening of the sixth century, apparently, the first attempts were made to lengthen the vigil of Christmas (*Adventus*) into a more formal preparatory fast, which in some places was developed into a full parallel to Lent. The usage at Rome, however, is at first obscure. Some lists fix the "pre-Christmas" Sundays at five and some at four, and certain evidence may indicate that Rome observed the season at first rather festally than penitentially until Gallican influence was effective. In any case Advent, as we now observe it, was not finally prescribed until *ca.* 1080 by Gregory VII, who also settled the present reckoning of the ember days.

Pre-Lent originated in 568 when Rome was threatened by the Lombards and John III appointed the three Sundays as times of special intercession. A similar danger in the time of Gregory I (590–604) led him to prefix four fasting days to Lent, thus creating Ash Wednesday.

The steady increase of saints' days had by 600 included some non-Italian martyrs, but it was not until Carolingian times that Rome developed an imperial self-consciousness which led to a general acceptance of foreign saints. But by the eighth century (apparently) confessors began to be canonized as well as martyrs.

After Gregory VII the Advent fast was reduced in the twelfth century to an abstinence period, even this being discarded two centuries later. In the thirteenth century Rome changed the opening of the church year from Christmas to Advent Sunday, following a custom already widespread in the West.

The actual term "Church Year" first appears in 1589 in a German Protestant work.

## LECTIONS

The Jewish synagogues, in their origin and early development, were simply assemblies where the Scriptures were read and expounded, and the Jewish precedent was inherited by the first Christianity. So I Timothy 4:13, "Give heed to reading, to exhortation, to teaching," takes for granted that an indispensable part of worship is the (public) reading of the Bible, followed by exhortation and teaching based on the passage read. An excellent example of the method is seen in the homily miscalled 2 Clement, which is a hortatory and didactic exposition of Isaiah 54:1. So Hippolytus (*ca.* 217) calls the weekday services of the Roman church simply "instructions in God's word"; if for any reason they could not be attended, absentees were bound "to take the Bible at home and read sufficiently in passages found profitable" (*Apostolic Tradition* 35-36). Hippolytus does not describe the Sunday eucharists, but Justin tells us (*Apology* 67) that these were preceded by services where the "reader" read and the "president" exhorted and taught.

In the earliest days of Christianity "Scripture" meant the Old Testament alone, but by the year 200 the canon included almost universally the four Gospels, Acts and thirteen Pauline Epistles, with additions that varied in different localities. And since to recognize a work as "Scripture" was to acknowledge its fitness for liturgical use, this growth of the New Testament was manifested

in practice by the increased number of books that could be read at
service time. But while in theory all Books of the Bible were
equally inspired, the Gospels had a special sanctity of their own. In
Justin's day these "memoirs of the apostles" were the only alternative to the "writings of the prophets" in use at the pre-eucharistic
services, and a close association between the Gospels and the eucharist was established everywhere. Nothing could be more natural, for at Christ's service when the Gospels are read Christ speaks
directly to His people.

In the early third century at Rome the sacred secrecy attached to
the eucharist was transferred to the Gospels as well; Hippolytus
(chapter 20) states that catechumens were permitted to "hear the
Gospels" only when they had reached the final stage in their preparation for baptism. So there must have been three parts in the Sunday service of his time. First came the regular instruction service,
open to all catechumens, in which the lessons could be taken from
any part of the Bible except the Gospels. Then the less advanced
catechumens were dismissed and a Gospel passage was read and
(presumably) explained. Finally the eucharist was celebrated, with
only full Christians present. So on Sundays there were always at
least two lections, the last alone being taken from the Gospels.

But in all probability at least three lections were commonly used,
one from the Old Testament, one from Acts or the Epistles or
Revelation, and one from the Gospels; such was the widespread
practice outside of Rome, while the Apostolic Constitutions go so
far as to prescribe readings from the Law, the Prophets, the Epistles, Acts and the Gospels; five in all. In the "Early" Roman Epistle list alternatives from the Old Testament are sometimes provided, while even in the present Roman missal certain penitential
days—whose services underwent less revision than those for the
feasts—have Old Testament lessons as well as Epistles and Gospels. But the practical piety of Rome eventually contented itself in
most cases with two lections, both from the New Testament.

## LECTIONARIES

Specialists are largely agreed that by the opening of the Christian era the Jews were already formulating lectionaries for the synagogues. The Law was divided into sections that provided for a continuous reading in a three years' cycle of Sabbaths. The arrangement for the Prophets seems as yet to have been more informal; apparently the synagogue reader was permitted to select a passage at will within the particular Book prescribed for the season. But there is no evidence that these schemes influenced Christianity; when Justin tells us that the reading of the Old Testament or the Gospels was continued "as long as time permits," it is clear that the Roman church could have had only the most rudimentary lection system.

The first traceable Christian plan may have originated in the third century, although very little is really known about it. It was simple enough. The whole Bible was to be read through each year; the Gospels at the Sunday eucharists alone, the remainder at the instruction services, weekday as well as Sunday. This is known as the *lectio continua,* or "continuous reading." At Rome Genesis was begun on the older New Year's Day in March and the reading went on in regular fashion throughout the year, paying no attention to feasts or fasts as they occurred. A memory of this is still preserved in the Roman Breviary's commencing the reading of Genesis on Septuagesima, the day that corresponds (after various readjustments) to the former New Year's Day.

The use of appropriate lections for special days developed very slowly. That Jerome under the direction of Damasus had anything to do with it is now discredited, but the beginnings were certainly made in his lifetime; Augustine tells us in his exposition of I St. John (written in 417) that the Easter season's special lections had interrupted the continuous (vernal) reading of the Fourth Gospel.

But the occurrences between his day and the scheme formulated in the first lectionaries that emerge in the seventh century are totally obscure. The festal lections in these lectionaries are so well chosen that they have largely continued to the present day, both in the Roman missal and the Prayer Book, but as to the stages they passed through we know nothing.

As regards the lections for ordinary Sundays, however, it is clear enough that the chief motive that led to abandoning continuous reading was the desire to shorten the services. When all four Gospels are divided into fifty-two pericopes, the individual sections are necessarily lengthy. Augustine's congregation perhaps did not find them excessive, but liturgies grew steadily longer and more elaborate, so that abbreviation became imperative. And, as the propriety of the annual cycle seems never to have been questioned, passages of necessity had to be omitted.

As regards the Epistles this was not serious; since the daily offices had an Epistolary of their own, the eucharistic lections could be shortened without disturbing the general scheme. The seventh-century table on pages 310 f. shows this clearly; the principle of continuous reading is preserved, while the lections are all of reasonable length; just so the present Prayer Book Epistles from Easter 1 through Trinity 4 reflect the old continuous readings from the Catholic Epistles.

The problem for the Gospels, however, was more complicated, since there was no corresponding lectionary in the daily services and since omitted passages could not be inserted elsewhere. So complicated, in fact, was the problem that it was given up as hopeless and a wholly new plan adopted, with appropriateness for the season as the ruling principle. For the Sundays after Epiphany a series of sections were assigned in each of which Christ's "manifestation" of Himself was the theme; in the seventh-century Evangelary nine such pericopes are provided. Septuagesima and Sexagesima look back to the old New Year's Day; Quinquagesima forward to Lent. Each Lenten Gospel has a definite purpose, which is explained in the commentary. Most of the Easter Gospels look toward Whitsunday. The present Gospel for Trinity 5 was originally that for the Sunday before St. Peter's Day; probably there are others in the Trinity cycle that at one time had some connection (now lost) with a fixed feast or fast. The Gospels for Advent 3 and 4, which are devoted to the Baptist, prepare for Christmas.

For Sundays to which no special significance attached it is very possible that at first considerable latitude was left to the celebrant; he may have been entirely free to choose for himself, or allowed to select at will any Gospel from a table like the Epistle table on pages 310 f. But information is lacking and, in any case, we are quite in the dark as to how the transition was made to the apparently arbitrary scheme of the seventh-century Evangelary. Here remnants of the continuous reading have almost vanished. Evidently in Rome, as in Africa, John was read in the spring, while Luke predominates in the summer and Matthew in the autumn. But no trace survives of Mark's original place, and the present Markan sections are inexplicable, as is much else.

From the seventh century on, however, the development is clear. Apart from Reformation and later changes, the Prayer Book pericopes are those of the Sarum missal, which in turn is derived from the Gallican use of the ninth century. And this Gallican use went back to the old Roman use, which in many regards it preserved better than does the present Roman missal.

A glance at the tables is enough to show that in most cases the association between the Epistle and Gospel of any ordinary Sunday is purely fortuitous. In the present work attempts are made to indicate how in these cases some unity may be established by the preacher, but such unity is of course derived from the material and was undesigned by the older lectionary makers.

PART TWO

EPISTLES AND GOSPELS
FOR SUNDAYS

# ADVENT

The character of the Advent season is the result of confusion between two different meanings of the Latin *adventus,* which are arbitrarily distinguished in the present work as "Advent" and "advent." *Adventus* denoted the Second Coming of Christ ("Advent"), which was the theme of the November-December sections of the old *lectio continua* of Matthew, and it was also an early term for Christmas ("advent"), and as such was used to cover the pre-Christmas weeks of preparation. But the exact duration of this season was fixed so late (Gregory VII) that corresponding lections for the Sundays were never fully supplied. Roman use finally provided proper Gospels for three of these Sundays but the Sarum use only achieved two, while none of the four Epistles is unmistakably "advent" rather than "Advent." So liturgical unity for the season as a whole can be attained only by an exposition that treats both the past Incarnation and the future Coming as eternally present facts.

# ADVENT

## INTRODUCTORY NOTES ON THE APOCALYPTIC ELEMENTS IN ADVENT PREACHING

APOCALYPSE is a Greek word of which the Latin equivalent is "revelation" and the English "a laying open." That which is revealed or laid open is the supposed will of God concerning the future, usually in the form of predictions of doom. The most notable instance of apocalyptic in the Old Testament is the Book of Daniel. The most notable instance in the New Testament is the Book of Revelation, which is often termed The Apocalypse. Both books were written under the pressure of violent persecutions, and both had as their aim to inculcate constancy under persecution by predicting divine intervention.

A study of apocalyptic in the Old Testament and more particularly in the period of Jewish history which intervened between the last of the Old Testament writings and the birth of Christ goes far to explain the survival of apocalyptic elements in the New Testament. It shows that the apocalyptic of the New Testament is not a Christian creation. It is an essential part of the heritage from Judaism, where it was the resultant of two contrary forces; on the one hand invincible optimism as to the success of God's plan, on the other hopeless pessimism as to the future of mankind. The world had grown so exceedingly evil, the times were so ruthlessly out of joint, that God Himself could now do nothing with His creation but destroy it and begin anew.

The real inception of this conviction among the Jews was caused by the persecution of Antiochus Epiphanes in B.C. 167, and it was nourished further by a long series of ensuing calamities. In the time of Christ Palestine's special tribulation was Roman tyranny. The oppression had become so unendurable that war sooner or later was inevitable, but no Jew was so deluded as to expect that Israel could by her own resources overcome the might of Rome: God would come to His people's rescue, destroy the oppressor and establish His eternal Kingdom. This belief was almost universal, and even those who did not share it in all details had little doubt that the course of this world was almost run.

It is against this background that the apocalyptic teaching of Jesus must be placed, if it is to be rightly understood. That a catastrophe was at hand no sensitively minded person could fail to see and, like every one else, Jesus depicted its horror in apocalyptic categories. But, unlike nearly every one else, He saw the issue at stake not as a conflict between righteous Israel and unrighteous Rome but between righteousness and unrighteousness wherever existing. In this conflict Israel could claim no prerogative and, except she repent, was face to face with destruction. Then a new power would go forth from God, in which Jesus himself would be the center.

All this would come to pass within a generation, as any one who would regard the signs of the times must see. But the precise day and hour no one could foretell; with the apocalyptist's computations Jesus had no patience: "the Kingdom of God cometh not with observation."

As has long been familiar, the fulfilment of these predictions took place in the events of A.D. 70. Not merely in the destruction of Jerusalem, tragic though this was. What was infinitely worse was that the collapse of all the Jewish Palestinian organization threw Judaism into the power of the Pharisees, who molded it into their own image. From that time on the Jews lost all interest in the world about them, divorced themselves from all sense of missionary responsibility, and settled down contentedly to worship a purely parochial God. And the place that might have been theirs was taken by Christianity.

Only the language of apocalyptic was adequate to convey to Jesus' hearers the extent of the approaching calamity and the religious transformation that was to follow. And, since even the most devout believer in Christ's Divinity realizes today that the assumption of a true manhood must inevitably carry with it the limitations of knowledge that are inseparable from humanity as such, it may even be that only the language of apocalyptic could express to Jesus Himself the magnitude of all that was so soon to come. But, in any case, the disciples at first made little attempt to distinguish between the predicted events and the conventional terms of a final judgment in which the predictions were cast, and the immediate effect was to heighten apocalypticism even beyond the fervour given it by the non-Christian Jews. So the experiences of Christ's resurrection and of the outpouring of the Spirit were taken by the first church as proofs of the immediacy of the end, when the Messiah, now at God's right hand exalted, would return to judge both the quick and the dead. This expectation continued unabated throughout the first generation, and was of course fanned to fresh heat as the predicted calamities drew near. In fact, as their imminence became unmistakable, Jesus' warnings were forgotten and the Christians turned once more to apocalyptic computations, some of which were even read back into Jesus' mouth; most of Mark 13 is a noteworthy example. The ten years from A.D. 70 to 80 saw the fever at its height, and during this decade conventional Jewish views of "the Last Things" were adopted wholesale, as is seen, for instance, in the sources used in the Book of Revelation.

But the orderly continuance of the world brought an inevitable reaction, and the apocalyptic hope receded more and more into the background. From time to time external pressure, such as

Domitian's persecution, caused temporary flare-ups, while there were always individuals fascinated by the curious lore of computations. But the great bulk of Christians were too much occupied with immediate problems to concern themselves with such matters, and what remained of apocalypticism gradually crystallized into a formal dogma of Christ's eventual return, a dogma unquestioned in theory but playing little practical part in men's lives. And so it has remained until the present time.

This history of the subject clarifies the task of the expositor. The first Christians universally believed that the world was near its end, but this fixing of the time has no more significance to us than the equally universal belief that the world was created around B.C. 4004. The Book of Revelation professes to set forth a detailed account of the events that will close history, just as the first chapters of Genesis profess to set forth a detailed account of the events that opened history, but neither account has practical authority for us. As a matter of fact, apart from the conventionalized prophecies in John 5:28–29 and II Peter 3, no apocalyptic prediction in the New Testament looks beyond the first century. II Thessalonians 2 predicts an end of the world around A.D. 70, Mark 13 sets it a little later, Revelation and I John redate the catastrophe not far from 95 —and in every case the prediction was untrue. To attempt to revamp these prophecies and to find their fulfilment in our own age, to identify, for instance, the seven seals with the events of Napoleon's day or of the European war, is folly. Geologists and astronomers tell us that instead of the few centuries recorded in the Old Testament the earth has existed for perhaps millions of years, and nowadays no believer is disturbed by such knowledge. The few decades to which in the New Testament the earth's continuance is limited have no greater authority and human life may endure for hundreds of millions of years yet to come. In any case about the actual end of our universe we can learn from the Bible nothing whatever. "It is not for you to know times and seasons."

Exposition of early Christian apocalyptic, consequently, must look beneath the external form to the underlying religious conviction; the judgment of mankind and of every individual human being consists in confrontation with the nature and person of Jesus Christ. This is of the very heart of Christianity.

And this transmutation of the eschatological hope has been woven into the very fabric of the Fourth Gospel. Formal deference to the older dogma is paid in 5:28-29, but everywhere else Judgment is viewed not as something to come but as something ever present and active: "He that heareth my word, and believeth on him that sent me, hath eternal life, and cometh not into judgment, but hath passed out of death into life" (5:24), "he that believeth not hath been judged already, because he hath not believed on the name of the only-begotten Son of God" (3:18). These and many similar passages take apocalyptic out of the realm of the bizarre and fantastic and bring home to the conscience the eternal significance and responsibility of life.

For concrete application various alternatives are possible. The simplest is "historical eschatology," where every crisis may rightly be regarded as a judgment; "judgment," in fact, is the etymological meaning of "crisis."[1] The Pharisees blinded themselves with selfish legalism—and they crucified their Messiah. A nation puts all its trust in material prosperity—and financial ruin overtakes it. A dominant social group grows indifferent to the misery around it —and revolution sweeps it away. A man allows himself to become lax and careless—and unexpected temptation turns him into a criminal. For the individual the supreme crisis is death. Such examples may be multiplied indefinitely, but the expositor must naturally be on his guard against picturing earthly disasters as final ills; the earthly events are only feeble representations of the deeper judgments of God. And it is important to make clear that, morally

[1]This treatment should not be confused with the "crisis theology" of the Barthians, which employs the axiological conceptions discussed below.

speaking, crises create nothing; they simply reveal the hidden strength or weakness that already exists. The parable of the Builders is the best possible illustration. If, individually or socially, we are to build a structure that can endure the crises that the future is bound to bring, it must rest on the rock of unselfish righteousness.

Or the appeal may be directly to God as the eternal background to every human action. To God, that is, not as the Judge who condemns or pardons by an act of His will, but to God as the perfect reality, in whose presence all that is unworthy shrivels into nothingness. (Isaiah 6:1-5 is the classic illustration.) In this conception the apocalyptic tension is transferred from time into—as it were—space, from the "horizontal" into the "vertical," but in the transfer the eschatological values can be maintained unimpaired. This method is known as "axiological eschatology." It requires more painstaking and delicate treatment than does the "historical" method, but it can be made extremely impressive and useful. For instance, the cross can be presented as in itself a true Advent symbol, whose contemplation lays bare—and so "judges"—the ignobility and meanness of our ideals.

In employing either method the tendency will be to emphasize condemnation rather than redemption. Generally speaking this is not to be regretted, for much contemporary preaching has reacted so far from the exaggerated "judicial" theology of an older day as to be in danger of becoming sentimentalized. When the divine attributes of goodness and love are dwelt upon too exclusively other divine attributes may be forgotten; and such are righteousness and holiness. Hence the advisability of regularly reminding ourselves that to say "God is love" in no way excludes saying "our God is a consuming fire." And Advent is a particularly fitting time for such reminders. None the less, either of the above methods may be applied with entire propriety to God's deliverance of His children. The well-built house will not suffer when the floods come. The soul in which dwells the image of the divine is strengthened, not destroyed, when the vision of God is revealed.

This last truth is capable of a special further elaboration. While a constant sense of God's presence is always to be cultivated, there are times when this sense should be particularly acute. And this is above all true of Christian worship. Where the traditional types of Western eucharistic theology are held this method is immediately simple and direct, while the act of Holy Communion can be regarded by practically all Christians as an "Advent" moment of unsurpassable significance. But the sacraments must not be so overstressed as to depreciate the truth in "where two or three are gathered together in my name, there am I in the midst of them." Whenever Christians assemble in the name of Christ they are in the divine presence, to receive from God according to their works; although, of course, in this "liturgical eschatology" the emphasis should be almost exclusively on judgment as redemptive.[1]

Finally, it must be borne in mind that while apocalyptic concepts undoubtedly are to be found in the teachings of Jesus, they do not determine its content. His ethic is never an "interim" ethic, where the expectation of the imminent end of the world makes pure other-wordliness the basis for conduct. On the contrary. Christ teaches men to be free from earthly anxiety not because the earth is about to be destroyed, but because God's care for the birds and the flowers proves that His care for men will be unfailing; a teaching that has nothing to do with apocalyptic. Indeed, He explicitly sets forth His "ethic" not as a new revelation now first given; He sets it forth as simply the true meaning of what had been revealed centuries before to Moses in the Law. When the followers of the Baptist, whose preaching was pure apocalyptic, were disappointed they were scattered. But the followers of Christ, despite

[1]For still further possibilities the works of the Barthian school will be found extremely suggestive, although it may be noted that Doctor Barth in developing his exposition often does less than justice to the ancient thought-world in which the Books of the New Testament had their origin.

whatever disappointment they may have felt, went forward with their work and their fellowship.

The one vital element in Christ's teaching that is really derived directly from apocalyptic is His assurance that in His lifetime the Kingdom of God was in a real sense actually present. But this truth likewise was soon seen to be independent of its historic source; the new and supernatural force that He brought into the world did not fail when the hope of the end grew faint; believers learned by their own experience that this gift to mankind will endure however long present creation may continue.

# THE FIRST SUNDAY IN ADVENT

## LITURGICAL NOTES

GOSPEL: Matthew 21:1-13. A Reformation lengthening of the Sarum section, which ended with verse 9. The passage was derived from the older (seventh century) Roman use; in the present Roman missal the pushing back of the Gospels for Advent 2-4 has resulted in the omission of this Gospel altogether.

EPISTLE: Romans 13:8-14. The Sarum and Roman missals begin with verse 11.

However the present selections may have been determined, they serve the Advent purpose admirably. The Epistle in the expectation of Christ's appearing sets forth the standard given by Him to men: love is the fulfilling of the law. The Gospel confronts men with that standard as embodied in Christ Himself: Behold, thy King cometh unto thee.

The Reformation lengthenings of both passages were great improvements. The Gospel is given a more definite Advent colouring by including condemnation (the cleansing of the temple) as well as redemption (the triumphal entry), while in the Epistle the standard of judgment is made fully explicit in the summary of the law.

## THE GOSPEL

In Advent—as distinguished from Palm Sunday—the details in this story should be passed over and attention concentrated upon the central fact, the coming of Christ as King. When it is thus used it affords the best possible example of the proper interpretation of apocalyptic: Christ comes to His people in the midst of their lives and His presence is their judgment. There are those who, as at the triumphal entry, run to meet Him and hail Him joyfully; in contrast to others who, as at the cleansing of the temple, are indifferent to His approach, unfeelingly immersed in the affairs of the money-changers.

For the Advent preacher this Gospel means that Jesus of Nazareth comes as the Christ of God (Luke 9:20), the fulfillment of the Messianic hopes of His people and of the universal longings of humanity for a Redeemer; and beyond this the embodiment of a divine authority to which all men are properly subject and of which earthly kingship is at best only a symbol (Revelation 19:16). The triumphal entry into Jerusalem and the cleansing of the temple were acts symbolic of the authority of the Messiah-King.

SERMON THEME: Christ's advent as His people's King has a threefold significance. Christ comes to His people as their King: in Him they are confronted with ultimate reality revealed as truth, beauty and goodness; and by their response they are judged.

(1) It was an advent in time. Christianity is a historical religion. In this respect it differs from the Greek Mysteries which it encountered at an early date and which it overcame. The Mysteries had nothing to do with history. They were concerned with myth. They gathered up reminiscences of a primitive nature-worship and dramatized them. They explored the religious significance of man's dependence upon his natural environment. They took account of his consciousness of sin and provided release by lustral rites of a symbolic character. Christianity too has its traditions and its sym-

bols, but they are not essential to it. What is essential is its hold upon history, its conviction that Jesus of Nazareth was a historical person, that He was truly born, truly suffered, truly died, and truly rose from the dead, and that these things constitute the Word and the Act by which the eternal God reveals in history His nature of love and accomplishes His purpose of redemption.

(2) Although the Advent was an event in time, it was a revelation of what was true from eternity (John 1:1-14). As a fact of the eternal world the Advent is timeless and belongs not only to the past but also to the present and the future (Hebrews 13:8). He who came still comes, in the events of history and in the personal lives of men, and always His coming is a "crisis," a confrontation of the eternal. His judgment of the world is not to be "viewed as a fixed event in the distant future, but as now forming part, an integral part, of the process by which the human race is educated under its divine Instructor" (A. V. G. Allen,[1] commenting upon the teaching of Clement of Alexandria). His judgment of individuals is inescapable, for men are judged by their response to the ultimate values, truth, beauty and goodness, which are revealed in Him, and indifference is not an escape but a negative response.

(3) The Advent is not only historical and eschatological but also sacramental. Christ comes where two or three are gathered together in His name (Matthew 18:20; see also Luke 24:13-35; and note the theory attributed to Fechner that in the spiritual world loving attention takes the place of gravitation in the physical world and brings into spiritual proximity those upon whom it is fixed). He comes in the sacraments of His church, especially in the Lord's Supper which is the sacrament of His realized presence. He comes in the preaching of the Word, whenever His gospel is proclaimed with saving power.

Note that the Advent has always social as well as personal sig-

[1] *The Continuity of Christian Thought*, p. 67.

nificance. The King brings with Him the kingdom, the realm of
God over which He rules in God's name.

## THE EPISTLE

This section is unified by two central ideas that permeate the
whole. From the ethical standpoint all is dominated by "love is
the fulfilling of the law." Hence "darkness" is the opposite of
"love" and is selfishness in general, of which the indulgences in
verse 13 are only special types. The full force of the contrasted
"light" is obscured in the English versions by the rendition "armour"
for the Greek "arms." Defensive garb is included but offensive
weapons are also very much to the point: compare the "sword" in
Ephesians 6:17. The Christian is summoned to an active attack on
the forces of evil, which beset others as well as himself.

In the second place the ethical imperative—let us walk as in the
day—is, as always in St. Paul, not the means to salvation but its
result. It is because we are already children of light, because we
have made a real beginning in putting on the Lord Jesus Christ,
that we can fearlessly take our place in spiritual combat. For the
same reason the challenge in verse 14, "pay no attention to the
flesh," is not impossibly idealistic but actually practicable. For a
famous and familiar illustration see *Confessions of Saint Augustine*
VIII:12. Christian biography abounds in similar records. Within
each of us there are unworthy desires that clamour for satisfaction,
but in the higher strength God has given us these can—and must
—be ignored.

Close exposition will follow St. Paul in illustrating by the evils
of sexual license; the shame which such practices arouse is one
striking proof of their anti-social character. But a less specialized
treatment of sins is quite legitimate.

The passage illustrates excellently how really superficial a part
the original apocalyptic expectation played in early Christian think-

ing. Unquestionably "now is our salvation nearer" and "the night is far spent" were meant quite literally by St. Paul to denote the approaching end of all things; indeed the very word "salvation" has here an apocalyptic colouring. But the temporal element does not enter into the deeper texture of the thought, and the contrast between the realms of light and darkness is independent of eschatology. The time element in verses 11–12 is therefore best disregarded. It emphatically must not be used as a promise that in this present world a change is close at hand when moral effort can be relaxed. Civilization may indeed advance, but each advance brings with it new problems and new dangers which must be met with new efforts and new vigilance. St. Paul's appeal to the sense of crisis is designed to give urgency to moral effort. It is as timely now as it was originally, since the Church again confronts a changing world order and faces a New Age.

SERMON THEME: The standard of judgment is love, known to the Christian as a spiritual principle of supreme authority by which all moral obligations are to be recognized, defined, and fulfilled.

St. Paul is here following the thought of Jesus in giving the "new commandment" (John 13:34). In expository preaching the preacher is greatly handicapped by the lack of words to distinguish in English, as in New Testament Greek the words do clearly, between love as a sentiment or emotion and love as the unalterable expression of character. Some circumlocution is required. C. A. Anderson Scott[1] suggests "caring for others is the fulfillment of the Law." Better, perhaps, "love like that of God" (Matthew 5:44, 45).

This "love like that of God," grounded in character and in consequence free from the fluctuations of sentiment and independent of the response of its object, is pre-eminently Christian and its origin is supernatural. It is a gift of God, the fruit of His indwelling Spirit, and the ultimate test of discipleship (John 13:35). It is

[1]*Foot-notes to St. Paul*, p. 61.

for all men the standard of judgment (Matthew 25:31–46). It is
the safeguard of Christian liberty (note St. Augustine's *Dilige et
quod vis fac*).

For an illuminating discussion of the relation between law and
love see *The Atoning Life* by Henry Sylvester Nash.

## THE SECOND SUNDAY IN ADVENT

### LITURGICAL NOTES

GOSPEL: Luke 21:25–33. So the Sarum and the older Roman
missals. Now used on Advent 1 in the Roman missal.

EPISTLE: Romans 15:4–13. So the Sarum and Roman missals. It
has no Advent significance, but was the closing section of a primitive continuous reading of Romans.

In any case the Gospel and the Epistle are unrelated, so that
attempts to connect them are usually over-ingenious. Perhaps the
best that can be done is to point out that the unity and forbearance
demanded in the Epistle should be immensely furthered by the
apocalyptic vision of the Gospel. In Christ's presence we realize
the pettiness of the causes that divide those who believe on Him.

From a different standpoint, if Advent 2 is chosen for a sermon
on the Bible, as is suggested by the opening verse of the Epistle,
the Gospel may be used to illustrate sound methods of exposition.

### THE GOSPEL

This is a difficult passage for the expositor, owing to a combination of disparate material. Verses 25–28 are a conventional Jewish
prediction of the last woes. The sea will leave its bed and a new
deluge will commence (verse 25), and the portents will be so ter-
rific that men will actually die of terror (verse 26). These verses
have no claim to be considered the historic teaching of Jesus.
(Harnack speaks of the Jewish Apocalyptic literature, eagerly read
by the first professors of the Gospel, as "an evil inheritance which
the Christians took over from the Jews, an inheritance which makes

it impossible to reproduce with certainty the eschatological sayings of Jesus.") It is to be remembered, however, that such language was not taken literally even by the apocalyptic writers; what they were endeavouring to do was to express their forbodings in terms dictated by literary convention. Otherwise words like these have value only in their declaration of the early Christian conviction that Jesus' Lordship embraces inanimate as well as animate creation.

The little parable in verses 29–30 is doubtless authentic, but the original context is lost. Probably, even though not quite certainly, it was used like the similar parables in Luke 12:54–59: if the Jews persist in a course dictated by religious pride and hatred, frightful calamity is certain. Verse 31 assumes this sense, and verse 32 warns that the respite will not be long; if the meaning given for verses 29–30 is correct, verses 31–32 may well be Dominical also.

Verse 33 as it stands is a conventional asseveration of the nearness of the end; compare, e.g., Revelation 22:20. None the less Jesus may actually have spoken it and with this significance. But the saying, if authentic, may originally have had a wholly different context, so that the attested "words" were not at all apocalyptic. In either case the saying voices the depth of Christian experience.

SERMON THEME: God's judgments are collective as well as individual; nations and other groups are answerable to the eternal standards of righteousness revealed in His word.

For practical exposition the passage as it stands must be treated frankly as an early Christian prophecy, embodying—although perhaps only in a general way—a truth actually taught by Jesus. And this truth is that God's judgments are not limited to individuals. To the Jews, who in their absorption in legalistic ceremonialism persistently neglected the eternal standards of righteousness proclaimed by the prophets, the Son of Man was revealed in shattering condemnation. But this judgment was not unique. The Roman Empire, which destroyed Jerusalem, was itself undone by inherent

and fatal moral evils; Spain's fall from greatness is to be associated
with the bigotry and cruelty of the Holy Inquisition; the selfishness of the aristocrats in France and in Russia and the indifference
of churchmen in Mexico and in Spain to agrarian wrongs brought
about the revolution in these respective countries; and so forth
through the whole field of history.

Moreover, these collective judgments cast their shadows before
them, creating "signs of the times" that are hidden only from
those who persistently close their eyes. Prophecy is "forth-telling,
not fore-telling," yet it makes prediction possible, not by a magical
anticipation of an undetermined future, but by an open-eyed reading of the signs of the times in the light of God's unchanging
laws. Because He is a God who hates iniquity and will by no
means clear the guilty, social injustice and oppression are as certain
indications of coming calamity as the new leaves on the trees
are evidence that summer is near.

It is the duty of the Advent preacher to sound this note of
warning, and it is especially called for at the present time. Civilization has entered a penumbra of pessimism in which human
thought finds itself inadequate to the high requirements of philosophy, human emotion inadequate to great expression in art, and
human purpose impotent in the face of impending disaster. We
see starvation in the midst of plenty, poverty in the midst of
heaped-up riches, and over all, gathering portentously, the black
clouds of imminent war. There is only one hope of escape from
the plight to which humanistic pride and self-complacency have
brought civilization, and that is that God will again confront man
with His reality and thereby shatter man's self-complacency, and
build His kingdom in humble and contrite hearts. For in Christian
apocalyptic the note of hope sounds more clearly than the note of
terror: "when these things begin to come to pass, then look up,
and lift up your heads; for your redemption draweth nigh." Calamity, while it confounds the worldly, is to be interpreted by the

Christian as the prelude to a new "coming" of Him whose advent forever brings redemption.

## THE EPISTLE

The opening verse so appealed to the Reformers as to produce a new collect for this Sunday, with the result that "Bible Sunday" is its popular title. But as a matter of fact this verse is wholly incidental to the theme of the section, which is the Old Testament's prediction of the extension of the Gospel to the Gentiles. And this theme in turn is merely subsidiary to the larger plea beginning in chapter 14: since God has so received you, be ready to receive one another. So verse 7 should receive the expositor's primary emphasis.

The motive given is that of verse 13; the divine gifts of joy, peace and hope through the Holy Spirit make mutual tolerance no longer difficult. (In the context verse 3 also uses Jesus' self-denial as an appeal.) And verse 4 assures us that these gifts are certainly ours, for God who cannot lie has promised them. The purpose of these gifts, moreover, is divinely directed, "that with one accord ye may with one mouth glorify God."

When the Greek text is not consulted the Revised Version is particularly necessary in this section, for the desire of the King James's translators to avoid repeating words has obscured the close-knit quality of the argument. It will be clarified if "this" be inserted before "patience" in verse 5 and before "hope" in verse 13. "Patience" is somewhat too weak a rendition; "endurance" is much better.

Little emphasis should be laid on the array of proof-texts. They are aptly chosen, but the controversy to which they apply, concerning the reception of Gentiles into the church, hardly outlasted St. Paul's life; by the end of the first century scarcely any Christian questioned the Father's willingness to "welcome" all His children.

For the expository introduction to the theme of this Epistle the situation described in chapter 14 may be outlined. Controversy had arisen between the "strong" and the "weak"; between those who felt that they had freed themselves entirely from legalistic restrictions and those who were still timid about giving up older sanctions. Both parties have abundant modern parallels. These will furnish illustrations for the sermon theme which follows.

SERMON THEME: Life in the Christian fellowship requires mutual forbearance, bringing diverse elements into organic union, and enabling Christians to receive one another in the new community as Christ has welcomed them.

In the expositor's appeal the religious basis and quality of the ethical demand must be kept insistently prominent. Central here as elsewhere in the writings of St. Paul is the assumption that Christians through their union with Christ are already living a new and supernatural life under the Reign of God. This new life in the Holy Spirit brings into organic union elements as diverse and apparently incompatible as Jewish and Gentile; to both it gives grace to rise above the ordinary jealousies, dislikes and misunderstandings of human nature.

The bearing upon ecclesiastical differences of the present time (*e.g.,* Catholic, Protestant, Modernist) is obvious. One can easily imagine what St. Paul would think of ecclesiastical journals subsidized for the express purpose of heaping obloquy upon fellow-Christians of different church affiliations! The allied theme of unity in diversity is fully developed in the Epistle to the Ephesians.

# THE THIRD SUNDAY IN ADVENT

## LITURGICAL NOTES

GOSPEL: Matthew 11:2–10. So the Sarum and older Roman missals. One of the original Gospels for "advent" in the first sense of the term; the story of John the Baptist was the proper preparation for the coming of Christ at Christmas. In the present Roman missal displaced to Advent 2.

EPISTLE: I Corinthians 4:1–5. So the Sarum and older Roman missals. Its original choice was probably due to the Advent atmosphere in verse 5, but it is also eminently appropriate for the Ember season with its ordinations. In the present Roman missal parallelism between Advent and Lent has caused an interchange of the Epistles for Advent 3 and 4; thus Advent 3 ("Gaudete") corresponds to Lent 4 ("Laetare").

Whatever was the original association of Gospel and Epistle, the Ember concept unifies them excellently. In the Gospel the work of Christ's ministers is set forth; in the Epistle the ideal of their characters. Compare the Collect; this was first introduced in 1661, in place of the Sarum-Roman Collect in the older Prayer Books: "Lord, we beseech thee, give ear to our prayers; and by thy gracious visitation lighten the darkness of our heart."

THE GOSPEL

Christ's estimate of the Baptist is the supreme apologetic for Christianity: only by contact with Christ can a soul acquire the spiritual power that reveals present membership in God's Kingdom. Morally the Baptist was faultless. His preaching of righteousness was declared by Christ to be "from heaven." His zeal for God led him unshrinkingly to martyrdom. Yet the revival of religion which followed his preaching had no permanent result, for he could not transmit to others the flame that consumed him. He could arouse contrition but he could not impart life. Christ's message voices this criticism by gentle implication; the acts set forth in verses 4–5 were beyond the Baptist's power. In this message, accordingly, the physical cures, while genuine, are cited with a higher significance, and it is the spiritually "blind," etc., that are really meant; compare the final clause, "blessed is he, whosoever shall not be offended in me."

Christ knew that the Baptist would not fully grasp the purport of His reply. Not because John was a weak vacillator, "a reed shaken by the wind." Not because he was a man whom only earthly pomp would impress, "a man clothed in soft raiment." John was pronounced to be the greatest of all the prophets: "among them that are born of women there hath not risen a greater." Yet he lacked just that last degree of spiritual vision that would have let him see the utter significance of Christ's modest-appearing work. He looked for the coming of the Messiah as Judge and Avenger: perhaps in verses 4–5 there is a contrast between the Baptist's proclamation of doom and Christ's works of mercy.

Certain able commentators prefer—with less probability—to read verses 7–8 non-allegorically: "Why did the Baptist attract such crowds? They did not cross the Jordan to see reeds—or courtiers!"

John the Baptist was pre-Christian, the greatest of the prophets because actually the Forerunner of Christ, but not himself a member of the new community. But it should be noted very carefully that Christ does not for a moment regard the Baptist as "lost," although He does describe him as less than "the least in the kingdom of heaven." The point is present utility, not future destiny. To make full understanding and acceptance of Christianity the sole possible road to salvation is to caricature our religion: compare the saying of Christ in Mark 9:40.

SERMON THEME: The work of Christ's ministers is to bring those to whom they minister into contact with Him, from whom alone they can acquire the spiritual power that reveals present membership in God's kingdom.

In expository preaching emphasis is to be laid upon the superlative importance which Christ attaches to this membership: the least of its members is more privileged than was its mighty herald. (For suggestive homiletic treatment see Phillips Brooks's sermon, "Nature and Circumstance.") Such members are more than "saved

souls"; they are "saving souls." The perfect expression of this truth
is set forth in the marvellous paraphrase in John 7:37-38. Here
Christ declares, "If any man thirst, let him come unto me and
drink." And what follows then? We expect to hear "And his thirst
shall be quenched." But this is not thought worth the saying; what
follows is infinitely more significant: "He that believeth on me, as
the scripture says, from his inmost being shall flow rivers of living
water"; such a one becomes in his turn a source from which the
thirst of others may be quenched. And such a one—but only such
a one—is truly "in" the kingdom. Compare John 4:14.

And as we follow the course of Christian history, we are impressed with the fact that this impartation of power increases instead of diminishes, changing men's natures, deepening their ca-
pacities, and confirming their abilities for good.

Nor is it merely upon individual men that Christ has set the
seal of His power. Contact with Him has leavened society in the
large. Hospitals and asylums are testimony to His pity for the
afflicted. Modern methods of dealing with crime show the hu-
manizing tendencies derived from His gospel. Free political institutions trace their origin to the self-respect, the love of liberty, and
the power of free origination that His teaching has imparted or
implanted. Human progress is not automatic: all hope of it depends upon the extension of Christ's realm.

### THE EPISTLE

This section is so closely connected with its context that it is
difficult to understand when taken alone. It is part of St. Paul's
long protest to those who are trying to set up oppositions between
the leaders of the church. As individuals they have no significance;
they are *only* ministers, *only* stewards. Yet Christ is their sole
judge, and human opinions are comparatively so unimportant that
they should be withheld altogether.

In verse 1 the "mysteries of God" are practically a synonym for

"Christ," in whom God is revealed. Historically there is here no allusion to the sacraments.

SERMON THEME: The personality of Christ's ministers should be submerged in their work; Christians, who share a universal priesthood, should not exalt their leaders into undue prominence but look to Christ as the sole Head of the church.

The opening verse is an admirable text for preaching on the ministry, although it is often egregiously misused as if it taught the dignity instead of the humility of the clergy. If used for an ordination sermon it should be taken in connection with 3:21–23 which it immediately follows. Christians share a universal priesthood; all things are theirs; they are not to forfeit their freedom and their self-respect by "glorying in men," *i.e.*, by exalting Paul, Apollos, Cephas (names of later religious leaders may well be added), into undue prominence. To do so is to dishonour Christ, the sole Head of the church, and to pave the way for all manner of party strife and factional dispute. Possibly Matthew 23:8 was in St. Paul's mind; at all events, the thought is here reproduced.

# THE FOURTH SUNDAY IN ADVENT

## LITURGICAL NOTES

GOSPEL: John 1:19–28. So the Sarum and older Roman missals. It is unmistakably a pre-Christmas, not an Advent Gospel, as it promises the historic, not the apocalyptic, coming of Christ. The present Roman missal after its transfer to Advent 3 replaced it with the somewhat similar passage Luke 3:1–6, originally assigned to Ember Saturday.

EPISTLE: Philippians 4:4–7. So the Sarum and older Roman missals; for the present Roman use compare notes on Advent 3. "Rejoice; the Lord is at hand!" may of course be construed in an Advent sense, but the joy of the approaching Christmastide was almost certainly the original reason for the selection of this passage.

## THE GOSPEL

The peculiar problems presented to the expositor by the Fourth Gospel are well represented here. Historically this section seems to have been composed as a sort of polemic against certain belated disciples of the Baptist, who were upholding their master as a rival to Christ. The Evangelist replies by citing certain purported words of John in which he abdicates all his personal pretensions in favor of the Greater One, whom he goes on to identify pointblank with Jesus (verse 20). Yet, as the Gospel for Advent 3 shows us, the Baptist never really advanced beyond a hope that Jesus might be "He that cometh," and was unconvinced by Jesus' reply. (To harmonize by arguing that the Baptist later lost faith that he once firmly held is to do him a grave injustice.) Yet in the realm of ultimate reality the Evangelist has seized the actual significance in the relations of Jesus and John; the latter's only true importance in religious history is that he prepared the way for Christ.

Incidentally the picture of the Pharisees as so completely the rulers of the people that they can be described simply as "the Jews" (verses 19, 24), and as so officially established that they have priests and Levites at their disposal as messengers (verse 19), is unhistorical for Jesus' day. It is, however, valid for the close of the first century, when the Fourth Gospel was written.

SERMON THEME: Condemnation of moral evil is useful chiefly as it awakens the conscience to a conviction of sin and need, so preparing the way for Christ as the only Saviour from sin and the unique and perfect Revealer of the counsel and nature of God.

Exposition must follow the general lines indicated for Advent 3. But the emphasis is now on the positive value of the Baptist's work. The ground must be cleared before a building can be erected. "Reformers" as such are often too destructive to accomplish much of permanent worth. But without their efforts creative geniuses may find their own task impossible. For an Old

Testament illustration consult the stories of Elijah and Elisha.

In more personal terms the war against sin is a negative thing. But until sin is known and hated even Christ can be of little aid to the soul. Not alone in heralding the Messiah, but also by the stern denunciations of moral evil which awoke in multitudes the conviction of sin, John the Baptist prepared the way for Christ. In the same goodly fellowship appear the names of preachers such as Savonarola and John Knox, more recently of Kierkegaard and Karl Barth.

For the Advent preacher all denunciations of moral evil must be associated with "crisis," confrontation by the God of judgment and of justice revealed historically in Jesus Christ. Measuring his individual morals against the standards set by society the average man feels little if any sense of sin. It is the business of the preacher to discredit and invalidate this standard, and to substitute for it an absolute standard of goodness. Men must be brought to see in the light of God's holiness the evil in their own hearts; in the light of God's truth the falseness of many of their words and deeds; in the loveliness that is Christ's their own ugly imperfection, that out of this contrast may come a genuine consciousness of shortcoming, and that through the gateway of penitence they may enter upon a new and higher type of life.

## THE EPISTLE

At the beginning "Rejoice" and not "farewell" is certainly right; it sets the keynote for the whole. "Moderation" is really "gentle forbearance," a joyful willingness to forego one's rights for the sake of others. (C. A. Anderson Scott[1] translates, "Let your graciousness be known unto all men.") In verse 6 the sharp antithesis between the two clauses must be given its value.

SERMON THEME: Christ frees His people from sorrow and anxi-

[1]Foot-notes to St. Paul, p. 197.

ety; expects graciousness of them in their dealings with one another; and enables them to face life with serenity and joy.

St. Paul does *not* say, "Take your troubles to the Lord in prayer," but far more uncompromisingly, "Worry is unworthy of you: let all your prayers be made with thanksgiving"; with that grateful recollection of God's past mercies which is itself the antidote to anxiety. ("Worry and prayer are more hostile to each other than fire and water." Bengel. Compare also William James: "the sovereign cure for worry is religious faith.") So God will give you peace beyond all human imagining ("understanding" misses the point). And note that this is a promise, not an aspiration.

The whole is unified by "The Lord is at hand," which to us becomes "The Lord is *here!*" Here in every significance of Advent: here as the season once more brings the Feast of the Nativity; here as the congregation gathers in Christ's Name; here in the preaching of the living Word; here in the sacrament of His realized Presence! And because the Lord of glory and of grace is here, we as His servants—and so His companions in His triumph—are raised infinitely beyond the reach of all that can possibly harm us. Note how much the apocalyptic note adds here to the reason for the injunction against anxiety found in the Sermon on the Mount. There the ground was dependence upon the care of God, like that of the lilies of the field: here Christ Himself is added to His message of trust.

So the preaching of Advent passes from warning to reassurance and at the threshold of Christmas ends upon a note of exultation. "The Lord is at hand; His 'coming' is cause for all rejoicing; that 'our redemption draweth nigh,' that we are found 'in Christ,' that being 'in Christ' we have His peace and are guarded by it against all adversity."

## CHRISTMASTIDE AND
## EPIPHANY SEASON

Christmas and Epiphany are in their origin identical seasons, whose present dual character is due to a compromise between the Eastern and Western calendars. The liturgical theme throughout is "epiphania": "This is the manifested nature of God." And this theme remains constant (except perhaps on Epiphany 5), no matter whether illustrated by the Nativity, the miracle at Cana or the Advent scene in the Gospel for Epiphany 6. It is particularly to be kept in mind on Christmas Day itself, where the danger of sentimentalizing over mother and child is very real.

# CHRISTMASTIDE AND EPIPHANY SEASON

## THE FIRST SUNDAY AFTER CHRISTMAS

### LITURGICAL NOTES

GOSPEL: Matthew 1:18–25. The Sarum and Roman Gospel for the Christmas vigil was Matthew 1:18–21; the passage which is concerned with events before Christ's birth is certainly better adapted to the vigil than it is to the Sunday following Christmas. The 1549 and 1552 Prayer Books used all of Matthew 1:1–25.

The Gospel for Christmas 1 in the Roman missal is Luke 2:33–40; the same section appearing in the Sarum missal (which, like the older Roman use, makes no special provision for the Sunday) for the sixth day after Christmas, "whether it be a Sunday or not."

EPISTLE: Galatians 4:1–7. So the Roman missal, and the Sarum missal for the sixth day after Christmas.

Liturgical unity of course comes in the Christmas message.

### THE GOSPEL

The expositor will receive no help from criticism in treating this passage, which moves entirely in the realm of faith; what *critical* conclusion can be drawn from a story which is explicitly only the description of a dream? Nor is exegetical assistance needed in interpreting so perfectly straightforward a narrative. About all that criticism can say is that the tradition comes from Jewish, not Gentile soil, but probably from Greek-speaking Jewish circles, since the Hebrew of Isaiah 7:14 has "young woman," not "virgin," and would certainly have employed another word (*bethulah*) to indicate virginity. Still, Greek-speaking Judaism may have influenced the Palestinian understanding of the passage in pre-Christian days;

or the Greek rendition (*parthenos*) may embody a Palestinian tradition.

Verse 19. "A just man," *i.e.,* a keeper of the law. According to Jewish law Mary was already the wife of her betrothed husband and the legal relationship could be dissolved only by divorce.

Verse 21. The name Jesus is the Greek equivalent for the Hebrew Joshua, which means "Jahweh is salvation."

SERMON THEME: Jesus is the Saviour of His people.

In Christmastide preaching the emphasis on Christmas Day will be on Christ as the "Word" in whom we have knowledge of God, while on the Sunday after Christmas the emphasis will be soteriological: He shall save His people from their sins.

As on Advent 1 the preacher will emphasize the historic character of the Christian religion. Accepting the Aristotelian principle that in every investigation of reality the fact or the actual is the proper starting point, he will present Christianity "not as a human faith, but as a divine fact,—an actual, present life of God upon the earth and among men."[1] It is not to a solar myth that we look for salvation, but to the Jesus of history.

The birth of Jesus was in an Hebraic setting. He was born of a young Jewish mother, born of the seed of Abraham, born the son of David in the land of David. He was born in fulfillment and vindication of Hebrew prophecy. In the whole range of human experience there is nothing more inspiring or appealing than the steadfastness with which the hope of their Messiah was cherished by the people of Christ's race.

"Jahweh is salvation." The very name of Jesus indicates the divine origin of the salvation which He brings: it is an act of God's love (John 3:16). He is Saviour because in a life lived among men, of which we possess the records, He conquered man's mortal enemy, sin (Genesis 3:15). He is Saviour because He imparts to those who are "in Christ" the same life and spirit and power.

[1] T. D. Bratton, *An Apostle of Reality,* p. 108.

Salvation means health, wholeness, integration; its positive content should be emphasized. It must be sought in Jesus because there are no other terms upon which human life can attain its full dignity of goodness, beauty and truth. Science cannot save men from their sins, for in the nature of the case it is devoid of ethical content: it can make men powerful but it cannot make them loving. Only the saving love of Christ and His redeeming pity, manifested in men and manifested by them, can overcome the centrifugal force of human selfishness and build a new community of co-operating wills.

## THE EPISTLE

Study of this passage must begin with Galatians 3:16–22 (Trinity 13); the "elements" here are "angelic powers," not evil but imperfectly good, who are the "guardians and stewards" of verse 2. The sun, the moon and the five planets, or the constellations of the zodiac, were believed throughout the Græco-Roman world to be the abode of such "elements," and superstitious fear of their influences was a very real "bondage," as it is for belated believers in astrology today. Even the purer faith of Judaism was not quite exempt from this bondage, shown not only in the older lapses into worship of the "host of heaven" (compare Acts 7: 42), but more generally in undue importance attached to Jewish fasts and fasts which were regulated by movements of the heavenly bodies. To "observe days, and months, and times, and years," is to turn again to the "weak and beggarly elements" and again to be in bondage.

In spite of the obscurity of the references to the "elements," St. Paul's essential meaning is clear. In modern terminology: Before Christ came the best religious vision of mankind was imperfect; men saw in God a despot and a taskmaster, whose favour was uncertain and whose demands were harsh. This discipline was necessary, if men were to learn even the rudiments of moral righteousness. But the vision of God which Christ has brought to us is that of a Father, releasing us from fear and slavery.

For verse 6 compare what is said in comment upon the Epistle for Trinity 8 referring historically to a baptismal custom.

SERMON THEME: Jesus' revelation of the Father releases us from every kind of bondage, and brings to us the confidence that we are children of God.

In expository preaching the stress will fall naturally upon verse 7. As the Gospel for the day presents Jesus as the Saviour from sin, so the Epistle presents Him as the Saviour from every kind of bondage. The Christian, no longer the slave of legalism or of superstition, is free as no other man is free. "In Christ" he becomes a son in the Father's house.

The preacher will note that a comparative study of religions shows religions of magic to be more primitive than religions of mythology, and both to be morally inferior to ethical religions; and that in the religion of the Hebrew prophets which culminates in Christianity magical conceptions, the basis of superstition, gradually disappear. The extent of the development of physical sciences on Christian soil and under Christian influence, though not always with the sympathy of the church, is also relevant.

"Christianity alone made possible both positive science and technique. As long as man had found himself in communion with nature and had based his life upon mythology, he could not raise himself above nature through an act of apprehension by means of the natural sciences or technique. It is impossible to build railways, invent the telegraph or telephone, while lying in fear of the demons. Thus, for man to be able to treat nature like a mechanism, it is necessary for the dæmonic inspiration of nature and man's communion with it to have died out of human consciousness. The mechanical conception of the world was to lead to a revolt against Christianity, but it was itself the spiritual result of the Christian act of liberating man from elemental nature and its demons."[1]

Childlike trust in God as the basis of freedom is of course characteristic of the teaching of Jesus. Father is His only name for God. Being "in Christ" the Christian comes to share Christ's knowledge of God as Father, and thereby to attain the dignity for which man was created, of a nature made in the image of God in respect of moral freedom, purposeful action, and the ability to love. God is infinite, but there is in the spiritual nature of man that which partakes of infinity. Thought is infinite: it is not stopped by boundaries of space or of time, but ranges the past in memory and the future with prophetic vision. In its highest expressions the human will has an element of infinity and men's purposes find far fulfillments. Above all, love as an expression of character betokens likeness to God, claims affinity and holds communion with Him.

No theme could be more appropriate to the Christmas season, or more truly express the purpose of Incarnation. Compare Athanasius' "God was made Man, that men might become sons of God."

## THE SECOND SUNDAY AFTER CHRISTMAS

### LITURGICAL NOTES

This service was first introduced in the American Prayer Book of 1928.

GOSPEL: Matthew 2:19-23. So in the Sarum and Roman missals for the vigil of Epiphany. The selection of it for Christmas 2 was not a happy one, as it makes the removal to Galilee precede the adoration of the Magi.

EPISTLE: Isaiah 61:1-3.

The liturgical season again gives unity.

[1] N. Berdyaev's *The Meaning of History*, p. 117.

THE GOSPEL

The section is dominated by the thought of the fulfillment of prophecy; just as the flight into Egypt was predicted in Hosea 11:1 (verse 15), so the removal to Galilee was foreseen centuries before (verse 23). Unfortunately, however, the source of the latter quotation is unknown. Isaiah 11:1 is out of the question, and the Evangelist must have had in mind some writing now lost to us; there is other evidence of prophetic associations attached to the word *Nazoraios*. The viewpoint of the Evangelist in searching for specific predictions of this sort is foreign to the modern mind, which does not so understand prophecy, but with his purpose we are in entire sympathy. He seeks to show that preparation for the Nativity was watched over at every instant by God's protecting care. Compare notes on Epiphany 2 (American).

Not much can be made of the chronology. If the indications in the Gospels are to be satisfied, the birth of Christ must be placed in the first half of B.C. 6. Herod died about April 1, B.C. 4. Archelaus did not succeed him as a matter of course but only by a special decree of Augustus, which took some time to secure.

In verse 22 the "notwithstanding" of the King James version makes the passage incomprehensible; "and" is right. The young child requires protection from Archelaus quite as much as from Herod and for the same reason: here is Israel's true though unrecognized King.

SERMON THEME: The appearance of Christ was no fortuitous event, but was prepared for in the long history of Israel and foretold in the hopes and aspirations of the prophets.

Homiletically the birth of Christ may be set against far more distant and inclusive backgrounds. Universal nature has its share in it; not man alone, but the entire creation finds meaning and justification and fulfillment in the coming of the Second Adam, the uncreated and eternal Lord of all created life. Man is the final form of creation, the goal of nature's æonic processes. "Cycles" ferried his cradle, "rowing and rowing like cheerful boatmen."[1] In Jesus the ultimate meaning of manhood is revealed.

For the Hebrew background compare notes on Epiphany 2 (American). It is the glory of the religion of the Hebrews that it gave the doctrine of creation to the world. In splendid contrast to the despairing and unmoral pantheism of the East, and to the cheerful but equally unmoral anthropomorphism of Greece and Rome, stands the religion of the prophets of Israel, that God created and that God redeems.

### THE EPISTLE

The expositor, fortunately, is not called on to concern himself with the critical discussions of this passage, about which Old Testament specialists are divided, and he need not even attempt to determine the original meaning assigned to the speaker, whether Israel, some righteous remnant in Israel, or some individual, actual or ideal. For liturgical purposes, exactly as in Luke 4:17–21, the speaker is Christ and no other. So the only expository significance of the Old Testament origin of the section is that in Christ all the earlier yearnings and aspirations are fulfilled. A similar application to the endless aspirations of the present day is more than justified. Of homiletical significance in this connection is the fact that in our Lord's quotation of the passage (Luke 4:18, 19) he stops short in the middle of Isaiah 61: 2: "the day of vengeance of our God" is not included in his appropriation of the words.

SERMON THEME: In the good tidings proclaimed by Christ all the best hopes of earlier days and of more primitive religions find fulfillment.

A sermon based upon a comparative study of religions would be appropriate.

[1]Walt Whitman, poem called "Walt Whitman" in *Leaves of Grass*.

# THE FIRST SUNDAY AFTER THE EPIPHANY

## LITURGICAL NOTES

GOSPEL: Luke 2:41-52. So the Sarum (for Epiphany 2) and Roman missals. A seventh-century Gospel. The reason for its choice is obvious: the story of the boyhood follows immediately that of the infancy.

EPISTLES: Romans 12:1-5. So the Sarum (for Epiphany 2) and Roman missals. The beginning of a continuous reading of Romans 12:1-13:7. As in the case with the other continuous readings it represents a survival from the older days and has no reference to the season.

Throughout the Sundays after Epiphany (with the exception of Epiphany 6), accordingly, the association of Gospel and Epistle is fortuitous. The most that can be done toward establishing liturgical unity is to point out the representation of the Christians' Lord in the Gospel, from whose nature the Christian duties described in the Epistle follow naturally.

## THE GOSPEL

Taken by itself this story would have little significance. It is a mother's memory (verse 51) of an attractively naïve happening in a boy's life. This particular boy took so deep an interest in religion that He not only forgot His parents but could not understand why they did not know what had become of Him: "Where else could I be but in my Father's house?" Just so boys the world over cannot see why what is perfectly clear to them should be less obvious to the rest of mankind. Equally characteristic of boyhood is the rest of the story. This particular lad is not credited with impossible achievements; all that is said is that—according to his mother's account—His teachers were surprised by His ability, while—again

according to His mother—he never again gave His parents any cause
for anxiety. Mothers tell such stories everywhere. (For homiletical
treatment of the mother's viewpoint see Phillips Brooks' sermon,
"The Mother's Wonder.")

None the less St. Luke deemed this incident fully worthy of inclusion in his Gospel, while the church has constantly seen in it a
true "epiphany." For the boy was Christ. His complete confidence
that God is His Father and His utter absorption in learning the
Father's will are wholly of the texture of His teaching and life
twenty years later. To this boy the Sermon on the Mount will be
inevitable. And so will Calvary.

As regards details. A Jewish boy was not bound to the full observance of the Law until he reached the age of thirteen, but his
parents were required to accustom him to the performance of legal
duties for at least a year in advance. The Rabbis taught that two
days (verse 43) in Jerusalem were enough to satisfy the Law's requirements. Palestinian boys of twelve are normally well grown
and able to take care of themselves. In Rabbinic schools both teachers and pupils sat. The Rabbis taught separately. But there were
many of them in the Temple, each surrounded by his pupils;
Luke's implication is that Christ had been going from teacher to
teacher. The method of teaching was highly catechetical, the instructor propounding questions to his pupils (note "his answers"),
who in turn were encouraged to engage in free discussions and to
carry on disputations among themselves. The notoriously generous
Jewish hospitality would be extended unquestioningly to a boy
visiting a religious school. In verse 49 "Father's house" and not
"Father's business" is right; the boy wonders why Joseph and Mary
did not know in what place to look.

SERMON THEME: Confident that God is His Father and absorbed
in learning the Father's will, the boy Jesus is found in His Father's
house.

A sermon on the boyhood of Jesus is called for. In a sermon on this topic Horace Bushnell[1] has some charming and suggestive speculations as to His mother's influence. It may well have been that watching her at work in domestic duties, kneading dough, patching clothes, looking for a lost coin, etc., "the glorious child" was "packed full of parable for his great preaching day." It is still more to the point that her dignity, graciousness and serenity formed in the boy the reverence for womanhood characteristic of His later ministry, and that He first learned from her sympathy with the unprivileged. Home influences had their part in providing Him with the analogy basic in His later teaching, that "at the center of the universe there is that which is more like a Father's loving heart than like anything else we know."

In application, the effect of the character of parents upon the preparation of children for life is obvious. "Far be it from me to limit the grace of God," said Jerry McAuley, "but I never heard of a saint who did not have a good mother."

### THE EPISTLE

In the opening verse "therefore" and "the mercies of God" resume nothing less than all of Romans that precedes, with especial emphasis upon the eighth chapter.

In verse 1 "reasonable service" to modern ears misses the point completely. "Service" here denotes "divine service" or "sacrificial worship." In Judaism the sacrifices were animals, unconscious of the purpose to which they were being dedicated; in Christianity the sacrifices are human lives gladly consecrating themselves. (Compare in the Communion Office: "Here we offer and present unto thee, O Lord, our selves, our souls and bodies, to be a reasonable, holy, and living sacrifice unto thee.") This self-offering takes the place of the material sacrifices common to pre-Christian religions. As no single English phrase is wholly satisfactory the expositor should explain and illustrate the conception. The more

[1]*Sermons on Living Subjects*, p. 19.

recent commentators generally note that since Christians are inspired by the Spirit the meaning is almost "worship such as is rendered in heaven."

The self-dedication naturally involves detachment from every unworthy ideal (verse 2), in order to give God's transforming power full play in us. (Note that St. Paul does *not* say "reform yourselves and thereby win God's approval.") In this way we shall learn by experience ("prove") how good and acceptable and perfect God's will really is.

These two verses offer ample material for an exposition of satisfactory length, and it may be well to stop at this point, leaving verses 3–5 to be treated in connection with verses 6–8. But on the other hand verses 3–5 can serve as an excellent concrete illustration of verses 1–2. One mode of being "conformed to this world" is especially dangerous, the self-assertiveness that injures social life. (Moffatt uses the term "self-important," and C. H. Dodd uses the psychological term "self-fantasy." The latter adds, "It is those who take themselves most seriously, and fix their ideal highest, who are most exposed to this danger." He might well have added also that the gift of humour is the best protection from it.[1]) We need not run to the opposite extreme and bewail our utter unworthiness. Self-estimate must be "sober"; *i.e.,* "judicious," "true to the facts," detached, objective, sane, as in the Greek precept "Know thyself." God gives to each one of us gifts that are real, which it is our duty to recognize, cherish and put to use, but not to boast about: since they are His gifts "boasting is excluded." And not only are they God's gifts but they are assigned to us in accord with our proportionate share in a still greater gift that all believers have in common—the gift of faith. (Here we are in the deep places of Pauline theology, and analysis of the full force of the last clause in verse 3 should be attempted only with students or a congregation already acquainted with it.)

[1] C. H. Dodd, *Epistle of Paul to the Romans,* pp. 193, 194 (Moffatt New Testament Commentary series).

The logical structure of this section is so admirable that the expositor cannot do better than follow it step by step. But detailed analysis of verse 5 should not be attempted at the end of so close-knit and taxing an argument; certainly not in an expository sermon. It should be postponed to Epiphany 2, where it will be essential to the analysis of the Epistle, or—still better—treated separately. In this case the fuller treatment in I Corinthians 12:12 will be a preferable point of departure. The essential fact to be remembered is that the metaphor of the Body is to St. Paul hardly a metaphor at all; it is the statement of a vital truth. Christ's activity on earth did not cease with the Ascension. On the contrary, with the Ascension it first began really to attain its power, now exercised through Christ's "members." That is, a member of Christ is one through whom Christ *works;* to be, let us say, the hand of Christ is to be one by whose means Christ performs tasks that otherwise will either not be accomplished or will be assigned to other hands. (Compare the prayer of the mystic, "Lord, I would be to thee what a man's hand is to the man.") So, while the figure of the Body as a social organism needs full and careful elaboration, the expositor must not stop there. A body should of course be properly co-ordinated or, in other words, "healthy." But health is not an end in itself. It is good to have, but is useless unless it leads to activity.

SERMON THEME: The fundamental motive for Christian conduct is thanksgiving: God having done for us what we could not possibly do for ourselves, Christian morality is our response to His undeserved mercy.

In stating what God has done for us the best approach is to recapitulate Romans 8. "God's mercy to you has been measureless and boundless. He has 'justified' you freely, reckoning to you the righteousness which is in Christ. He has poured His Spirit upon you without limit. He has predestined you for Himself. *Therefore* in grateful love and awe respond without reserve."

For an Old Testament parallel of the argument, note the prophetic conception of a covenant relation between God and His people: their response to His grace, manifested in the deliverance from Egypt, is to be obedience of a Law which requires of them holiness like His own.

Christian morality is always social as well as personal. The gifts of God can never serve to glorify their possessor; their purpose is for the common good, and the common good is to be co-extensive with a redeemed humanity. A church may be never so well organized, and never so devout in its sacramental life, yet if it is not engaged in missionary enterprise it is failing to fulfill its proper function as a member of Christ's Body.

# THE SECOND SUNDAY AFTER THE EPIPHANY

### LITURGICAL NOTES

GOSPEL: Mark 1:1–11 (American; first introduced in 1928) and John 2:1–11 (English and the earlier American Prayer Books). The former is found as an alternative in Carolingian evangelaries; the latter is that of the Roman missal. The Sarum Gospel was Luke 2:41–52.

For the English Gospel see Epiphany 3.

EPISTLE: Romans 12:6–16a. So in the Sarum (for Epiphany 3) and Roman missals. Compare on Epiphany 1.

No real liturgical unity exists between the Epistle and either this or the former Gospel.

### THE GOSPEL

The primary "Epiphany" motive is contained in verses 9–11, but to the Evangelist all that precedes is an integral part of the story: the fulfillment of prophecy and the preaching of the Baptist were likewise "manifestations" of Christ's hidden nature. Probably, as in the Revised Version, verse 1 is a quasi-title. Then the "as it is written" in verse 2 has its correlative in "John did baptize" in verse 4, but in any case verses 4–5 insist that the appearance of Christ was no accident in history. He came at the fullness of time long since predicted by the divinely inspired prophets, whose record was so precise that John's very garb and food testified to his character as the promised voice in the wilderness (verse 6). He, too, had a prophetic message to deliver, bearing his testimony to the Mightier One about to reveal himself, to bless all his followers with the gift of the Spirit. This prophecy of John's was fulfilled immediately. Jesus came; and after His baptism Himself received the Spirit, while the heavenly Voice proclaimed, "Thou art my Son, the Beloved One; thee have I chosen."

Such is the sense in which the Evangelist meant the passage to be understood. The expositor, however, will realize—and be ready frankly to admit—that much of the material employed does not really admit the interpretation placed upon it. In verse 2 he attributes to Isaiah a verse of Malachi (3:1); to correct this error later Greek manuscripts (followed by the King James Version and the Prayer Book) changed "Isaiah the prophet" into "the prophets." In this verse, moreover, the Old Testament "my" has been altered to "thy" in order to apply it to Christ. Similarly in verse 3 "Lord" (originally "Jehovah") is made Christ's title, while the description of the Baptist is gained by transferring "in the wilderness" from "prepare" (its place in Isaiah 40:3) to "crying." If the Baptist's message in verses 7–8 is compared with the fuller form in Luke 3:16–17=Matthew 3:11–12, it will be seen that the Evangelist's abbreviation has converted an apocalyptic prediction into a description of Jesus as an historical figure. Compare further notes on Advent 3 and 4.

But when all this has been recognized, the fact remains that the coming of Jesus was the event that gives history its value. We appreciate that the Baptist did not grasp the significance of his own task, but God can work through men's ignorance as surely as through their knowledge, and John builded far better than he knew by preparing the Jews for Christ's message. Nor will the expositor find difficulty in showing that there was a true "fullness of the times"; there is a myriad of illustrations both within Israel's borders and beyond them.

Verses 9–11 are so inseparably connected with the supremely significant and revealing Temptation stories (compare notes on Lent 1) that there is every reason to accept them as an authentic recollection of Christ's own words: it was in this form that He explained His commision to the disciples after they had explicitly acknowledged his Messiahship. These verses consequently embody His inner experience after His baptism, told in intensely Hebraic imagery (perhaps slightly elaborated in transmission). The essentials are the sense of the inrush of the Spirit (Ezekiel 2:2, etc.) and the proclamation of the Voice, the sense of whose words is given in the paraphrase above. (The dove, emblem of harmlessness, may indicate a contrast to the popular expectation of a Messiah who should break his enemies with a rod of iron: Psalm 2:9).

A textual sermon on verse 11 would give opportunity for detailed analysis, but in an exposition of the entire Gospel for the day only a rapid summary should be attempted.

SERMON THEME: Jesus is the Christ of God to whom the prophets have witnessed; His coming was no mere incident in history but the event that gives history its value.

That Jesus is the Christ of God to whom the prophets have witnessed is the secret which the Evangelist shares with his readers, using historic facts to set forth his doctrine. We may not read the Old Testament prophecies with the literalness of former generations, but the gigantic experience that we call "the religion of Israel" none the less led forward irresistibly to a supreme revelation.

For a masterly discussion of the extraordinary connection between Christianity and history, see N. Berdyaev's *The Meaning of*

*History,* chapter vi. "The exclusively historical character and dynamism of Christianity are the result of the Coming of Christ, which constitutes the central fact of Christian history. This fact is unique and non-recurring,—the essential quality of everything historical. And it focuses the whole of world history."

### THE EPISTLE

To make this section comprehensible the expositor must preface it with verses 3–5, noting particularly that "the proportion of faith" in verse 6 simply resumes "the measure of faith" at the end of verse 3. In the illustrations that follow, "prophecy" to the first church meant a revival of the Old Testament charisma, a preaching that was so literally inspired that God's will for men could be declared immediately. There is no precise modern equivalent, but instruction given from the depths of a rich religious experience is fairly analogous. "Ministry" was primarily personal care for the sick, poor, etc. "Teaching" and "exhortation" are self-explanatory. It is suggestive to observe how Saint Paul treats "giving" as itself a "gift," and even co-ordinates it with "exhortation" and "ruling." (Compare Chrysostom: "Almsgiving is the first of all trades.") "With simplicity" means "without any desire except to give." "Ruling" savours a little too much of officialdom, so that "taking the lead" may be preferable. In the context "he that showeth mercy" is presumably "he who pardons offences committed against him"; Christians must do this "cheerfully." With Paul as with his Lord vindictiveness is looked upon as so injurious to the "body," the new social organism, that warnings against it abound.

To modern readers this list seems to contain a curious combination of "clerical" and "lay" duties, but it must be remembered that Saint Paul made no hard and fast distinction between them, such as emerged at a considerably later period. In the first church almost every one at times would figure as a prophet, teacher, exhorter or even ruler; the passage consequently is quite as available for general application as for pastoral exhortation to the clergy. It is even possible to find more or less satisfactory ways of rendering the precise terms used—for instance, a chairman of a church committee can be described as a "ruler"—but other illustrations of varied activities are perfectly legitimate. In any case the connection with verses 3–5 must be rigorously maintained.

At verse 9 the metaphor underlying verses 3–8 is dropped, and Saint Paul passes to a more general exhortation that continues unbroken to the end of the chapter. Hence, and since no real unity can be established with what preceded, exposition is best postponed until Epiphany 3, *q.v.*

SERMON THEME: It is faith in God that gives all His gifts their proper worth: social action is defective unless it proceeds from an outlook that finds its values in God revealed as love.

For a sermon at a meeting of guilds or parish societies the homilectical values here are unsurpassable. If each member of the social organism would ask always, "How can my own special talents be made socially most fruitful?" the parish would indeed become "a colony of heaven!"

Note also that the faith which Saint Paul describes is the creative element in social life, and that Christians must try themselves by this element of creativeness, the characteristic quality of Christian ethic.

# THE THIRD SUNDAY AFTER THE EPIPHANY

## LITURGICAL NOTES

GOSPEL: John 2:1–11 (American; transferred here in 1928) and Matthew 8:1–13 (English and the earlier American Prayer Books). The former is that of the Sarum missal; the latter that of the Roman.

For the English Gospel see Epiphany 4.

EPISTLE: Romans 12:16b–21. So in the Sarum (for Epiphany 4) and Roman missals. Compare notes on Epiphany 1.

There is no true liturgical unity.

## THE GOSPEL

The early association of this section with Epiphany is due not only to the bald language of verse 11 but to the structure of the story as a whole. A deity mingles with men incognito, but his veiled "glory" is suddenly made manifest by a marvellous miracle; this is the essence of the Greek "epiphania" legends. So the Evangelist frames his account in such a way as to leave no possibility for lesser explanations. The wonder was performed by Christ's sheer fiat, for He never even left His seat. The quantity of water transmuted was extremely large, amounting to something like 130–140 gallons (the Greek "measure" held about seventy-two pints), and (verse 10) the wine so produced was of extraordinary quality. Nor was there any doubt about the facts, for the (many) servants testified to what happened under their very eyes (verse 9). Verses 3–5, moreover, accent still more sharply the sheer divinity of the Logos. He is omniscient. So to offer Him a suggestion, no matter how humbly or with what good motives, shows a lack of faith that must be sharply rebuked.

This last feature—a characteristically Johannine adaptation of the tradition in Mark 3:31–35—is assuredly unhistoric, but probably no more so than the story as a whole; that so tremendous a miracle should be wrought to save the bridegroom from mere embarrassment is altogether out of proportion. And that it should be done as a "sign" or "portent" to convince men of His Messiahship is entirely out of keeping with Christ's character as revealed in the story of the Temptation as well as directly contrary to His own sayings (Mark 8: 12; Luke 11: 29).

Such are some of the difficulties which a literal understanding of the story must encounter. But a deeper insight into the meaning

and structure of the Fourth Gospel shows that the Evangelist
never meant his impressive narrative to be so understood. To him
the events in chapters 2–3 are of a piece; the change of the water
into wine, the purging of the Temple, the insistence to Nicodemus
that men must experience a supernatural birth, all teach the same
thing: Christ changes Judaism into Christianity. In other words
the section is written and meant to be understood as an allegory
and must be so explained. "The Jews had only water—but Christ
gave them wine—so He manifested His glory—and His disciples
believed on Him." So the "wine" is positive spiritual life as contrasted with the "water" of negative ceremonial lustrations "after
the manner of the purifying of the Jews." The expositor will note
that not only Judaism but far too much of historic Christianity has
been content with the water-pots of ritual cleansing, centering
religion around abstinence and taboos. But a genuinely Christian
experience is something wholly different; it is to have life and to
have it abundantly. This life is gained through contact with
Christ; thus He "manifests His glory." And he who experiences
this life can have not the slightest doubt that its Source is divine:
"His disciples believe on Him."

When the Evangelist chose this particular type of miracle and in
this particular setting he did so with full deliberation. Christ turns
water into *wine*—and at a *marriage*. Historically this was a thrust
at the contemporary teachers who were "forbidding to marry and
commanding to abstain from meats" (I Timothy 4:3). "How
precious is his witness here against an indolent and cowardly
readiness to give up to the world, or to the devil, aught which, in itself innocent, is capable of being drawn up into the higher world
of holiness, even as it is in danger of sinking down and coming
under the law of the flesh and of the world!"[1] Possibly also a
contrast is indicated between Christ's ministry and that of John
the Baptist: Christ "should not be as another Baptist, a wilderness

---

[1] R. C. Trench, *Notes on the Miracles of Our Lord*, p. 85 n. (in substance).

preacher, withdrawing Himself from the common paths of men. His should be at once a harder and a higher task, to mingle with and purify the daily life of men, to bring out the glory which was everywhere hidden there." (Compare Saint Augustine *Serm.* xcii. *Appendix.*) And for this he was dubbed by the unco guid "a gluttonous man and a winebibber!" (Luke 7:34=Matthew 11:19.)[1]

A word on the Jewish use of wine may not be out of place. Its cost was extremely high; the Talmud tells how a poor man might have to sell his garment to obtain the cups of wine needed for the Passover feast. Hence it was used highly diluted with four or more times its bulk in water. Intoxication, consequently, was necessarily rare and habitual drunkenness was a vice for the rich alone.

SERMON THEME: Christ changes Judaism into Christianity, turning the "water" of negative ceremonial lustrations into the "wine" of positive spiritual life in which the gifts of God are accepted with joy.

Note that in so doing Christ "took definite part with the West against the East in making the distinctive note of life not *apatheia* but *energeia.* Thought, desire, will, were not to be abjured and disowned in despair, through the overpowering sense of their futility. Life was not to be reduced to zero through their renunciation, but raised to infinity through their affirmation and satisfaction."[2]

The common problem is to transmute life, to find inspiration for it, to change not its content but the meaning of its content, to take its "two or three firkins of water" and make wine of them: that is, to turn what is commonplace and prosaic into what is beautiful, good and true. For illustrations, consult the Synoptic Gospels *passim. E.g.:* Jesus transformed poverty. Silver and gold He had

---

[1]Certain recent scholars find the eventual source of John 2:1–11 in the "epiphania tales" about Dionysius, whose presence caused even the rivers to run wine. If this is true, it means that in his indignation at the negativism of the ascetics and their denial of good to God's creatures the Evangelist has not hesitated to couple together the two most unlikely names conceivable, Christ and—Bacchus!

[2]See T. D. Bratton, *An Apostle of Reality,* pp. 142, 143.

none. But in His very poverty He came close to the poor, and dispensed spiritual gifts of mercy and of service like a king. Jesus transformed loneliness. "The Son of man hath not where to lay His head." But He made the countryside of Galilee His home, and had His sanctuary in the hearts of those who loved Him. Jesus transformed suffering by the way He suffered, and tasted death for every man by the way He died. Here is the answer to the question, Who was Jesus? He was and is the "hidden Deity" of the Fourth Gospel, the eternal Spirit manifesting in human nature His creative and transforming power, that men may learn of Him the meaning of free personality.

Of all Gospels of the Church Year this is the most appropriate for a sermon on marriage, the dignity and honour of the family, and the need of sublimating human relationships through love.

## THE EPISTLE

As was said on Epiphany 2 the section for this Sunday is a fragment, and continuity can be gained only by taking verses 9–21 as a whole. The theme is "love" (verse 9), regarded as the central and constructive principle of Christian social ethics. The theme is illustrated in manifold aspects by a series of independent sayings skilfully linked together but with no attempt at logical development; they might equally well stand in any other order. There are no real exegetical problems, but in verse 11 "fervent in spirit" is better rendered as "glowing in the Spirit." In verse 16 "things that are lowly" is much better than "men of low estate"; making the meaning "be content with humble tasks." (Compare George Herbert's making "drudgery divine" in *The Elixir*.) The sense of verse 18 is: "Any breach of the peace must come from others; never from you." The "coals of fire" in verse 20 are a figure for "a burning sense of shame." Verse 20 is strictly in accord with the teachings of Jesus in the Sermon on the Mount, of which verse 21 is almost a summary.

SERMON THEME: Christians are to live peaceably with all men, letting any breach of the peace come from others, never from themselves.

Exposition is reduced to the simplest possible form; it is enough to read the passage slowly and to intersperse it with illustrations.

# THE FOURTH SUNDAY AFTER THE EPIPHANY

## LITURGICAL NOTES

GOSPEL: Matthew 8:1–13 (American; transferred here in 1928) and Matthew 8:23–34 (English and the earlier American Prayer Books). The former is that of the Sarum missal; the latter that of the Roman (8:23–27), lengthened.

EPISTLE: Romans 13:1–7. First introduced at the Reformation; not in the Sarum-Roman sequence. The Roman missal (and the Sarum for Epiphany 5) has Romans 13:8–10. Compare notes on Epiphany 1.

Neither Gospel has real connection with the Epistle.

## THE GOSPEL

(English and the earlier American Prayer Books.) Again the "Epiphany" motive is double; Christ manifests His glory by His power over nature and over demons.

No generalization from the Gospel tradition of nature miracles is possible; each presents a special problem of its own. In the present case, the older form (Mark 4:35–41) relates the following facts. It takes for granted a knowledge of the Sea of Galilee, which is exposed to violent gales from the Hermon range to the north and north-east. When the storm strikes the small and comparatively shallow lake, the water is rapidly lashed into violent waves, which subside with equal rapidity as soon as the wind ceases. Such a gale occurred on one occasion when Christ and the disciples were in a boat. They awoke Him, clamoring for aid. He cried "Peace, be still!" The storm ceased. Whereupon He rebuked them for their lack of faith.

Obviously this account can be read as it stands as an eye-witness' story of a "non-miraculous" occurrence, the only error being the assumption that Christ's rebuke was addressed to the waves instead of to the excited disciples. In this case the section exhibits Christ's faith in the midst of danger; while the Father has work for Him to do, the Father will preserve Him. And, probably, this teaching will be the most generally helpful nowadays. (Compare Saint Augustine: "In corde Christiano et tranquilitas erit et pax, sed quamdiu vigilat fides nostra: si autem dormit fides nostra, periclitamur.")

Matthew has heightened the story by transposing the rebuke for lack of faith and the command to silence.

For the problem of the exorcisms compare notes on Lent 3.

Verses 28–34 are a condensation of Mark 5:1–20. Mark's version may be read as a somewhat coloured account of an exorcism in which a herd of swine was frightened into a panic; Matthew has heightened the miracle by making the swine feed "far off." Both Evangelists saw in the event Christ's glorious victory over an immense demoniac host, "legion," but the idea can hardly be made to appear anything but grotesque to moderns; it is for this reason that the American Prayer Book has eliminated the section. The most fruitful theme for exposition is the contrast between Christ's benevolence and the terror of the inhabitants at His act. In this way connection with the preceding section may be established. The disciples, too, were terrified at Christ, but they obeyed Him, while the Gerasenes drove Him away in fright.

### THE GOSPEL

(American Prayer Book.) The "Epiphany" motive is once more double; Christ manifests His glory by miracles of healing, and

He also manifests Himself to the Gentiles as typified in the centurion.

The cures wrought by Christ are divided by the Evangelists into two sharply distinguished classes, the healing of the sick and the expulsion of demons. For the latter compare Lent 3. As regards the relief of bodily ailments the expositor's attitude should naturally be as closely as possible that of Christ Himself, who demanded as a primary and indispensable element faith from the sufferer; where this was absent Jesus "could" not help (Mark 6:5). "Thy faith hath made thee whole"; with this declaration Jesus explicitly puts His healings into the class of faith-cures, such as are familiar the world over. Nor are the essentials of the problem changed by the fact that some cures were wrought at a distance; in both the recorded instances—here and in Mark 7:25-30—there were believing intermediaries who had assuredly aroused corresponding trust in the afflicted ones. Real difficulty is created only by the accounts of the raising of the dead, but in neither Mark 5:35-43—where the power of faith is sharply accented—nor in Luke 7:11-17 —in its present form a secondary tradition—are the details recorded with such historic precision as to permit objective generalizations to be drawn.

In the second place, Jesus treated His cures as so subordinate to His real task that He usually directed those healed to preserve silence, while on at least one occasion (Mark 1:35-39) He hurriedly left the city, where the demand for physical help was too insistent. Consequently to overstress these miracles is to be untrue to His attitude; while they had significance, it was only secondary (compare on Advent 3).

In evaluating this secondary significance a fundamental fact is that the "faith" that produces cures need have no moral content. Faith in Christ heals, but so does faith in Aesculapius, in a human charlatan, or in an amulet. And, so far as we can tell, the healings in the latter cases may be just as striking and just as efficacious as in the former. In other words, Christ's physical cures belong to a general class, and since this class is really general it must illustrate the workings of equally general laws. But as to these laws our ignorance thus far is almost complete, despite the common occurrence of the phenomena. A facile division of all ailments into "functional," in which mental suggestion may help, and "organic," in which it is useless, is not really scientific. No doubt it contains elements of truth—there would appear to be no possibility, for instance, of faith instantaneously healing a broken limb—but that "mental" factors may really influence "organic" conditions is beyond question. From the strictly scientific standpoint psychotherapy is an almost unexplored field. Yet there are individuals who have an intuitive understanding of its resources and who are able to accomplish extraordinary results. And of these Jesus was one.

So the cures at least help us to gain a better conception of His personality: He had a power that so stirred men's hearts as to evoke a concentrated faith that broke down even physical barriers. We need not hesitate to say that in the cures the power of Jesus was even more active than the sufferers' co-operation, that actual power "went forth" from Him. Yet, after all, this is a theme on which true reverence will not dwell too long, for even savage medicine-men have the same power to a very real degree. Far more important to the understanding of His character is the fact that Jesus subordinated His ability to cure to His power to "cast out demons" and to fill men with the life of the kingdom of God.

The story of the leper in verses 1–4 is taken by Matthew from Mark 1:40–44, being made more straightforward by omitting Mark's puzzling verse 43. Verse 4 refers to Leviticus 13:6, etc. "For a testimony to them" means "for a public proof." True leprosy is an "organic" disease in the fullest sense of the term, and an instantaneous cure would not only involve the removal of the diseased portions—which are very deep-seated—but their replacement with healthy tissue. But the very fact that Leviticus provides for cures shows that other diseases were confused with it by the Jews.

Verses 5–13 (*Cf.* Luke 7:2–10; 13:28–29) are from the Sayings source. Here, in contrast to Mark, the cure is made only an incident in a far more important event: this Gentile's faith and the praise Christ gave it. From the earliest days this story was taken to prefigure the extension of the gospel to the whole world; Matthew, in fact, makes this explicit in verses 11–12 (Luke has for these a more original context where, perhaps, the words may not mean quite so much).

Faith is faith, whether in "orthodox" circles or outside them; indeed a more vital faith may be present where traditional modes of thought have not dulled spiritual apprehension. No one was quicker to recognize this than Jesus (verse 10).

The Fourth Evangelist's handling of this same story (Trinity 21) is worthy of special study.

A matter of detail often forgotten is that this centurion was not in the Roman service; as long as Herod Antipas was tetrarch no Roman troops were stationed in Galilee. But Antipas had his own constabulary, which was officered partly by Roman veterans, so that the actual status of this man may be defined accurately enough as "chief of police in Capernaum." In verse 7 Jesus' words are best understood as an astonished question: "Do you ask me to come and heal him?"

SERMON THEME: Health of body is a by-product of Christianity. Jesus never permits His ability to cure to become an end in itself, but subordinates it to His power to free men from ignorance and sin and to fill them with new and supernatural life.

On miracles in general, W. P. DuBose had an argument which may be summarized as follows:[1]

First: miracle has gradually disappeared, not assuredly because

[1]See T. D. Bratton, *An Apostle of Reality*, pp. 152, 153.

facts have changed, but because our understanding and interpretation of facts have changed. We assume that if we understood all facts, all facts would be natural. Second: We are learning to see God less and less in transcendences of nature, and more and more in the perfect unity and order and wisdom of nature. We feel that the whole work of God is one. Third: The true supernatural is only the truer and higher natural. The life of Jesus Christ, because it is higher than nature can carry us, is not therefore contrary to nature. It is our own highest nature not to be completed by nature, nor to be able of ourselves to fulfill the law of self-completion, but to find the completion at once of our nature and of ourselves in highest union and association with God. Fourth: There are psychic and spiritual forces as yet latent in human nature of which we know not whereunto the future development may reach.

If this line of approach is adopted, the expositor will be on firm ground as he develops the implications of Christ's "mighty works" of healing. If faith in an amulet or in a charlatan avails to heal the sick, how much more should reasonable faith, trust in the love and power of the Father whom Jesus has revealed. And with this inestimable advantage, that thereby soul as well as body experiences healing. Moreover, since the spiritual Christ is ever-present, the power which He manifested during His early life is as available for healing as ever it was. The expositor may justly promise his hearers that steadfast faith may often reap even a "miraculous" physical reward (compare well-authenticated cases of healing at Lourdes and elsewhere), while in any case it creates a serenity of mind that makes for physical well-being.

### THE EPISTLE

This section is in no wise an essay in Christian sociology that endeavours to depict the ideal state and the Christians' proper place in it. It is simply a realistic attempt to deal with things precisely as they were. Under the Roman Empire private individuals were subjects and nothing more. They had no part in the administration, their opinions as to policy were not desired, and even to petition was dangerous. To the Christians, the state was something entirely apart, ruled by officials who were without exception pagans, and headed by an Emperor (Nero!), who was not only a byeword for viciousness but—what to Christians was even worse— who actually claimed divinity for himself. It is no wonder that many members of the church regarded the Empire as wholly diabolical, whose behests were to be resisted and evaded at every opportunity.

This attitude Saint Paul sharply rebukes. Whatever faults Romans and Roman rule may have, they none the less are accomplishing a necessary good. They preserve the world from anarchy and enable society—and with society the church—to function. So, since attempts to reform them are unthinkable, they must be admitted to fulfill a divine purpose, and to this extent are to be accepted with gratitude.

There would be no exegetical problems here were it not for the King James Version's perverse use of "damnation" for "judgment" at the end of verse 2. The judgment Saint Paul means is primarily human and only indirectly divine: "To transgress the civil law incurs a civil penalty, which can also be regarded as God's chastisement." The King James rendition represents a truly seventeenth-century conception of the divine right of kings.

"Tribute" and "custom" are probably "direct" and "indirect" taxes.

SERMON THEME: In their relation to the state Christians should be good citizens; selfish lawlessness is definitely irreligious.

In applying this teaching to the present age full regard must of course be paid to our wholly different conception of the state. Now, except in countries where political freedom does not yet exist or has temporaily been eclipsed, each individual is in a real sense a ruler as well as a subject, so that the old irresponsibility for the state's conduct no longer exists. "Ye, too, are God's ministers." There are easily imaginable circumstances under which persistent disobedience to an unjust law in the expectation of forcing its repeal or "passive resistance" shown in a determined refusal to pay certain taxes, may become wholly justifiable.

Yet such circumstances are exceptional, and the essence of Saint Paul's teaching is as applicable today as ever it was. The state performs an indispensable duty for us and it is entitled to our support. Christians should be good citizens. When things are wrong we should try to change them in orderly fashion, but no system can operate efficiently when its citizens keep only such laws as they see fit. The harm done, especially in America, by an exaggerated individualism is perfectly familiar: to cite a single instance, disregard by selfish motorists of the laws providing for public safety is responsible for the deaths and mutilations of more innocent victims than have occurred in any war in which our country has been engaged. The expositor must not hesitate to emphasize the fact that lawlessness of this and similar types is not only reckless; it is definitely immoral and irreligious. Smuggling, for example, is to be regarded as a contemptible vice.

Saint Paul's elevation of tax-paying to an almost sacramental height is in full accord with the broad principle he has laid down. There may be an echo here of Jesus' "Render unto Cæsar the things that are Cæsar's."

# THE FIFTH SUNDAY AFTER THE EPIPHANY

## LITURGICAL NOTES

GOSPEL: Matthew 13:24-30. So the Sarum (for Epiphany 6) and Roman missals. Its "Epiphany" significance is not evident, and it may be a remnant of some older sequence.

The return at this point of the new American Prayer Book to the traditional section has caused the omission of the old Gospel (Matthew 8:23–34) for Epiphany 4, used (without verses 28–34) in the Sarum missal for Epiphany 5.

EPISTLE: Colossians 3:12–17. So the Sarum (for Epiphany 6) and Roman missals. On Epiphany 4 the continuous reading of Romans in the Roman missal reaches 13:10 but 13:11 begins the Epistle for Advent 1. Apparently the continuation of Romans after Epiphany 4 was moved back to Advent, leaving a gap filled by the somewhat arbitrary selections now used in the Roman missal for Epiphany 5 and 6; they are not ancient.

Liturgical unity can be established by noting that the Epistle sets forth the true characteristics of the "wheat" in the Gospel.

## THE GOSPEL

This "parable," as the detailed explanation in verses 36–43 shows, is more properly an allegory. Its purpose is unmistakable. Admission to the Christian community in the first generations was universally held to be not the way of salvation but the privilege of the redeemed; the "saints," despite all their faults, were actually saints, that is, saved persons, "members of Christ, children of God, and inheritors of the kingdom of heaven." Yet the church became uneasily conscious of members unworthy of their vocation, and their presence was a problem that tormented Christians well into the third century. How could they be explained? And what should be done about them?

Our allegory attempts to answer these questions. Truly the Sower (Christ) sowed only good seed (faithful believers). But Satan in his malice introduced evil seed (false brethren). At first immature tares and wheat are very much alike (the initial zeal of many converts seems perfectly sincere), but time manifests the difference. No doubt separation is desirable but to weed a well-grown wheat-field is quite impracticable; we must wait until the harvest (excommunication is a dangerous remedy—and the Parousia is close at hand!).

Evidently this allegory must belong to a somewhat advanced stage of first-century development. The elaboration of details (verses 36–43), in striking contrast to the simplicity of the parables of Jesus, and the fact that it deals with a situation which did not exist in His time, make it difficult to believe that as it stands it came from Him, though it may be based upon one of His remembered sayings. The literary imperfections, too, are obvious; no farm-servants would ask the question or need the instruction of verses 28–30. And the representation of the church as a field into which Christians must be sown is very awkward, while the equation of this field with "the world" in verse 38 has produced some astonishing theological conclusions. The confidence in the nearness of the Parousia, moreover, proved illusory, while the tares (Gnostics!) were found to be not only worthless in themselves but positively dangerous to the wheat, so that excommunication was absolutely unavoidable (I John 4:4, etc.).

None the less the supreme resort to excommunication became frightfully abused; too often in the course of church history the wheat has been rooted out by fanatical religious persecutors who were themselves the tares.

SERMON THEME: Church members who are unworthy of their vocation are not to be excommunicated except as a last resort, but left to the just and final judgment of God.

If the advice given in this allegory had not been forgotten, church histories would be less cheerless reading and the disunity of Christians today a less deplorable spectacle. Saint Augustine was nobly right when he used the allegory against the Donatists who maintained that holiness was the only "note" of the true church, themselves being the judges! Catholicity is a "note" no less true, and the Donatists have their modern counterparts in many obscure sects which by losing sight of the fact have cut themselves off from the fruitfulness of Christian fellowship.

As things stand at the present time the allegory regains its full rights. Heresy trials have become of infrequent occurrence, and in the freedom of thought now permitted an honest search for truth usually brings its own correctives of theological error: one of the most distinguished of American theologians acknowledged that his own mind, "like that of the church, and under the guidance of the church, passed successively, and in the same order through all the heresies." Really unworthy members of the church usually excommunicate themselves, while the comparatively few who remain cause indefinitely less harm than is done by attempts to expel them. The broad tolerance of the Evangelist is not the specious tolerance of moral indifferentism—at all times he is ready to expose and denounce evil—but a patient waiting for the judgments of God. As such it is perfectly in accord with the mind of Christ. "Let both grow together until the harvest"; but let no one doubt that the harvest will witness the separation of wheat from tares upon a principle which ecclesiastical tribunals too often ignore. (Compare Matthew 25:31-46.)

## THE EPISTLE

The initial "therefore" looks back to verses 1-4, which should be read as the proper introduction to the passage. It is because they are "risen with Christ," and because their life is "hid with Christ in God" that Christians can and must show the fruits of the Spirit: pity, kindness, humility, consideration for others, forbearance. The directions, then, will be seen to be very much the same as those in the latter part of Romans (compare on Advent 1 and 4 and Epiphany 1-3); or in other words are typically Pauline. Note that in verse 15 "peace of Christ" is the correct reading; "peace of *God*" in the late Greek texts and the King James Version spoils the argument. Verse 14, "love which gives coherence to the perfect life."[1] With verse 16 compare on Advent 4: emphasis again upon the joy of redemption. "Christ's teaching should become so integrally a part of your nature that it expresses itself naturally in poetry and melody." Saint Paul himself could not have defined the precise distinction between the "psalms," the "hymns" and the "spiritual songs," particularly since in the Pauline communities the "psalms" were not those of the Old Testament—sometimes most unsuited to Christian use—but Christian compositions (I Corinthians 14:26).

SERMON THEME: Christian experience should find expression in Christian hymnology.

The magnificent poetical interludes in Revelation are the best examples of the first Christian hymnology. The emotions they expressed are those of awe, wonder and exaltation of spirit when comfronted by God's grace and glory, together with thanksgiving for His mercies. There is no subjectivism in them; consequently nothing of the sentimentality and "infantilism" of too many modern hymns. If Saint Augustine is right in defining the Christian hymn as "praise to God in song," how far Christian hymnology has fallen below that lofty standard! It can be restored only through the realization of what is implied in verse 16.

Although strict exposition scarcely warrants it, the preacher may find occasion here to speak of the association of music and religion. When the instinct of worship seeks expression, often it finds music best adapted to its need. When music reaches its highest point of artistic perfection, as in the grand surges of orchestral harmony, the feeling which it arouses is almost invariably religious. This association of music with religion is not accidental. It indicates a true and deep relatedness, through which worship finds its natural expression in the language of noble music, and music has as its

[1]C. A. Anderson Scott, Foot-notes to St. Paul, p. 206.

highest and ultimate achievement the interpretation and expression of the deep-lying emotions which are evoked by faith in God.

# THE SIXTH SUNDAY AFTER THE EPIPHANY

## LITURGICAL NOTES

GOSPEL: Matthew 24:23–31. As the sections in the Sarum missal for Epiphany 2–6 were all moved back one Sunday in the 1549 Prayer Book, its compilers were left with no section for this day. But, since six Sundays after Epiphany are of infrequent occurrence, they did not think it worth while to fill the gap and directed repetition of the sections for Epiphany 5. The 1552 Prayer Book gives the same rule, but in 1661 the present Gospel and Epistle were chosen, evidently on the principle of closing the Epiphany season with the supreme eschatological "manifestation" of Christ.

The Roman missal continues the passage for Epiphany 5 by assigning Matthew 13:31–35 for Epiphany 6. This is not ancient; the early lists provide Mark 6:47 ff. for this day.

EPISTLE: I John 3:1–8. The Roman missal has I Thessalonians 1:1–10; compare on Epiphany 5.

As is noted above, the present apocalyptic liturgical unity is deliberate.

## THE GOSPEL

The critical problem is much the same as on Advent 2. In the present case verses 26–27, 28 (Luke 17:23–24, 31) are from the Sayings source and are authentic. "Do not be deceived by pretenders. True judgment is unmistakable when it takes place. And (verse 28) it will take place wherever it finds an object."

Verses 23–25 and 29–31 are from Mark 13:21–27, slightly expanded: verse 30a (from Daniel 7:13 and Zechariah 12:10; compare

Revelation 1:7) is added by the First Evangelist, as is the conventional "with a great sound of a trumpet" in verse 31. Of these verses 23-25 represent a parallel but secondary tradition of the warning in verses 26-27, while verses 29-31 are pure inherited apocalyptic. Exegetical difficulty is offered only by "the sign of the Son of Man" in verse 30. There are possibly second-century traces of an interpretation (traditional in later days) of this sign as the cross, but Matthew gives no hint that he so understood it. Perhaps the sign is conventional, such as a lightning flash; perhaps (more simply) the genitive is appositive ("the sign which is the Son of Man").

SERMON THEME: Christ and His redemption are an unmistakable experience.

For the expositor the accent is on verses 26-28. Christ and His redemption are unmistakable to every one who has experienced them:

> Whoso hath known the Spirit of the Highest
> Cannot confound or doubt Him or deny—

and the byways of religion attract only impatient seekers after sensations. Christ is not to be found in the "secret chambers" of the religious charlatan, no matter how great "signs and wonders" he may show! All else in this Gospel is to be treated as merely illustrative, the most notable illustration of the fate of those who reject the true Messiah being found of course in the destruction of Jerusalem by the Roman legions.

## THE EPISTLE

The First Epistle of John, despite its unearthly beauty, can really be understood only when its background is known. It is directed against the tenets of the Gnostic Cerinthus, who taught that his disciples were "spiritual" beings, supermen raised wholly beyond good and evil. To them sin was of no consequence and they might commit it with entire impunity, just as long as they took pains to observe the Gnostic "laws" (verse 4: the Revised Version is much clearer). That is, Saint John's passionate declaration in verses 6–7 is not directed against all "sinners," since, as he states explicitly (1:8–10), no one is free from sin. What he is attacking is Cerinthus' doctrine that sin does not matter and that believers may indulge themselves as they please; whoever, Saint John indignantly retorts, holds such a theory "knows" (a play on "gnostic") nothing about God. To be a son of God does not yet make us perfect, but it gives us a perfect ideal and goal.

Saint John, like Saint Paul, bases his appeal not on the hope but on the possession of salvation; it is because we already *are* children of God that we can confidently attempt to purify ourselves ever as our Father is pure. Peculiar to Saint John, however, is the intense mysticism of verses 2–3. "Our destiny is beyond all imagining, for it will bring us the open vision of God, and he who can endure that sight will be like the angels."

In the Johannine writings (compare John 8:44) the devil is not a fallen angel but an Ahriman, evil from the beginning. This conception, of course, is simply an unanalyzed inheritance.

SERMON THEME: Christian experience gives us an ideal in which acceptance of sin can have no place.

The theme may be richly illustrated by instances gathered from Christian biography. Note for example the religious experience indicated in a letter which John Wesley wrote to John Newton in 1785: "But how came this opinion into my mind? I will tell you with all simplicity. In 1725 I met with Bishop Taylor's *Rules of Holy Living and Dying.* I was struck particularly with the chapter upon Intention, and felt a fixed intention to give myself up to God. In this I was much confirmed soon after by the Christian Pattern (à Kempis, *The Imitation of Christ*), and longed to give

God all my heart. . . . In 1727 I read Mr. Law's *Christian Perfection* and *Serious Call,* and more explicitly resolved to be all devoted to God in body, soul and spirit . . . I saw that only one thing is needful, even faith which worketh by the love of God and man, all inward and outward holiness."[1]

[1]*Letters,* V. 4, p. 298 f.

# PRE-LENT AND LENT

When the Lombards entered Italy in 568, John III appointed the three pre-Lenten Sundays for supplication against the impending peril. On the first two the extra-mural churches of Saint Laurence and Saint Paul were made the stations, while on the third the populace gathered at the shrine of Rome's patron, Saint Peter. The collects for Septuagesima (probably) and Sexagesima (certainly), with their petitions that we may be "mercifully delivered" and "defended against all adversity" were framed at this time, together with certain minor propers still retained in the Roman missal, while the Epistle for Sexagesima is due to the day's station. The Lombard threat continued for many years, so many, in fact, that the prayers against it became fixed in the liturgy and were not changed when the danger finally ceased. The collects were accordingly re-interpreted as prayers against spiritual foes, and pre-Lent was assimilated to Lent as a preparatory "semi-penitential" season.

Liturgically this conception found expression in discontinuing the use of "alleluia" at all services and of the *Gloria in Excelsis* at all but saints' days services, a use that can be traced back into the ninth century. Indeed, during the Middle Ages a special service was held on the eve of Septuagesima known as the "Farewell to Alleluia"; compare the hymn "Alleluia! Song of Gladness."

The names of the three Sundays were established in reverse order, "Quinquagesima" and "Sexagesima" being accurate enough and "Septuagesima" being added for symmetry.

Unfortunately the Gospels and Epistles are of so diverse origin that the expository preacher cannot find in them any common liturgical theme for the season.

# PRE-LENT

## SEPTUAGESIMA

### LITURGICAL NOTES

GOSPEL: Matthew 20:1–16. So in the Sarum and Roman missals; a seventh-century Gospel, and certainly much earlier than the seventh century. It is best explained as originally selected for the traditional beginning of the year, which in Rome came in March; then farmers began to prepare their vineyards and (Sexagesima) fields. The eventual extension of Lent pushed the section back into (normally) late winter.

EPISTLE: I Corinthians 9:24–27. In the Sarum missal the passage is continued through 10:4, in the Roman through 10:5a. The Reformation shortening produces greater concentration. Apparently a New Year selection, instilling good resolutions for zeal.

Although the Gospel and Epistle were chosen for wholly different reasons they supplement each other admirably. In the parable of the labourers the theme is God's goodness; He gives men far more than they can possibly earn. Yet (Epistle) this does not dispense us from our utmost efforts.

### THE GOSPEL

This is a true parable and not an allegory. The master of the house does not represent God directly and the comparison is to be found in the moral as a whole, explicitly stated in verse 15: "Are you envious because I am generous?" (the traditional English renderings of this question are needlessly obscure). When workers receive an agreed and adequate wage, they have no right to grumble because others who are less fortunate are treated liberally. Con-

78

sequently "just" persons should not complain when God welcomes penitent sinners. Compare the parables in Luke 15, noting that the complaining labourers here parallel the irritated elder brother in the parable of the prodigal.

Otherwise the details must not be stressed. The labourers hired at different hours do not represent specific classes of Christians, and what they were doing before they met the master of the house is immaterial. The first group were legally entitled to the covenanted pay, but it does not follow that any human beings can similarly claim salvation from God. The manner of payment in verse 8 has no deep significance; it merely explains why those first hired felt aggrieved immediately. Each man in the parable receives the same amount, but this in no way proves that in the kingdom of heaven all rewards are equal, nor can the denarius be equated directly with "salvation." The lesson is simply that earthly conceptions of individual achievement cannot be carried over into the heavenly realm. Where work of any sort has been faithfully performed for God, He does not haggle about the recompense. The conception of contracts may do on earth—but not in heaven!

Verse 16a, however, "so the last shall be first, and the first last," should be ignored by the expositor. In the Synoptic tradition sayings of Jesus were not infrequently associated only by external similarities, and this clause was appended through the influence of verse 8. In late Greek texts and the King James Version matters were confused still more by the further addition of the completely irrelevant "for many be called, but few chosen."

SERMON THEME: Since God's goodness gives men far more than they can possibly earn, the standards of the market-place can have no place in His kingdom.

If the expositor will bear in mind that neither here nor anywhere else did Christ give specific instructions in regard to economic and industrial matters, he may then point out that indirectly and by implication this parable gives support to those who are working for such reforms as the living wage, unemployment insurance, old-age pensions and the like. Men should deal with one another as God deals with them, upon a more generous principle than that which governs the hard bargaining of the market-place. The standards of the market-place are "So many pennies for so much work," irrespective of human needs. The standards of the Realm of God are those of family life, by which father deals with son, and brother with brother. The welfare and the needs of persons are to be regarded as of more importance than the acquisition of wealth.

For contemporary recognition and application of the principle, note the pronouncements on social and industrial problems by the Lambeth Conference of Anglican Bishops, by the Federal Council of the Churches of Christ in America, by representatives of the Russian Orthodox Seminary in Paris, and in the papal Encyclical, *Rerum Novarum*. Social reconstruction is bound to come: the ferment of unrest throughout the world makes it certain. The question is whether it is coming accompanied by the indescribable horrors of the "class war," or by gradual, peaceable, willing reform of social abuses, in which the followers of Jesus will lead the way by practice and example.

### THE EPISTLE

The expositor should study carefully the place of this section in the whole argument of chapters 8–10. In part it looks back to Saint Paul's practice of self-denial in 9:1–18 and (in a lesser degree) 9:19–23, but rather more concretely it looks back to the warning in 8:9–13 and forward to what the Corinthians are asked to do in chapter 10. "He who would do Christ's work must train his whole nature for the task." In verse 27 the meaning is "I make my body my servant by refusing to indulge it." Matthew 5:29–30 is a splendid parallel. The means used by the Apostle to "buffet" his body are illustrated in the Epistle for Sexagesima; he forced himself to endure hard work and privations uncomplainingly.

The imagery of the section is taken from the arena, a device so common among contemporary orators and moralists that special reference to the Isthmian games of Corinth is hardly to be looked for. Allusions found in the writings of the Church Fathers to martyrs as "athletes of God" provide historic backgrounds of stern fortitude. Real difficulty is offered only in verse 24, and here the expositor had best admit frankly that the figure is unfortunate; in a race only one man can win but in the Christian struggle no earnest soul can lose. In verse 27 "castaway" is too strong a word. Continuing the metaphor a better translation would be "disqualified."

Liturgically the Epistle can fitly be used as the first warning of the approaching Lent.

SERMON THEME: God's goodness does not dispense us from our utmost efforts, and the Christian must train himself to endure hard work and privations with the cheerfulness of an athlete preparing for the contest.

For notable instances of cheerful and effective self-discipline consult John Wesley's *Journals* and the *Life of William Ellery Channing;* also in general the lives of the saints. But note that "ascetic" practices, in the ordinary sense of the word, find no justification from this passage, and the self-torture which in the mediæval and even in some branches of the modern church often has been regarded as a mark of sanctity warranting canonization comes directly from heathen sources and is to be counted anti-Christian. It derives from Egyptian deserts, not from the primitive church.

# SEXAGESIMA

## LITURGICAL NOTES

GOSPEL: Luke 8:4–15. So the Sarum and Roman missals. Compare on Septuagesima.

EPISTLE: II Corinthians 11:19–31. In the Sarum and Roman missals the section is extended through 12:9. This was first chosen as a "station" Epistle, the Station at Rome on this day being at Saint Paul's-Without-the-Walls, the lesson being in honour of the Apostle.

In this case no natural liturgical unity seems indicated. Nor does either Gospel or Epistle lend itself without artificiality to pre-Lenten purposes.

### THE GOSPEL

The parable is so familiar to all and is so free from difficulty that correct exposition is almost inevitable, provided only that no attempt is made at radical novelty. It may be noted, however, that the interpretation that follows the parable in all three Synoptics is not quite primary, nor is it wholly consistent with the parable: in verse 13, for instance, "those on the rock" ought to be "those who are like the rocky ground." The expositor, consequently, is at liberty to reinterpret the various classes, if he find it helpful, omitting verses 11–15.

Verse 10 should be omitted in any case. The Second Evangelist (Mark 4:11–12, 21–25) has inserted a theory of the parables that is definitely unhistoric: These stories were mysterious allegories, whose key was deliberately withheld by Jesus from the people lest they be converted; it was only after His death that the truth could be proclaimed without reserve. Verse 10 in St. Luke reproduces this Markan theory in a softened form; perhaps without wholly understanding it.

SERMON THEME: Although some seed is lost in sowing, the seed that falls on good ground bears fruit an hundredfold.

This may well have been the original meaning of the parable; if so, it comforted the disciples and the early church for their first apparent lack of success. When conditions are similar, the same comfort is still valid and should bulk more largely in preaching.

Warnings, and occasionally denunciations, have their place, but if they are given too large a place, preaching degenerates into nagging, and sometimes into scolding the faithful few who are present for the faults of the absentees. It is better to dwell particularly on the class represented by the good ground in the parable: "It is true that in sowing some seed is lost, but when it falls on good ground it brings forth an hundredfold."

For illustrations, consult the lives of missionaries generally. *E.g.,* Bishop Schereschewsky was many years in China before he made a single convert to the Christian religion, yet later the Chinese church which he helped to found showed the steadfastness exemplified by the native martyrs during the Boxer rebellion.

## THE EPISTLE

When this section is read apart from its context it is apt to impress hearers as voicing an overweening egotism. So the expositor must be at pains to explain how only the direst necessity could have wrung such boasting out of the Apostle. In all the time he had spent at Corinth he had talked so little about himself that his converts knew almost nothing of his achievements. So when others came, who had no such reticence, the Corinthians were impressed: "Paul never accomplished such wonders or went through such trials!" Hence in the ensuing conflict of authority, when his very gospel was at stake, he was obliged to assert himself in a way that he describes as the way of "a fool." But he had no choice: "ye compelled me!" (12:11).

In any case the passage must be read beginning with verse 16, for verse 19 opens practically in the middle of a sentence.

The adversaries at Corinth represented Jewish Christianity. Although not so radical as the Judaizers in Galatia, who insisted on circumcision, Jewish Christians generally taught that Gentiles must consider themselves as inferiors, who ought to order themselves lowly and reverently before their Jewish betters: this is the meaning of the sharp sarcasm in verse 20. The traditional English renderings of the difficult verse 21 are impossible, but the sense is approximately "I say this to shame you, because you say that I have been weak! There will be an end of weakness now; if other people can boast, so, at a pinch, can I!"

The triple asseveration in verse 22 shows the basic point at issue; no one knows more about Jewish privileges than Saint Paul. Verse 23: To boast at all is foolish but to boast of one's accomplishments as Christ's servant is madness. So even under this extreme provocation the Apostle cannot bring himself to record his "successes," such as the number of churches he has founded or the number of souls he has converted; he confines himself to his "weaknesses" (verse 30), *i.e.,* his sufferings and privations. The "stripes above measure" (*i.e.,* "far more than my opponents") are specified in verses 24–25 as five Jewish and three Roman floggings, while the "deaths" (*i.e.,* "danger of death") are set forth in verses 24–27. Deuteronomy 25:3 allowed forty stripes to be given a culprit; the reduction to thirty-nine was a Jewish "fence about the law." There is no record of the Jewish punishments in Acts, but one of the Roman beatings is told in 16:22f. Legally Roman citizens were exempt from this punishment (Acts 16:37), but provincial officials were not always law abiding. The "stoning" appears in Acts 14:19. The "shipwrecks" are not described in Acts (the one in Acts 27 took place long after II Corinthians was written); presumably they belong to the period mentioned in Galatians 1:21. "In the deep" means "on a raft" or perhaps "clinging to a spar." In the ancient world all "journeyings" by an unprotected traveller were dangerous, and Saint Paul's examples show how manifold these dangers were. "Waters" should be "rivers," whose fords were often perilous in the extreme. That "false brethren" ever made the Apostle run in danger of death is unlikely, but they could—and did—cause him endless vexation. "Watchings" means "loss of sleep." "Fasting" sums up "hunger and thirst" (voluntary fasts would not be "weaknesses"). Every clergyman knows what "anxiety" for even a single church involves. Able commentators, incidentally, note that "that which cometh upon me" can be rendered "the throng of people who want to talk to me." And verse 29 may support this, "I use up my last energies in sympathizing with them all!" Verses 30–31 sum up the whole.

SERMON THEME: What Saint Paul willingly endured in the service of Christ makes all boasting appear foolish.

The preacher will make it plain that this Epistle, which was chosen in the early middle ages to illustrate the greatness of Saint Paul, is one which he himself would have relegated to obscurity. After this explanation, to apply the passage he need only ask, "What do men usually boast about?" and compare with it the Apostle's "Iliad of woes" endured for Christ's sake. "Men do not gamble with their lives, nor stake their souls, on abstract truths and systems; but a great love is different. They will do it, Paul did it, for that."[1]

# QUINQUAGESIMA

## LITURGICAL NOTES

GOSPEL: Luke 18:31–43. So in the Sarum and Roman missals; a seventh century and almost universal Western Gospel.

EPISTLE: I Corinthians 13. So in the Sarum and Roman missals.

The unity of Gospel and Epistle appears to be deliberate, both looking forward to the Lenten season now so close at hand. "Behold, we go up to Jerusalem," to a time of penitence and searching of heart, praying that our blinded eyes may be opened. Yet it is a time of *Christian* penitence in which we have only a single aim, that our recovered sight may be more closely fixed on the ideal of love.

## THE GOSPEL

The choice of this entire passage may have been due originally only to the feeling that verses 31–34 by themselves were too short,

[1] James S. Stewart, in *A Man in Christ*, pp. 7, 8.

although there is a real connection between the blindness of the disciples and that of Bartimæus. None the less, the first four verses will probably be found ample by most expositors. Men hold persistently that the way to success must be through "successes," and to the higher values that Christ saw in the cross they are blind. To learn the truth is often a fearful trial for His disciples, yet sooner or later they come to realize that He was right.

Critically the passage is taken from Mark 10:32–34, somewhat edited and perhaps supplemented from a special source. In both Mark and Luke (verses 32–34) the details of the Passion have been added after the event, for no disciples, no matter how stupid, could possibly misunderstand so precise a prediction. Perhaps the historic form consisted only of verse 31, or it may be even better preserved in 12:49–50.

Historically Jesus' choice of the road to Jerusalem was deliberate. Although Galilee had become unsafe for Him, He could have lived and taught without interference in Philip's domains (3:1) or outside of Palestine. But to do this would be a renunciation of duty. His mission was to the Jews and the Jews must make the final decision, even though He knew in advance what that decision would be (13:33–35: compare on Palm Sunday).

Verse 32. The Gentiles' share in the Passion appears for the first time, while the Jews' responsibility retires behind "delivered." It is well to bring out this point, as attributing the crucifixion solely to the Jews has stimulated anti-Semitism and has sometimes led to barbarous "reprisals."

Verse 34. The disciples' inability to understand is stated with extreme emphasis; Luke impresses the lesson on his readers.

Verses 24–43 are from Mark 10:46–52, the variations being insignificant. Historically the section has special value through the fact that Jesus, now face to face with death, does not rebuke the blind man for hailing Him as "Son of David." This is the only instance in Luke of "Son of David" as a title for Christ. Its only meaning can be "Messiah," for descendants of David had no power to work miracles because of their ancestry. The Messianic secret is now so near public revelation that one voice more or less no longer matters. How Bartimæus acquired his belief we do not know, nor do we know the nature of his blindness; all we are told is that his faith was strong enough to heal it.

Verse 42. In "saved" Luke doubtless saw more than physical healing; cf. 7:50, 8:48, 17:19. Gregory the Great comments nobly upon the concentration of the petition "that I may receive my sight." "Non falsas divitias, non terrena dona, non fugitivos honores a Domino, sed *lucem* quæramus."

SERMON THEME: Christ determines to go up to Jerusalem, knowing what awaits Him, because His mission requires that His people be given the opportunity to accept or to reject Him.

The sermon should be expository of Christ's purpose in making this decision. It was the willing choice of hardship and deadly danger in the way of duty. He could have carried on His work outside of Jerusalem and no one would have interfered with Him—nor should we ever have heard of Him! As a prophet He taught the word of God, but as Messiah He was the one whom God had appointed to bring in the kingdom: the Messiah not only teaches but does something; Messiah and kingdom are absolute correlatives. The moral teachings of Jesus are not the primary power of Christianity; the pull which brings men back to God is the Redeemer's death, which He regarded as filling an essential purpose in God's plan. There is very definite Atonement theology here.

## THE EPISTLE

The great obstacle to real understanding of this celestial chapter is an over-familiarity that contents itself with superficial sentimentalities; Bishop Christopher Wordsworth's familiar hymn, "Gracious Spirit, Holy Ghost," has had a particularly unfortunate influence in this regard. The expositor must therefore emphasize unsparingly that Saint Paul does not say one word about love as an emotion but centres everything on love as a motive. It is not how love feels but what love does that counts.

Yet it is equally true that, externally, almost everything that love can do can also be done through less worthy motives. Love of God may lead to ecstasy ("tongues"), but so may sheer emotionalism (verse 1). Love of God should bring deepened knowledge and spiritual power, but pure intellectual curiosity may also bring real knowledge, while savage medicine men may possess inexplicable gifts of wonder-working (verse 2). Love of God of necessity makes us ready for self-sacrifice, but a passion for notoriety may lead to reckless giving or even to fanatical self-immolation (verse 3), as every psychologist knows today. How then can we distinguish? Verses 4–7 give the answer in unmistakable terms: the motive for an act must be unselfish: these verses, in fact, are simply a rejection of selfishness in its manifold forms.

The rhetorical arrangement is worth study: after two positive statements there follow seven negations, then (verse 6) a negative and a positive clause in parallelism, the whole being closed with three positive declarations. "Doth not behave itself unseemly" is rather more than "is not guilty of discourtesy": the Apostle is thinking, e.g., of "speakers with tongues" who exercise their gift to the disturbance and discomfort of others. "Seeketh not her own": i.e., "her own advantage." The King James "thinketh no evil" in the Revised Version becomes "taketh not account of evil," the sense being "does not cherish a list of other peoples' misdeeds"; a common failing. Verse 6 carries on the same thought, "is not glad to detect faults in others but rejoices at their virtues." In verse 7 for "beareth" the "covereth" of the Revised Version margin is preferable; "love avoids making injuries public." (The reference of course is to personal injuries and does not contemplate a "hush, hush" policy when honesty demands exposure of wrongdoing.)

Verses 8–13 return to the concrete question raised in chapter 12,

"What is the most desirable spiritual gift?" And the answer is, "The gift that is permanent." Men usually think of the "saint" as one endowed with supernatural inspiration or power—but in heaven these gifts have no place. Only children should love display (verse 11): adults should be more wise. The enduring gifts are those that are not ostentatious, faith, hope and love—and the greatest of these is love.

Does Saint Paul in verse 13 mean that not only love but faith and hope will last on in heaven? The contrast of "abideth" here with "shall be done away" in verses 8–10 certainly supports the possibility. And such an interpretation may be defensible. Even though we "know as we are known," yet we shall continue finite and cannot know everything, so that there may still be room for faith. And, if the heavenly state is one of progress, hope may look forward to fuller and fuller life. Yet all this may be overliteral and certainly goes beyond the text.

SERMON THEME: Love, not as an emotion but as a motive for conduct, is the most desirable spiritual gift, and the Christian must aim to make progress in it.

The Epistle is itself the sermon; all that is necessary is to bring it out in modern terms. Prophecy is better than the gift of tongues because it has social value. The gift of tongues was an ecstatic experience: "Groanings that cannot be made intelligible." In the ancient world the gift was prized to an extraordinary degree: the more unintelligible the sounds uttered in ecstasy, the more spiritual they were thought to be, as it was believed that human intelligence was superseded by the divine. The point to be made by the preacher is that mystic gifts and virtues, like everything else, have to be Christianized. In themselves ecstatic experiences have no moral significance: they are found in fullest fruition in lowest types of religion, such as those of degraded South African tribes.

It is sometimes asked whether by "love" Saint Paul means chiefly "love of God" or "love of man." The question is meaningless, for the love he describes is the Christian fruit of the Holy Spirit, in which the love of God and the love of man are inseparable, for both are our response to God's love for us.

The application to the approaching season of Lent is obvious: "if you want to make your Lent profitable, plan to come out at the end of it with greater patience and affection for other people."

# LENT

THE GROWTH of a penitential preparation for Easter from a single day in the second century to nine full weeks (including pre-Lent) in the eighth is revelatory of the change of the ethos of Christian worship from joy in redemption to fear of perdition. But since the Reformation a counterchange, in practice if not in the liturgy, has taken place in the Roman Catholic Church by a radical relaxation of the Lenten rules; nowadays only the more devout among the laity make much attempt at Lenten observance. And in the contemporary Anglican Communion there is a similar mitigation of the strict Lenten practices that came in with the nineteenth-century liturgical revival; the Anglican Church thus agreeing with the Roman Catholic that the mediæval rigour was a mistake.

Lent, consequently, will generally be viewed as a season of special spiritual opportunity rather than as a penitential period in the older sense. But some continuity with the past can be retained by regarding this opportunity particularly as one for seeking out the hindrances and obstacles to spiritual progress. The Lenten Epistles and Gospels are admirably suited to this purpose; they emphasize at the beginning the need of effort and at the end effort's greatest incentive, Christ's death as the cost of sin; while between the two periods Lent 4 gives a welcome break of "refreshment."

## THE FIRST SUNDAY IN LENT

### LITURGICAL NOTES

GOSPEL: Matthew 4:1–11. So in the Sarum and Roman missals; a seventh-century and almost universal Western Gospel.

EPISTLE: II Corinthians 6:1–10. So the Sarum and Roman missals. Also seventh century.

The Gospel must have been appointed even before the seventh century, during the period (from the late fifth to the late sixth century?) when Lent began on this day. The Epistle was presumably chosen at the same time on account of verses 4–7 and (especially) verse 2*b*. Liturgical unity is therefore deliberate.

## THE GOSPEL

Compare Luke 4:1–13. Luke's order for the three temptations is better and is followed below.

Divested of its imagery the Temptation story may be retold as follows. At John's baptism Jesus received His call to Messiahship. It came to Him as an overwhelming experience in which the sudden inrush of the Spirit and the Father's voice (compare on Epiphany 2) seemed actually visible and audible. So He emerged from the baptismal waters in ecstasy, moved to the depths of being by the realization "I am Messiah." To grasp the implications of so shattering a vocation solitude was imperative, and He sought it at once in the wilderness. (Compare Mark 1:12, the spirit *driveth* Him into the wilderness.)

What must God's Messiah do? All the popular religious expectation of the day had an immediate answer: the Messiah must manifest Himself as a wonder-worker, confirming his authority with marvellous miracles. And: the Messiah is the Captain appointed by the God of Battles, leading Israel's armies to victory over the hosts of the Gentiles, and reigning over the world as the triumphant conqueror. These expectations, all the more poignant because they were soundly based on Old Testament teaching, formed the first two temptations, which were resisted by Jesus as unworthy of the Representative of the God whom He knew. The third was to ask "Is this 'call' I have experienced really to be trusted? Am I actually Messiah at all? May I not put God's message to the test by a reckless experiment?"

In more detail: Verses 1–2 describe a period (the "forty days" are of course conventional) of exaltation ("full of the Spirit") in which care for the body was ignored. The inevitable reaction brought a corresponding depression and perplexity, while an overtaxed nature cried out for food. Verse 3: "As I am God's Messiah, I can work all miracles, and so can satisfy my hunger here and now." Verse 4: God's ordinary providence is always sufficient to give men what they truly need; to demand a miracle from Him would be to question His goodness (compare Matthew 6:25–34, especially verse 33). Verses 8–10 hardly need explanation. No doubt the Messiah must rule the world, but God's rule cannot be established by an appeal to men's instincts for war. About verses 5–7 there is difference of opinion. Frequently they are taken as a proposal to convert the nation by an irresistible display of divine power, and this interpretation can no doubt be made practically fruitful: God never forces men's consciences. But the text says nothing about the effect of the miracle on other persons; hence the sense adopted above is better. Nearly every one who is conscious of a call to special service is tempted to test it in some self-devised fashion.

In any case the Temptation story is an account of Jesus' refusal to compromise with the highest possible ideals. On God's road there are no short-cuts.

The simple directness of the spiritual lessons in this section and their perfect accord with Jesus' teaching as a whole and particularly with the actual fulfillment of His Messiahship make exceedingly difficult any hypothesis of origin other than from Jesus Himself. The story was probably told by Him, in conjunction with that of the baptismal experience, in the last part of the Ministry. The perfect naturalness of the narrative is inimitable; exaltation on discovery of the Messianic vocation, retreat into solitude without a thought of care for the body, waning of the ecstasy, and resultant hunger and depression, which gave a fit moment for the intrusion of diabolic suggestion. And the temptations exactly summarize the Ministry. They exhibit the refusal to take thought of self, or to accede to demands for a sign, or to seek popularity through lowering the moral standard. The Temptation story may be received as a fragment of autobiography of inestimable interest and significance, deeply embedded in the oldest part of the New Testament record (its source is the Sayings), and faithfully transmitted by those who received it from their Lord.

SERMON THEME: Christ meets and overcomes the temptation to be the Messiah of popular expectation and accepts instead God's call.

(1) The first temptation arises directly out of the physical situation. Christ externalizes an internal experience: "If I am Messiah, I can relieve My hunger." He had been taught that the Messiah would be a miracle-worker like Moses, who had confounded the Egyptian magicians by surpassing their magic (Exodus 7:8-10); brought water from the rock (Exodus 17:6); and wrought many similar wonders. (Note that belief in magic is characteristic of primitive religion.) Christ regarded the desire to work such a miracle as an indictment of the way in which God has ordered the world. "Every word that proceedeth out of the mouth of God" (verse 4) means all God's laws. To turn stones into bread is not part of God's plan: there is something blasphemous in the suggestion. Having received the Spirit, Christ now experienced its guidance: being Messiah did not mean being a miracle-worker. Being Messiah meant being the Son of God, and being God's Son meant trusting the Father's love, the Father's care, the Father's providence as expressed in the natural order of the world which the Father Himself had given. (Compare Matthew 6:24-34, and note the implications with respect to prayer.)

How little many of the first Christians understood the mind of Christ in this matter! Being Jews, they wished to see their Messiah in the part which He disclaimed, as a wonder-worker, a second and greater Moses, one who could and would and did turn stones into bread. And their wishful thinking coloured to some extent their account of what He said and did: *e.g.*, the shekel in the mouth of a fish (Matthew 17:27), the cursing of the fig tree (Mark 11:21). But the fact remains that Christ Himself, when asked for a sign from heaven, such a sign as Moses was supposed to have given Pharaoh in the plagues of Egypt, replied with indignation, "This generation is an evil generation: it seeketh after a sign; and there shall no sign be given to it but the sign of Jonah" (*i.e.*, the *preaching* of Jonah, Luke 11:32).

3. (2) Popular expectation demanded that the Messiah should be not only a second Moses but also a second David, a military conqueror. Milton in *Paradise Regained* described with historic accuracy the meaning of this second temptation:

> Victorious deeds flamed in thy heart, heroic acts—one while
> To rescue Israel from the Roman yoke,
> Men to subdue, and quell o'er all the earth
> Brute violence and proud tyrannic power.

In the Old Testament there is no suggestion that war waged for so good a purpose as this would be wrong; and in Catholic theology it would probably meet the requirements of a "just" war. Christ Himself is responsible for the conviction now slowly forming throughout the church that war is incompatible with His teachings and gospel. He was expected to drive out the Roman invader, to reign in Jerusalem, and from Jerusalem to conquer the world for God. He knew that if He appeared in this rôle, all Israel would rally to Him with fanatical devotion. He knew also that if He refused this rôle of military conqueror which was thrust upon Him, His own end was certain. He would be despised and rejected by a disappointed people, and would suffer the vengeance of their disappointment. Here was the paradox: (*a*) His certainty of Messiahship; (*b*) His certainty of approaching death. In Jewish thought the two were irreconcilable: a crucified Messiah was a contradiction in terms. But in Jesus the stream of Messianic consciousness rises and overflows the obstacle of impending death, and in the wilderness, with the shadow of Calvary already across His pathway, He repels the second temptation and in so doing chooses martyrdom.

The temptation to bring in the kingdom of God by coercive measures exerts its greatest pressure upon the young. It is the young who today are leaders in the communist movement, the fascist movement, the nazi movement, and most of the coercive measures of our time which so terribly endanger all civil and religious liberty. Youth is eager, impetuous, ardent, idealistic, and forever tempted to use short cuts in order to obtain its objectives. It is prone to believe that only by coercive measures can it establish the better social order the vision of which has set it on fire. The Jesus of history, the Jesus of the first century, was young too. He knew the power of this temptation; He also knew its diabolic origin. We can all but hear the "young Prince of glory" crying with anguished intensity, "Get thee hence, Satan!"

2. (3) The third temptation is more obscure. Renan's suggestion that it was a temptation to suicide originating in the reaction from elation to profound depression may be dismissed as preposterous: the man whose sanity is the standard by which mental health may be judged, the one completely normal man who has appeared in the course of universal history, was not a manic depressive! Doubtless there was in His mind a recollection of having been in the Temple, stood upon its towers, possibly felt there the instinctive impulsive to jump off which most persons experience when standing on high places; in which case the recollection now brought the temptation to go back and give the sign from heaven which would dazzle and convince all Israel—a variant of the first temptation. Or, more probably, this was the supreme temptation of the three: to doubt the Messianic vocation itself and to put it to a test. This He refuses to do. Magic is again repudiated: how tragic the misunderstanding of the mind of Christ that ever made wonder

miracles part of the Christian apologetic! Knowledge of vocation is not to be determined by "signs," such as that of opening the Bible at random, placing the finger on a text, and finding thereby a divine guiding. God gives us reason and conscience, and the guiding of His Spirit: by these we are to determine our vocation even as Christ did in the wilderness.

## THE EPISTLE

The relation of this section to that used on Sexagesima is unmistakable; it is explained best by the hypothesis—now very generally accepted—that chapters 10-13 of II Corinthians were written before chapters 1-9. So what is there told for the first time in a fiery polemic is repeated here as a comparatively gentle reproach to the readers for their lack of affection. Exegetically the section is a highly personal appeal from a much-enduring Christian leader: "When you remember what I have suffered for Christ's sake are you not ashamed of your neglect of what I taught you?" A direct transfer of this appeal from the Apostle to the expositor is, naturally, legitimate only in very exceptional cases, but the values can be not only preserved but greatly heightened by applying verses 4-10 to the long prospect of Christian leaders by whom the faith has been spread and preserved.

Verses 1-2 are properly a missionary appeal to the unconverted, but the wavering attitude of the readers made it once more appropriate. Such renewed elementary exhortations are frequently required everywhere—compare the revivals and "great awakenings" of a former day—but they are especially adapted to the beginning of Lent; so giving a peculiar emphasis to the "now" in verse 2. In verse 1 "the grace of God" is the opportunity of salvation (verse 2) divinely extended.

The rhetorical construction of verses 1-3 is so harsh that some commentators suspect that something has been dropped out of the text, while others speak of an abrupt change of theme. But in any case the subject of "giving" in verse 3 is St. Paul, not the readers; the grammatical agreement is with "we" in verse 1. For verses 4–6 compare on Sexagesima. Verse 7*b*: "holding a sword in the right hand, a shield with the left"; "armour" is an impossible translation (compare on Advent 1). "By" in this verse—not the same Greek word as that used in verses 4–6—expresses not the means but the situation: "with" is a better rendering. In verse 8 "amid" would be clearer. The two contrasts in verse 8*a* introduce a striking list of seven paradoxes in verses 8*b*–10, in which men's judgments are contrasted with God's. "Chastened" is much too weak a word; "viciously punished" by scourgings under which men often die.

SERMON THEME: In the service of Christ earthly trials and rewards are unimportant: it is the service alone that counts.

The section is ideal for an *ad clerum* address, or for an ordination sermon: if this use is made of it, consult Henry Newbolt's *Speculum Sacerdotum,* which is a classic treatment from this viewpoint. But if used for a pre-Lenten meditation, the section should be cut down to the first two verses and made textual rather than expository, as the remainder is for the most part entirely irrelevant to Lent. It is not the ordinary life of the Christian which is described, but the devotion of the greatest of the Apostles.

# THE SECOND SUNDAY IN LENT

## LITURGICAL NOTES

GOSPEL: Matthew 15:21–28. So the Sarum missal. It is used in the Roman missal for the first Thursday in Lent; for the Sunday Gospel compare below.

EPISTLE: I Thessalonians 4:1–8; the Sarum and Roman sections end with verse 7.

Originally the service for the preceding day (Ember Saturday) was a vigil, terminating with the eucharist after midnight. So no further eucharist was held on this Sunday, which the Gregorian sacramentary, *e.g.,* describes as "vacant." And even the present Roman missal still lacks a special Gospel, the one printed (Matthew 17:1–9) being really only the Saturday Gospel repeated. The Western lectionaries differ greatly, but the Sarum Gospel appears as an alternative in Carolingian lists.

Both Gospel and Epistle appear to have been chosen to parallel those for Lent 3; compare the note there.

## THE GOSPEL

In this Gospel the problem of demoniac possession and the exorcisms appears. The first-century Jews, like the ancient world generally, divided diseases into two sharply distinguished classes (Mark 1:32–34), those produced by evil spirits and those due to other causes, a division corresponding fairly well to the modern popular distinction between "mental" and "physical" ailments. In the former a demon was supposed to have obtained control of the mind and body of the sufferer, so that every word and act came from the demon and not the man. If the demon could be expelled by exorcism a cure would follow, otherwise the evil spirit would end by slaying his victim (Mark 9:22).

The conception was wholly without moral content; this cannot be too strongly emphasized. Or, to put it differently, the belief in its primitive origin is medical rather than religious. To be possessed by a demon was not the result of sin but was a misfortune that might happen to any one. Christian moralizings on mental degradation due to persistent evil living are beside the mark; in particular the mediæval theory—probably responsible for our present collect—that made possession specifically due to impurity. To the world of the New Testament a mental affliction was due to the powers of evil; and this was all there was to it.

That Jesus, in this, as elsewhere, shared the scientific concepts of His age cannot be doubted. Like His contemporaries He distinguished rigidly between the "sick" and the "demoniacs." His attitude toward the former class has been discussed on Epiphany 4, and it is very different from that taken toward the other. To Him sickness lay outside the immediate problems of His work; He avoided excessive demands for cures, normally enjoined silence about them, and used His healing power only indirectly as evidence for His authority. In the exorcisms, on the contrary, the injunctions to silence do not occur; indeed, the healed demoniac of Mark 5:19 is told to publish his release abroad. And in the very oldest Gospel source (Luke 11:20 = Matthew 12:28: compare on Lent 3) He cites His successful exorcisms as a vital proof for His message. That is, while sickness is only indirectly evil, demoniac control is wholly Satanic and must be attacked on every possible occasion.

It is of course impossible to transfer this estimate directly from the first century into the twentieth; much mental aberration, for instance, is due to causes that are merely physical. Yet the first-century belief embodied a genuine element of permanent truth. We of today are learning abundantly that the minds of only too many men and women are truly possessed by "demons" who must be "exorcised." In the commonest types of improper mental co-ordination, the neuroses and psychoses, no corresponding physical disturbance can be detected. The mind of the patient has become dominated by unreality—usually in the form of fears—which it is the psychiatrist's task to detect and expel. And in the expulsion the creation of a wholesome religious faith is of the very greatest value; in a heart really assured of God's Fatherhood the insidious demons called "phobias" cannot lurk.

So a healthy mind that is fixed on God need never dread disturbance of this sort. True religion is a perfect prophylaxis against such unbalance. It is naturally only under unusual conditions that a clergyman should be called on to treat a mental disorder, but it is his unceasing duty to guard against its occurrence by setting before his people perpetually what Christ is and what He does for the soul. In this way Jesus is, now as ever, the victorious conqueror of demons.

Matthew 15:21-28 is a revision of Mark 7:24-30, and the First Evangelist's only significant alteration is to accent the woman's faith by making it withstand three rebuffs. As a whole the story is modelled extraordinarily like the Gospel for Epiphany 4; a Gentile approaches the Messiah of the Jews and wins His help by steadfast faith. Real difference in treatment, in consequence, is hardly possible. The distinctive element here is the contrast between the "dogs" and the "children"; this distinction in itself is no longer of interest but it can be used as a starting point for a study of the value of humility. As an illustration of the value of persistence compare Luke 11:5ff; 18:1ff.

SERMON THEME: The mission of Christ was primarily to the Jews, but from the first its universal implications were shown in His response to faith.

The motive which led to the insertion of this Gospel was to show Christ's approval of Gentile missions, which were "foreign missions." It is a very interesting passage as showing the Evangelists' reverence for their material. They do not rewrite, even when it does not give them just what they want: here, for instance, the story leaves the impression that true Christianity is Jewish Christianity and that Gentiles come in for "uncovenanted mercies." The mission of Christ was to "the lost sheep of the House of Israel"; so be it: the Syro-Phœnician woman accepts the fact. But in every divinely appointed mission there is an overplus of grace, crumbs from the Master's table, wheat for gleaners after the reapers have done their work; for this she asks, and this in response to her faith she receives.

Historically, Christ did regard His mission as to the House of Israel. A Messiah who would treat Old Testament prophecies with disdain would have been an historical monstrosity. The Messiah is first of all the Saviour of the Jewish nation, the people of the covenant. It is from the Jews that Christianity should have proceeded; they had the unique opportunity of religious history and threw it away, defeating Christ's purpose to utilize the religious possibilities of Israel. But the ultimate purpose, to bring in the Realm of God, was not thereby defeated. The Syro-Phœnician woman, the outsider who nevertheless displayed religious faith, is the type of the Gentile world which was ready to accept what Israel had rejected. Faith, covenanted or uncovenanted, is rewarded at once.

This self-limitation of Christ's mission is significant. His gospel is universal. His salvation is for all mankind. And yet as the Messiah He Himself limits it at the outset to His own race. But it must be remembered that His was an *historic* mission, that the time was short, the place circumscribed. He was not called to preach the gospel to the Gentiles; that would be the task of His apostle Paul. His mission was to His own countrymen, in order that through them the Gentile world might be converted and saved.

This aspect of Christ's earthly life has a definite meaning for Christians today. It suggests that racial consciousness is a right thing, and a fruitful thing, provided that it is inspired by the realization of mission, vocation, beneficently related to the Realm of God in its universal aspect. The life of every race and nation, like the life of every individual, is a plan of God who made them different for His own purpose, and His purpose is fulfilled when universal brotherhood is sought through race and nation, not apart from them. There cannot be internationalism without nations. The bearing upon the work of foreign missions, to make Christianity indigenous is evident. See R. E. Speer's *Christianity and the Nations.*

In this story the miracle is incidental and taken for granted: what is important here is the mission of our Lord, not His ability to cast out demons. Discussion of the latter topic should be postponed until Lent 3, unless it is used as an illustration of the nature of His mission.

## THE EPISTLE

The standard English versions—the Revised Version even more definitely than the King James—take the whole section as a warning against impurity, in accord with an expository tradition reaching back into the Patristic age. Then the "matter" in verse 6 is a euphemism for "sex relations" and the verse is a warning against adultery; so "vessel" in verse 4 would probably mean "wife," a sense supported by some Jewish (not Greek) evidence. But this interpretation is unsatisfactory. Adultery, which is one of the gravest sins, would scarcely be treated in so incidental a fashion. Nor would it be regarded as a common temptation, particularly in this congregation with which Saint Paul is so well pleased.

It is consequently much preferable to limit the warning against impurity to verses 3–5, giving to "vessel" the more natural sense of "body." "Matter" in verse 6 may then be taken as "quarrel," as in I Corinthians 6:1. In any case "uncleanness" in verse 7 is too narrow a rendition of a Greek word that means "sinfulness" quite generally.

Neither of these exegetical alternatives presents any real expository difficulties. But the expositor must remember that "sanctification" in verse 3 is God's act, not ours.

SERMON THEME: The Christian must learn to direct his instincts in holiness and honour.

For practical suggestions, consult books on psychology written from a viewpoint sympathetic with religion and note especially what is said on "sublimation." "It is not enough to condemn sex aberration, selfishness, or the sins committed under the impulse to win a place in one's group, as wicked; we must go farther to help the unfortunate to understand what has happened; and then, by instilling unquestioned ideals help them to cultivate the psychological functions through which we grow up. Instincts need control and direction in the interests of the personality as a whole."[1]

Note especially that God, who has called us "unto holiness," has "also given unto us His holy Spirit"; our part is so to order our lives that the work of the Spirit in them be not hindered.

# THE THIRD SUNDAY IN LENT

## LITURGICAL NOTES

GOSPEL: Luke 11:14–28. So the Sarum and Roman missals.

EPISTLE: Ephesians 5:1–14; a Reformation lengthening of the Sarum and Roman section ending with verse 9.

This Gospel and Epistle were selected to prepare for the baptismal "scrutiny" which in the sixth century was fixed for the following Wednesday; in earlier days it was held a week later. On this day such catechumens as were deemed worthy of baptism on Easter Eve were segregated from the others, and were brought into church for the first of the exorcisms that continued daily until baptism was administered. Exorcism, consequently, is the direct theme of the Gospel, while the Epistle sets forth the transformation of life that baptism must entail.

In the present Roman missal the mass for the Wednesday before Passion Sunday is still the old scrutiny service of the fifth century, although the day was later changed to the week before, while the scrutiny itself has been discontinued for something like a thousand years. The collect, secret and postcommunion, however, are still older and are not concerned with the scrutiny.

## THE GOSPEL

Verses 14–26 (= Matthew 12:22–30, 43–35) are from the Sayings source. Verses 27–28 are peculiar to Luke; they may or may not be a milder version of 8:19–21 (from Mark 3:31–35).

[1] J. G. Mackenzie, *Souls in the Making*, p. 122.

Verse 20 (Matthew 12:28) is the essential saying in this section. That in Jesus there was revealed to men a sinless being was only the beginning. In Him there was revealed a goodness the essence of which, like God's, is activity, a power which gives life to dead souls. In kind, no doubt, this activity was not unique. Others than Jesus had—and have—real success in "casting out demons," for God has never left Himself without witness. But wholly unique was the degree to which this power was present in Jesus; so extraordinarily so as to prove that through Him a new supernatural force was among mankind: the long-awaited kingdom of God was *there* ("is in contact with you").

This is the central fact in Christianity. In Jesus Christ the truth about God is revealed. But there is more. By contact with Him we are given the strength that makes it possible to follow the truth, the strength that drives out the demons of fear and selfishness. They cannot resist the power of Him who came that we might have life and have it abundantly.

The introductory verses 14–19 (except verse 16 which prepares for verses 29–36 and should be omitted) are the reply to those who refused to recognize goodness when it threatened to disturb their prejudices. Difficulty is offered only by verse 19, which is an appeal to "expert testimony": "Among you are those ('your sons') who succeed now and then in banishing demons; ask them if this can be done by Beelzebub!" The frightful lengths to which Christ's enemies carried their malice—"*Jesus* is possessed by Satan!"—would be incredible did we not constantly meet modern examples of the bigoted hatred that can fill professedly religious men.

The little parable in verses 21–22 emphasizes verse 20. The "strong man armed" corresponds to Satan and the "stronger than he" to Christ or (perhaps) the Kingdom. But the details must not be allegorized further.

Verse 23 carries on the thought of verses 21–22: no one can treat the conflict between good and evil as indifferent to him: here is no room for spectators for all are actors and not to choose the good is itself a contrary choice. So understood, the old controversy about the relation of this verse to 9:50 (=Mark 9:40) is not worth reviving; the latter passage does not deal with the inner attitude at all but with external conduct. From the critical standpoint verse 23 is rather out of place in this context, however, for the adversaries of verses 15–16 had no thought of neutrality.

Verses 24–26 are a parable told in extremely popular terms, and on the surface relating only to a fact of common observation: mania, after an interval of quiescence, often bursts out with extraordinary fury. If a connection with verse 23 is to be established the vacant house must represent the soul of a man who has turned from sin but suspends his judgment about Christ. This seems to narrow it unduly, however, and these verses are best treated independently, to teach the familiar lesson that a superficial reformation may be worse than none at all. Expositors since time immemorial have pointed out the fatal mistake in leaving the spiritual house "empty"; if Christ had been welcomed in the demon would not have dared to return. This is scarcely in the text, but is a legitimate enough homiletical application.

That demons fear water, will not cross a stream, etc., is a common belief among primitive people.

To weld all of verses 14–26 into a unified exposition is difficult, but to add to this the unrelated further verses 27–28 is practically impossible. The expositor, in consequence, had best divide the section into three parts to be taken separately: verses 14–23, 24–26 and 27–28. For the last the theme is obvious, "My kingdom is not of this world!" The kingdom of God takes precedence of even the most intimate earthly relationships. The words do not necessarily contain a reflection upon the character of Christ's mother: she was herself one of the blessed ones who "hear the word of God, and keep it." Yet there may be a hint here of temporary alienation. Even Christ's mother did not understand His Messiahship.

SERMON THEME: From the person of Christ radiates a force that expels "demons" of mental and spiritual disorder, and contact with Him gives life and health.

For the problem of demoniacal possession see on Lent 2. Being true man, the Jesus of history shared the scientific concepts of His age. He distinguished sharply between those who were sick merely in body, and those who were sick in mind and soul; He regarded the latter as possessed of demons, and He drove the evil spirits out of them in the name of God and of God's kingdom. He uses His success here as a very definite "sign," but a moral sign of a moral thing. His success in curing sick souls is a sign that a moral power is at work.

This power is still at work. The psychiatrist of today does not, of course, accept the theory of possession as he explores the depths of disordered personality. Yet he does find repressions, he finds complexes, he finds obsessing ideas, he finds what he terms maniacal monoideism, prolonged fixed attention upon one idea, with resulting mental disorder. Anti-Semitism provides an illustration. In times of great strain and tension, disorders born of fear are bound to occur. Whatever their cause is, the cure for them is exactly what it was in the first century, contact with the life-giving, fear-dispelling goodness of Christ and His religion.

Not all mental diseases are moral inflictions, but some are. We speak quite naturally of slaves of drink, of drugs, or of forms of sexual perversion; we say of a man that he is insane with jealousy or beside himself with anger. This is bringing the "demons" back with twentieth-century names. Christ Himself first gave them their true names. "From within, out of the hearts of men, proceed evil thoughts, adulteries, fornications, murders, thefts, covetousness, wickedness." Psychology reveals that there is in the unconscious something of the sub-human, something of the bestial, Tennyson's "ape and tiger"—and he might have added the donkey! In mental disorders the unconscious casts up something of its sub-human content and presents the appearance of demoniacal possession.

The cure is the same as of old. It comes from Him who with the finger of God casts out "demons." To know Him is to find safety from our own baser selves. To follow Him is to make life positive and noble and sane. To be in contact with Him through sacrament and prayer is to build up an integrated personality. This in turn will manifest His creative life, and drive "demons" out of other men. And so we come close to what is the very heart of the Christian religion, the religion of spiritual power derived from Christ.

## THE EPISTLE

Verses 1–2 are properly the conclusion of the appeal in 4:25–32. They are not well adapted as an introduction to verses 3–14, although "walk in love" can suggest the perversions and debasements of love treated in what follows. But the pair of verses taken by themselves are admirable: note the bold "imitation of God" as in Matthew 5:45, where the apostolic writers are usually content with "imitation of Christ."

Verses 3–14 are a warning against impurity and particularly against the specious excuses urged in defense of moral laxity.

A slight incongruity in verses 3–5 needs explanation. To the Jew the primary triad of Gentile vices was "impurity, covetousness and idolatry," and so closely were these associated that to name any of them inevitably suggested the other two. Hence the appearance of "covetousness" in verses 3 and 5 and of "idolatry" (compare Colossians 3:5) in verse 5, where they are really out of place ("covetousness" is not a sin that "ought not to be named," like sexual vices). Exegetical attempts to justify their presence—e.g., that "covetousness which is idolatry" means prostitution for pay, such as was practised in the Venus cult—are over-complicated.

The English versions obscure the argument in verses 11 and 13 by translating as "reprove" a verb that means "expose," carrying on the thought in "light." The source of the quotation in verse 14 is not known (Isaiah 60:1 is out of the question), but it may well be an early baptismal hymn. In Clement of Alexandria (Protrep. ix, 84) the same citation is continued:

> The Sun of the resurrection,
> Rising ere the morning-star,
> Bestowing life with its beams.

Sermon Theme: Purity is one of the fruits of the Spirit; a Christian life draws from God strength which enables it to walk in the light.

Excuses for impurity always leave the conscience uneasy. No matter how much sexual indulgence may be palliated, men know perfectly well that such things cannot endure the light, that despite all pretence they are and must remain "unfruitful works of darkness." A wholesome life contains nothing that it seeks to hide; a Christian life draws from God strength which enables it to walk in the light.

"Reprove" should be "expose"; if we can bring the light on evil things, men will stop doing them. This is psychologically sound. Psychiatrists emphasize the "talk cure" and the importance of bringing things out into the open. It is even more important to show that deterministic conceptions are disappearing in science and to make men realize that they are not determined by their past mental states but that a new faith may set them free. Illustrations may be drawn in abundance from Christian biography, showing "the expulsive power of a new affection." The vision of Christ upon the cross freed Raymond Lull in an instant from a guilty passion with which before he had been unable to cope. Harold Begbie, in *Twice-born Men,* gives modern instances of similar emancipation.

Pauline theology is implicit here: purity is not urged as a way to win salvation, but clearly recognized as one of the fruits of the Spirit which mark those who are "light in the Lord." "Let no man deceive you with vain words!"—the expositor need not hesitate to apply the warning to those deceived by the type of psychologist who advocates sexual laxity as a means of avoiding "repressions."

## THE FOURTH SUNDAY IN LENT

### LITURGICAL NOTES

Gospel: John 6:1-14. So the Sarum and (with verse 15) the Roman missals; a seventh-century Gospel. On this Sunday the Lenten fast was relaxed, and at Rome the Pope distributed bread to the poor; hence the choice of this section. The source of the custom is unknown, but conceivably it was originally a sort of pre-Lenten carnival in the period (fourth or early fifth century) when Lent began on the following day.

Epistle: Galatians 4:21-31, a slight Reformation change from the Sarum and Roman 4:22-5:1a. The section was chosen because on this Sunday the Roman station was at the Church of Holy-Cross-in-Jerusalem.

Although the Gospel and Epistle were chosen for wholly independent reasons, the heavenly food in the former and the heavenly destiny in the latter are themes that can be brought into a real unity. Jesus is the "bread of life," imparting and sustaining life eternal.

As titles for this day "Refreshment Sunday" is derived from the Gospel and "Mothering Sunday" from the Epistle (verse 26).

"Rose Sunday" comes from the fact that on this day the Pope blesses the "Golden Rose," a superlative honour to be sent to some Catholic prince. This rite is of sixteenth-century origin and has no liturgical significance.

### THE GOSPEL

The feeding of the 5000 is related by all the Gospels and that of the 4000 by Mark and Matthew as well. This popularity of the section is due to the great importance in early Christianity of the agape or "love-feast," which the believers (rightly) understood to be prefigured in these stories.

One significant purpose of these meals was charitable. Sometimes the food was provided by a single individual, sometimes all who were able brought what they could afford, but a large part of the company normally consisted of the very poor, whose needs were thus supplied. But a still deeper meaning was found in these feasts; each was the common act of a group whose social unity came from the Lord, in whose name the feast was held. Hence in the first century the agape was intimately associated with the eucharist, so much so that in the combined agape-eucharist *all* the food was conceived to have a supernatural quality. At each such meal Christ was present, and all that His disciples received they took from His invisible hands.

The lesson that the Evangelists found in these stories was consequently complex. Through Christ's power it is possible to care for those in want; it is possible even for a congregation whose resources do not seem to be more than five loaves and two fishes. In a community where the spirit of Christ's love really touches every heart no sufferer will go hungry and neglected. Sacrifices may be needed on the part of those who have anything to give, but in such sacrifices Christ feeds those who make them as well as those who profit from them; He feeds them all in a common unity where there is no distinction.

It should be noted that the Evangelists do not record the name of the donor or donors of the loaves and fish. It would never occur to first-century Christians that they deserved particular credit for their generosity; they took it for granted that any believer would be glad to do the same. Verses 10–13 are liturgical, describing the procedure at agapes; these details are given more fully in Mark 6:39-43.

Verse 13: "Not only through Christ's blessing were their efforts successful, the believers could rejoice in an overplus."

SERMON THEME: Jesus is the "bread of life," imparting and sustaining life eternal. Through His power it is possible even with scanty means to care for those in want by sharing.

Before attempting an exposition of the present Gospel, the preacher should summarize for his hearers the original moral of the passage, and particular attention should be called to its place in John as the introductory scene for the discourse on the Bread of Life, showing that the feeding has wider implications than satisfying physical hunger.

To the early disciples the "great multitude" were the poor of the church. Philip and Andrew represent the church authorities, almost in despair at the responsibility imposed upon them. Exposition may be strained somewhat, but homiletical treatment may distinguish between the "practical" Philip who is pessimistic because he overlooks the tiny available resources, and the inspired Andrew who notes the "five barley loaves, and two small fishes" which Christ can use. The moral is plain: if the power of Christ comes, we can manage; the trouble is not that we have not the money but that we have not been sufficiently touched with the spirit of Christ to give it up. Handled in this way the story means what the Evangelists meant it to mean; otherwise it becomes a mere wonder and portent story.

Basic in this story is the compassion of Christ, which is the origin and cause of all that happens. This compassion was characteristic of Him. He advised the well-to-do of His day to make feasts and call in—not other well-to-do people who could reciprocate their hospitality—but the poor and the maimed and the blind, the whole neighbourhood of needy folk. He repeated the (Jewish) story of Dives and Lazarus (compare on Trinity 1) to warn rich men that if they allow their fellowmen to starve on their doorsteps unregarded they themselves will one day awake and find themselves in hell. People sometimes speak of "mere philanthropy," yet philanthropy, though by no means the whole, is so essentially a part of Christ's religion that in His account of the Last Judgment our Lord makes it the criterion of judgment by which men's final destinies will be determined.

Note also the wider social implications. Hospitals and asylums for the aged and the homeless are found chiefly in Christian lands, or in lands that have been influenced by Christian example, and almost all modern institutions for the alleviation of human need were in the first instance sponsored by the church.

In applying the lesson the expositor will remember that although the agape has disappeared the essential feature of it, provision for those in the Christian community who are in material need, survives in the eucharist in the Communion alms. And the spirit of the agape will not be content today with almsgiving alone, but will press for solutions of the problem of poverty along the lines of a more humane, fraternal and equitable social order. Of course the application is not limited to the sharing of material goods. There are other possessions that may be even more important, such as sympathy, intellectual attainments, leisure time, etc. "Whoso seeth his brother hath need" is bound to share with his brother and so help to meet the need.

## THE EPISTLE

This section stands alone in Saint Paul's writings as a deliberate piece of virtuosity. It is a refutation of the Judaizers with their own exegetical weapons; he says, in effect, to his readers: "You like the allegories that they have been using: very well, I can allegorize too!"

The standard English versions of verse 25a are incomprehensible. If the clause is not a marginal note that has crept into the text, it must be translated " 'Hagar' is the name they give in Arabia to Mount Sinai" . . . an assertion for which there appears to be real evidence. This fact explains how the apostle comes to equate Hagar with the Law, and so with Jerusalem the centre of the Law's observance. "In bondage" means slavery to Rome. Possibly (not very probably) in verse 25 there may be a further allegorical equation, obtained by counting the numerical value of letters ("gematria"). The doctrine of the two Jerusalems in verses 25–26 (compare Hebrews 12:22; Revelation 21:10) had been developed in Jewish thought before the Christian era, and is conventional Jewish apocalyptic. In verse 27 the application of Isaiah 54:1 to the heavenly Jerusalem—approximately the original sense of the passage— is likewise pre-Christian. In verse 28 "ye" (not "we") is the correct reading. The "persecution" of Isaac by Ishmael in verse 29 is still another Jewish tradition: Abraham was supposed to have had to cast out Hagar because Ishmael tried to kill Isaac. The reason for the reference is that the Jews were causing trouble for the Christians; Saint Paul has in mind events like those described in I Thessalonians 2:14–16. Verse 30 cites Genesis 21:10 (compare Genesis 21:12, where God approves Sarah's request). "Wherefore" in verse 31 summarizes the whole.

Since Saint Paul nowhere else uses such elaborate allegory, it may be doubted if he himself took the method very seriously. But in any case the modern expositor cannot think of arguing that the old Testament passages have any such meaning as is here thrust upon them. Detailed exposition is accordingly out of place in a sermon, although it can be made very interesting in a classroom. So for homiletic treatment this section can be utilized only as the enshrinement of a general truth in terms that belong to a bygone era; modern practical concern is only with the truth, not with these terms.

SERMON THEME: Our relationship to God is one of sonship, not of bondage; it is not bound up with detailed observances of codes of rules.

In using the passage the preacher should begin by making it plain that it was written by Saint Paul deliberately as a *tour de force;* he has taken a method from his opponents to show that it can be just as easily reversed as work straight forward. "Which things are an allegory" means "can be allegorized," and when the allegorical method is used the Bible can be made to prove anything.

The method is ironic, but what Saint Paul seeks to prove is plain, and important for all time. The controversy was between religion as legalism and religion as a thing of the spirit. The Jews regarded the Law as necessary for full spiritual perfection. (For their historic reason in doing so, also for the revolt against legalism within Judaism itself, consult Lewis Browne's *Stranger Than Fiction*.) Saint Paul's reply is, "Full spiritual perfection is that of those in heaven where these laws do not hold. To exact them actually harms spiritual progress." To ceremonial practices by individuals, however, he had no objection in principle; his point is that neither observance nor mere non-observance has any merit: both are equally unimportant, for neither is the heart of Christianity. Most ecclesiastical controversies are concerned with matters that are in essence legalistic and not Christian. It was by following the track of Saint Paul's thought that Martin Luther led the Protestant Reformation, and by leaving it that Puritanism relapsed into the bondage of which "Blue laws" were the symbol.

## THE FIFTH SUNDAY IN LENT

### LITURGICAL NOTES

GOSPEL: John 8:46–59. So the Sarum and Roman missals; seventh century.

EPISTLE: Hebrews 9:11–15. So the Sarum and Roman missals; seventh century.

The actual title "Passion Sunday" ("Dominica de Passione") is first found in the Micrologus (late eleventh century), but over two centuries earlier Amalar of Metz (d. *ca.* 850) wrote "The days of the Lord's Passion are counted for the two weeks before Easter."

Possibly a reminiscence that the pre-Easter fast was originally in honour of Christ's Passion, not of His fast, may have been of influence.

"Passion Week," as a title for the following week, is a nineteenth-century Anglican innovation; the term properly means "Holy Week."

## THE GOSPEL

This section opens abruptly in the middle of an argument, and to understand the situation it is necessary to begin at least as far back as verse 31. As the Evangelist puts it, many Jews had believed in Christ but, when they learned that He would not recognize their nationalistic prerogatives, they turned against Him savagely. Saint John here describes a painful situation of his own day which of course had not arisen during the life-time of Jesus. Christianity had at first been under the control of Jewish believers, who felt that their Abrahamic descent privileged them to direct the church. But by the end of the first century the church not only rejected this claim but summoned the Jewish Christians to lay aside their nationalism. The result was apostasy; rather than give up their pride of race they turned back to their old beliefs and to historic Judaism which offered safety and privilege. Such apostates constituted a terrible danger to the church, for they knew who its leaders were and could—and did—denounce them to the Romans. Hence the bitterness of the passage. The Evangelist writes as a pastor, who has seen members of his flock taken to torture and death through the instigation of men who had rejected Christ after having once accepted Him; such men were actually "murderers."

This terrible experience is clothed in the form of the dialogue in this Gospel. Christ demands personal righteousness, to which the Jews reply that no legitimate Israelite needs anything. The case of such men is hopeless; for the man who knows he is a sinner, pardon is free, but for the man who gives thanks that he is not as others, pardon is not possible since he is not ready to accept it. So when Christ tells these men that their spiritual state is desperate, they see in His warnings only the ravings of a madman. They treat His appeals to His own character with contempt, while the further appeals to His supernatural authority goad them into insensate fury.

While the background of this controversy is late first-century, it really does summarize in miniature the historic controversy between Jesus and the Jewish leaders. Their conceptions of God were irreconcilable; the Father whom Jesus preached and the legalistic deity of His enemies had nothing in common. And when the Jewish leaders realized that behind Jesus' preaching there lay claims of supreme personal authority, they seized on these claims as an excuse to destroy Him.

By concentrating on the central theme the expositor can avoid distractions produced by the historical problems involved. Yet it is usually helpful to point out that the Christological terminology is that of Christian experience and not that of Jesus himself. And when it is taken as expressing the mind of the early church about Jesus, then the claims made so coldly explicit by John are found to be implicit in the Synoptic Gospels. Verse 51 needs but little verbal modification to convert it into Synoptic form. Verses 45, 46, 50, 54-55 merely translate into theological language the facts that His consciousness of the Father was really free from the impediments we call "sin" and that His devotion to His mission was genuinely devoid of selfishness.

Verses 56-58, however, advance beyond the possibilities of Messianism and state a theological conclusion: He who could truly claim apocalyptic Messiahship must belong by nature to the supernatural world. In verse 58 "I am" gathers past, present and future together in a single phrase, like Psalm 90:2; it contains no metaphysical reflection on the extratemporality of eternity.

What is least sympathetic in this section—and throughout the

Fourth Gospel—is the dualism that insists men are either wholly the children of God or wholly sons of the devil. Here the consciousness of the church at the end of the first century is speaking: the Christian communities were rigidly isolated from the pagan world about them. Within all was light, without all was darkness; there was no half-way. In the twentieth century this is no longer the case: much that is of Christian origin has influenced directly or indirectly the world outside the Christian community, while on the other hand the church itself has often been secularized by its closer contact with the world.

SERMON THEME: Spiritual blindness, due to spiritual self-satisfaction, is a fatal obstacle to the recognition of God in Christ.

In one respect the original setting of this Gospel is being reproduced in the history of our own times. Communism as the religion of class, Fascism as idolatrous exultation of the state, and Nazism as the religion of "blood and race" all tend to produce a fierce and exclusive pride which challenges the catholicity of the Christian religion. Already there is widespread apostasy in lands hitherto regarded as Christian, giving rise to betrayal and bitterness, and the stark and uncompromising oppositions depicted in the Gospel. Such oppositions are unavoidable, for no compromise is possible between the teachings of Christ and the claims of the totalitarian state. *Hora novissima, tempora pessima sunt; vigilemus.*

More generally, the theme of the Gospel is spiritual blindness due to spiritual self-satisfaction. Strictly speaking, the blindness in this section comes from an orthodoxy so obstinate as to believe that every contrary opinion comes from the devil. Such blindness unquestionably persists today and is sometimes exhibited in arrogant ecclesiastical exclusiveness coupled with contempt for those outside. To combat this modern Pharisaism the expositor's best weapons are appeal to the universality of the Christian religion and warning against the ecclesiasticism which caricatures it or is offered as a substitute.

Happily, however, such blindness is less in evidence than in former times and may be ignored unless specific examples of it call for exposure and condemnation. There are other and equally dangerous types to be dealt with today; particularly blind economic selfishness—a vice never more detestable than when coupled with lip-service to Christ.

## THE EPISTLE

The basis of the argument in Hebrews 9 is the conviction that the Old Testament is totally inspired in its every word and letter. So by God's decree the blood of bulls and goats was actually efficacious for the appointed purpose. "It has been appointed by the Holy One, and men must not inquire into His reasons!" Therefore, since Christ was an infinitely more precious victim, His blood was infinitely more efficacious.

That is, the writer has no *theory* of the Old Testament sacrifices, they were effectual purely because they were divinely ordained. No more has he a theory of the effect of Christ's atoning death; it is efficacious to the writer because it corresponds to the efficacious types. Faithful exposition must be content with a similar restraint. No theory of the Atonement has been accepted as final by the Christian consciousness. Yet the atonement is an immutable fact: Christ's death has actually changed the universe. And in so asserting we assert only what is an axiom to religious consciousness everywhere, that in the relations between God and man sacrifice occupies an essential place. It is to this unshakable realization that Christ's death makes its irresistible appeal. What we cannot do, He has done for us; through Him our conscience has been cleansed from dead works to serve the living God.

The details of the argument in Hebrews, however, are best ignored in the pulpit. The correspondence which the writer establishes between the Pentateuchal worship and the Passion are ingenious but are not even true to the facts. In the context of the present section there are at least three blunders (verses 4, 10, 19) in citing the Old Testament. No exegetical ingenuity can extract any comprehensible meaning from verse 23 (how was heaven defiled?). And in verses 15b–17 the hesitation of the translators between "covenant" and "testament" comes from the writer's equating two incompatible meanings of the same Greek noun.

SERMON THEME: All the real values found in ancient religions are perfectly fulfilled in Christ. The atoning significance of His sacrifice lies in the nature of His relation to God and man. Sin and death are conquered by the entrance of God into humanity.

In preaching from this Epistle it is all-important that the Atonement be interpreted by the Incarnation, and not *vice versa.* "It was because Jesus was what He was by nature that His sacrifice had such final value; its atoning significance lay in His vital connection with the world of absolute realities; it embodied all that His divine personality meant for men in relation to God."[1] What is needed is a return to Nicene theology, in which the doctrine of the Incarnation is "the essence of the Christian faith, from which other beliefs and convictions must spring, and with which they must correspond." "The tenets of original sin and total depravity, as expounded by Augustine, and received by the Protestant churches from the Latin church; . . . the idea of a schism in the divine nature which required a satisfaction to retributive justice before love could grant forgiveness, the atonement as a principle of equivalence by which the sufferings of Christ were weighed in a balance against the endless sufferings of the race, find no place in the Greek theology, and are irreconcilable with its high spirit."[2] "God was in Christ, reconciling the world unto Himself," and God's is the atoning love, the redeeming energy, given in Christ for the winning of a lost world back to sonship and obedience.

[1] J. Moffatt, *Hebrews*, p. 124.
[2] A. V. G. Allen, *Continuity of Christian Thought*, pp. 19, 20.

# PALM SUNDAY

## LITURGICAL NOTES

Gospel: Matthew 27:1–54. The Sarum and Roman missals have all of Matthew 26–27—the "Matthew Passion"—in accord with a practice presumably much older than the seventh century. The Prayer Book of 1549 shortened this slightly by the omission of 27:57–66, which formed the (new) Gospel for Easter Even. In 1661 chapter 26 was transferred to Morning Prayer, while verses 55–56 of chapter 27 were further omitted to give a better ending. Liturgical purists lament these changes from the traditional use, but the two whole chapters are impossibly long in practice.

Epistle: Philippians 2:5–11. So the Sarum and Roman missals. The liturgical unity is obvious.

The observance of this day as "Palm Sunday" originated at Jerusalem, where the services during Holy Week were highly dramatic, copying as closely as possible the final events of Christ's life: on this Sunday all who were able met on the Mount of Olives, and, escorting the bishop, carried tree branches in a procession into Jerusalem. The first origins of the custom are not recoverable but the *Pilgrimage of Etheria* (*ca.* 390?) describes the Holy Week ceremonies in a highly developed state. It was in the sixth century that the procession of palms was introduced into the West, as a frank imitation of the Jerusalem precedent. A form of blessing the branches—still today unknown in the East—appears a century later in a Gallican sacramentary (Bobbio), while the present Roman office attained practically its completed state in the ninth century.

## THE GOSPEL

An exposition of all of Matthew 27 is impossible in the time allotted to a sermon. For it, however, may profitably be substituted, as is very commonly done, an account of the entry into Jerusalem, preferably in its oldest form as told in Mark 11:1–11.

Historically the Palm Sunday procession is to be interpreted as our Lord's deliberate and premeditated challenge to the Jewish authorities. "Behold, we go up to Jerusalem" (Mark 10:33, see on Quinquagesima) expresses the intention: this is the arrival. Every one knew that for Jesus to place Himself in the power of the Sanhedrin was certain death, and no one knew this better than Jesus. On reaching the city He is not going to enter inconspicuously. He rides for the only time in His life. He makes His entry as aggressive as possible, and in order that the challenge of it may not be ignored, He follows it immediately with the still more polemical act of cleansing the Temple. The Jewish authorities might be glad to let Him alone. He will not let them let Him alone. He forces them to act, and to act at once, sweeping away any indecision.

In choosing an ass for His mount Jesus may very well have had Zechariah 9:9 in mind, but the main purpose in riding into the city was to compel men's attention. Matthew's account, through a misunderstanding of the prophetic passage, has made two animals of the original one. That the ass was one "whereon no man ever yet sat" is probably a deduction of later reverence. The purpose of Mark 11:2-6 is partly to explain how the animal was available (by prearrangement with the owner), partly to show Christ's supernatural knowledge; it is best passed over in exposition. The steeds of kings were decked with rich trappings and their routes were spread with carpeting and flowers; the disciples did the best they could with the homely resources at hand. It should be carefully noted that the acclamations in fact fall short of being definitely Messianic: Jesus heralds the approaching Kingdom but is not directly identified with its King. Here Mark (compare Matthew 21:11) is undoubtedly historic, for Jesus' Messianic claims were closely reserved; the enlargement in the other Gospels reflects the Christian conviction. "Hosanna" means "Salvation (is at hand)." "Hosanna in the highest" means "Salvation is prepared for us in heaven."

The weeping over Jerusalem in Luke 19:41–44 may represent historic fact or may be the Evangelist's reconstruction (compare on Trinity 10): in either case it represents in a deeply moving way the prophetic reality of the situation. In Mark 11:11 the "looking on all things" is hostile: "viewing the abuses to be purged on the morrow." According to Mark the Palm Sunday entrance was in the afternoon and Christ did nothing more on this day. The cleansing of the Temple was on Monday.

It is well to remember that because of the high altitude of Jerusalem the palm grows nowhere for miles around; the branches plucked by the multitude were from less tropical trees. *Palm* branches appear only in John 12:13 as *"the* (well-known) branches of the palm trees"; presumably the palms kept from the Feast of Tabernacles, which were preserved by all Jews in their homes until the feast came again.

There is little probability that those who cried "Hosanna" were to any significant degree identical with those who five days later cried "Crucify." The latter constituted the Jerusalem mob; the former, a crowd that went with Christ to the city and there suffered one disappointment after another—to be rewarded finally by Easter.

SERMON THEME: Christ will not let men let Him alone, but challenges them in a manner which compels them to accept or to crucify Him.

The note of challenge here is central, and should be kept central in the expository sermon. In an evil course of action hope is often entertained that the worst results can be avoided by temporizing. But God does not permit this. For judgment came Christ into this world (John 9:39). A merely critical, non-committal attitude towards Christ is impossible. He embodies the ultimate values, and to be indifferent to ultimate values is to be judged by them; not to choose becomes contrary choice, and not to decide is an adverse decision. So the lesson is plain: When men least expect Him Christ thrusts at their consciousness in some crisis comparable with

that of Palm Sunday, leaving them only the choice of abandoning
their selfishness and accepting Him—or of crucifying Him.

Appeal to the will, however, is not enough: there must be the
presentation of Christ in His irresistible goodness, truth and beauty,
winning the allegiance of men's hearts, as with the faithful on
Palm Sunday. "Constant appeals to the will merely increase either
self-righteousness or the despair of impotence. Wherever men really
fulfill the law of Christ they do it not by the strength of their
will but by some strength which has entered their will. Whenever
self-love is transcended it is by a force which can only be described
by the words, 'I, yet not I, but Christ that dwelleth in me.'"[1]

### THE EPISTLE

Specialists are largely agreed that in verses 6–11 Saint Paul quotes
an early Christian hymn that was familiar to his readers. In any
case its strophic arrangement is clear and has determined the verse
divisions. Three stanzas (verses 6-8) describe Christ's humiliation
and three (verses 9–11) His exaltation, and each of these stanzas
contains three elements; only the last clause of verse 8 is out of the
scheme and is probably a Pauline addition. The passage therefore
is to be explained as an immediate appeal to the heart, not a series
of exegetical enigmas.

Traditional miscomprehension has created the only real difficulty
by taking "the name of Jesus" to mean "the name which is Jesus"
instead of "the name which Jesus received" at His exaltation. This
name is "Lord"; it is in recognition of his Lordship that every knee
bows. This explains "equality with God" in verse 6: from the
hymn's standpoint this equality is the Lordship, the receiving men's
explicit adoration. Before the Incarnation men did not address
worship to the Son, but He did not "grasp" after it; instead, He
humbled Himself and so received it. The phrases "in the form of

[1]Reinhold Niebuhr, *An Interpretation of Christian Ethics*, p. 81.

God" and "emptied himself" are pictorial and no attempt should be made to define them too closely.

SERMON THEME: Jesus received the name of LORD through His humiliation, giving us the example of self-realization in the service of others.

The context determines the sermon and its application. Saint Paul was addressing a church with no glaring faults, such as incurred his reproaches in certain other epistles, but in which there was, as everywhere, desire for personal pre-eminence and rivalry for position. For this purpose he quotes a little Christian hymn, which voices the language of devotion, not of theology, and must not be treated as rationalized theology. Probably the best exposition is a simple telling of the story of the humiliation, reserving verse 5 to the end: "So Jesus did. Let the same mind be in you!"

For Holy Week verses 6-8 should undoubtedly receive the primary emphasis. But to forget—as preachers at this season often seem to forget—that Christ's sufferings were not the end, is unChristian. Even Good Friday addresses should remember Easter. The obedience willingly rendered to what He knew to be the Father's will carried Christ to death upon the cross, but the justification of it followed immediately; it is the living Christ, not the dead Christ, in whom the Christian religion finds its author and to whom Christians in worship give the Name that in the Old Testament was given only to God—the Name of Lord.

# EASTERTIDE

The oldest Christian season was the "pentecost" from Easter to Whitsunday, kept as a time of unmixed rejoicing, in which all fasting and even kneeling in prayer were prohibited; believers even while still on earth should regard themselves as risen with Christ. The Middle Ages failed to preserve this spirit. The Friday fast was intruded into the whole season and even into the Easter octave. Fasting was further exacted on the Rogation days and on the eve of Whitsunday, and the custom of standing in prayer was abolished. As a result the later mediæval church developed an unrelieved penitential season without an unbroken festal season to correspond, and Lent assumed an importance that was denied to Easter. It is imperative today to redress the balance; to recall that, although Christ endured the cross, He endured it for the joy that was set before Him, that, while we must suffer with Him, we shall also be glorified with Him, that we are already raised up with Christ and made to sit with Him in the heavenly places.

The Epistles for the Easter season, as remnants of an older *lectio continua,* are not especially useful for this purpose, but the Gospels, except perhaps for Easter 2, are well adapted to it.

# EASTERTIDE

## EASTER DAY

### A

LITURGICAL NOTES

GOSPEL: Mark 16:1–8. So (without verse 8) the Sarum and Roman missals; a seventh-century Gospel.

EPISTLE: I Corinthians 5:6–8. So (without verse 6) the Sarum and Roman missals.

This Gospel and Epistle in the 1549 Prayer Book were appointed for the *second* celebration. In the 1552 and subsequent English Books they were dropped but were introduced into the American Book in 1892.

### B

GOSPEL: John 20:1–10. This section has little precedent for Easter Day, although it is used in the Mozarabic rite. But in the Sarum and Roman missals John 20:1–9 is the Gospel for Saturday in Easter week.

EPISTLE: Colossians 3:1–4. The Sarum and Roman Epistle for the Easter Vigil (compare below). The corresponding Gospel is Matthew 28:1–7. In all the English Prayer Books and in the American Books until 1928 verses 5–7 are added.

The older Roman service for Easter was that of the Vigil, centering around the solemn baptismal ceremonies and closing at daybreak with the eucharist; these rites are still largely preserved in the Roman Office for "Holy Saturday." When in the early fifth century this service was moved back to Saturday morning a new service for Easter had to be devised.

During Easter week services were held every day, in the course of which the accounts of the resurrection were read through. Hence the Gospels for Easter Day itself contain only the preliminary sections, describing the discovery of the empty tomb but not the appearances of the risen Christ. Thus both the present Easter Gospels end on a note of sheer perplexity, something that is most unfortunate. In any future revision of the Prayer Book this defect is entitled to primary attention.

## A

### THE GOSPEL

Something may perhaps be made of the confusion and terror of the women when first confronted with the truth that was about to bring them eternal joy. But a regular expository treatment of the section in an Easter sermon would be inadvisable, since it would divert the attention of the hearers from the main theme of Easter.

For the critical problems in the story here—which are more complicated than appears on the surface—the special treatises on Christ's resurrection must be consulted. In any case apologetic treatment of the evidence should begin with I Corinthians 15, not with the empty tomb narratives, which have passed through revision and editing before they reached their present form. Saint Mark's version is devotionally the least helpful of all; the risen Lord does not appear; the women found nothing and they said nothing. The empty tomb is negative evidence; apart from the record of the appearances of the risen Christ it would present a problem but not a gospel. Mark 14:28 properly translated—"After I am raised up I will lead you onward into Galilee"—shows the priority of a Jerusalem tradition which verse 7 converted into a Galilean tradition.

SERMON THEME: He who was crucified, dead, and buried, rose again the third day and was seen of His own. This faith, vindicated by experience, is the "gospel" of the church, the secret of its power, and the only explanation of its history.

When the apostolic preaching began, it proclaimed more than

that Jesus had gone to the Father, that His Messianic work was transferred from earth to heaven, and that in a few years He would return as the glorified Messiah. It proclaimed that Jesus was *risen*, that He was in contact with earth as well as with heaven, at first in a visible presence, and then universally and for the ages through the Spirit.

The details of the first resurrection visions are no longer recoverable. The Gospels take the facts so completely for granted that they are quite unconcerned to marshal evidence; it is from Saint Paul that we receive a list of the appearances to Cephas, to the twelve, to "about five hundred at once," of whom the greater part were alive when he wrote, to James, to all the apostles. The visions were many; they correspond to no known psychological laws; they were crowded close together over a large territory, but in a very few days they suddenly ceased—leaving the visionaries fully conscious that they would not occur again; those who shared them were filled with a sense of inexhaustible and invincible power. What made possible the apostolic preaching was the confidence of the first believers that they had actually seen Jesus—not as a ghost, not as a visitant from the heavenly world, but as risen.

To this must be added a further fact; those who throughout the centuries have shared the faith of the disciples have found themselves in contact with the same source of power and life. They know Him as Simon Peter knew Him, as One who forgives, cleanses, restores, strengthens, and bids them feed His sheep. They know Him as the travellers on the road to Emmaus knew Him, as the Companion of their journeyings, the Teacher who explains life's mysteries, the Guest whose entrance brings blessedness and peace. In great moments of spiritual intuition they know Him as Saint John knew Him, the Friend whose fellowship is eternal life. History has no parallel to the conviction shared by every generation of Christians that they enjoy a real and blessed intercourse with Him who is the object of their faith.

THE EPISTLE

The choice of this section was due to "Passover" and "let us keep the feast," both being applied directly to Easter Day. To Saint Paul, naturally, "the feast" is the whole of life, but this very divergence of concept admits a most practical application: the spirit of Easter is the spirit in which a believer should live continually. And the context, which equates "leaven" to "sin" defines this spirit as a steadfast refusal to acquiesce in evil.

The imagery, however, is presumably due to the fact that Saint Paul was actually writing around Passover time (16:8). The Christians may well have had special observances of their own, but the Apostle's mind reverts to the well-remembered customs of his pre-conversion days. Before the feast every orthodox Jewish family conducts an almost ludicrously painstaking search of their home for leaven, since even the tiniest crumb of ordinary bread is regarded as defiling, and not until every suspicious fragment has been collected and destroyed do they feel ready for the festival. Christians, says Saint Paul, have a similar duty, although on an infinitely higher plane. Not until they have freed their souls from all condoning and acceptance of wickedness—compare verse 2—and malice are they fit for the joy that Christ brings them. "A little leaven leaveneth the whole lump"—"a single unpurified nook in our nature is a focus of infection." The preacher will think of psychological analogies. As always in Pauline theology the ethical demand is based upon the religious experience: it was because of their standing as redeemed persons that they were called upon to act as became that free and joyful status and "keep the feast" of their emancipation by remaining free from sin.

In the "sacrifice" of "Christ our Passover" there is no allusion to the Atonement as ordinarily understood. The death of Christ here —as often in Saint Paul—is His transition from this world where sin rules to the sinless world of heaven. That it is called a "sacrifice" is due to the Passover setting. Yet being "in Christ," spiritually identified with Him, makes His people sharers in this transition, and so there is still "atonement," though not in the sense in which the word is generally employed, but as indicating the power to begin a new life without continuity with the old sinful life.

## *B*

### THE GOSPEL

Compare what is said on the Gospel under *A*. That the "other disciple" "believed" on superficially inadequate evidence may be evaluated practically, if no attempt is made to laud mere credulity. Verse 9 implies that if the disciples had known the "moral necessity" that Christ must rise again from the dead they would have needed no further proof.

### THE EPISTLE

A perfect section for Easter, superb in its concentration, and one that has gained immensely by the omission of the verses (5–7) that were included by the Reformers.

SERMON THEME: The mystical union of the believer with the risen Christ gives power to begin a new life without continuity with the old life of sinfulness.

Saint Paul's soteriology is based on the mystical union of the believer with Christ. He teaches that in Baptism there is an actual fusion of the two lives; as a result, what is left of our old life or "old man" is an atavistic remnant of no great importance. We have acquired a new personality which is "heavenly"; the life that we are now living is already victorious over death, and there is something in us that cannot be harmed or buffeted by the transient things of earthly life, something in us that changes not.

No doubt the mysticism that underlies its terminology is not easy to explain to many congregations. So it is quite sufficient to interpret our death and resurrection here as our renunciation of selfishness in order to serve Christ, and His gift of spiritual life to us. And he who identifies himself with God's ideal of righteousness is invincibly identified with God's eternal triumph. Let us live accordingly. And not only in the hope of a better life to come but in the full possession of spiritual power now. We are *already* risen with Christ. And the life which we share with Him is the life of God.

## THE FIRST SUNDAY AFTER EASTER

### LITURGICAL NOTES

GOSPEL: John 20:19–23. A Reformation shortening of the section in the Sarum and Roman missals that continued to the end of the chapter, so including the events of the original first Sunday after Easter, which alone is commemorated in the ancient section (verses 24–31 only). Verses 26–29, in fact, are so obviously appropriate to this day that their use seems to be almost universal outside of Anglicanism; this is one of the very few instances where the Eastern and Western churches agree in their selections.

EPISTLE: I John 5:4–12; the Sarum and Roman missals close with verse 10*a*. The last of the "baptismal" sections.

With this day the prolonged baptismal rites were brought to their final conclusion. On this morning in Rome the newly baptized resumed their ordinary clothing, laying aside the white robes they had worn during the week. These they now brought to the altar of Saint Pancras, a youthful martyr, the patron of innocence and the sanctity of vows; there they took a solemn oath to preserve their baptismal promises inviolate. Hence in the Gregorian Sacramentary this Sunday is called "Dominica post albas"; in the later Roman use less correctly "Dominica in albis."

"Low Sunday," the traditional English name for the day, appears to mean simply "the lesser Sunday in the great octave."

Liturgical unity can be gained by taking Christ's resurrection as the foundation of "the victory that overcometh the world." Or the old baptismal application of the Epistle can be maintained by taking each Easter experience as a fresh beginning in the life of the Spirit.

## THE GOSPEL

The account in verse 22 is a parallel version to the familiar story in Acts 2. John's version here is, like everything else in his Gospel, dramatically interpretative rather than literally historical, but in this instance he seems to be nearer the actual facts than Acts; the ecstasy that the first church recognized as the gift of the Spirit was surely produced by the presence of the risen Master and could hardly have been delayed for over seven weeks. Verse 23 expresses the primitive conviction that membership in the community confers the immediate possession of salvation; forgiveness for each believer was complete, for each had passed out of death into life. Therefore to "forgive" a man's sins was to admit him to membership, and to "retain" them was to exclude him (*i.e.*, the conception of absolution here is social, since only in a moral society can man be truly moral). Then if verse 23 is to be given any meaning deeper than a legal fiat, it must be taken as defining Christians' duty to the church, just as verses 20–21 define the church's duty to the world. As things are today no part of Christianity—outside, perhaps, of some very small sects—dares claim such a fullness of spiritual life that membership therein is *ipso facto* an absolution. But until such purity is regained the missionary vocation will be correspondingly weakened, and missionary success correspondingly diminished.

SERMON THEME: As God sent Christ, so Christ sends His disciples to proclaim the gospel; a Christianity that is not missionary is not Christian.

The "Great Commission" is the only invariable element in all the resurrection traditions. No matter what else the first Christians desired to tell about their risen Lord, they felt this to be wholly indispensable. "Do you believe that Christ is risen? Then spread the glad tidings!"

The contrast between "the fear of the Jews" and Jesus' "Peace be unto you" is extraordinarily fertile. The risen Christ, conqueror of death, becomes for His disciples the conqueror of fear: compare John 16:33. Fear of death is the deepest of all fears. Life has no meaning unless its meaning is eternal. Disbelief in its continuance palsies or makes trivial every human exertion. No one who is living a man's life, who cares for his work, who cares for his friends, who cares that truth and goodness and beauty be found enshrined at the heart of things, can afford to be indifferent to the question of immortality. He needs the peace and reassurance that the risen Christ alone can give, of the victory of life over death. He needs peace of mind before he can be entrusted with great tasks.

But having been assured of immortality, how that conscious immortality should compel him, and make him ready to receive the Great Commission! To believe in immortality and then to live an earth-bound, trivial, inconsequential life, a life devoid of mission, is moral shipwreck. "As my Father hath sent Me, even so send I you." The risen Christ makes sure that His resurrection will be a message, a commission, an incentive, a commandment, a gospel to be carried into every sphere of human knowledge, of human labour, and of human hope.

Men needed one thing more. They needed inspiration for the task, and the disciples received it. "Receive ye the Holy Ghost." There is a mystery, a grace ineffable given in the gospel, making all things possible to him that believeth. It is the power to become the sons of God. It is the life of God within the Christian soul.

## THE EPISTLE

For the general purpose of I John *cf.* on Epiphany 6. Cerinthus taught that Jesus and Christ were not the same. Jesus was (only) a good man, Christ was a heavenly æon. When Jesus was baptized Christ entered into Him, but left Him before His death; *i.e.,* Christ "came by water" but *not* "by blood": hence the indignant contradiction in verse 6.

Lying behind the controversy were two different philosophies. Cerinthus was a dualist, teaching that matter is irredeemably evil and that spirit alone is good; Saint John was a monist, insisting that the visible world is also God's creation. So to Cerinthus the only way of "overcoming the world" was to escape from it; to Saint John the victory comes through a faith that confronts evil and triumphs over it (compare John 17:15-19). Faith can do this; he who believes that in Jesus we find the ultimate reality in the universe (verse 5) will face life as fearlessly as Jesus did, in a life that (verse 6) was as truly human as our own.

In verse 7 the appeal to the Spirit is what we nowadays call "the appeal to religious experience," which in verse 8 is widened to include the sacramental experience of "the water and the blood," baptism and the eucharist. (Gnostics who held that Christ did not really die either modified the meaning of the eucharist out of recognition or abolished the rite altogether.) All this experience is uniform. The constant inner testimony of the Spirit, the meaning of baptism, the perpetually reiterated message of the eucharist all teach the same thing: the revelation of God is to be found in a true human being, and above all in His death.

Verse 8 probably explains the allegory in John 19:34-35, but to reverse this relationship only produces confusion.

The saying about the "Three Heavenly Witnesses" in the King James Version's verse 7 is no part of the original text.

Verses 10-12 point the polemic in terms of characteristic Johannine antitheses between believers and non-believers. The expositor must be careful to explain that the harshness is due to Cerinthus' defence of moral laxity and selfishness.

A homiletic exposition of this section as a whole is difficult, partly because of the complexity of the historical references, partly because of the strangeness of Cerinthus' system. Much that is really useful can, however, be made of the contrast between Christianity as a religion of social activity and the various "escape" religions, including certain forms that profess themselves Christian. But in this case the polemic must be softened; the sincere theosophist, for instance, may be mistaken, but he certainly does not merit such condemnation as is implied in verse 10.

SERMON THEME: The victory that overcomes the world comes not from "escape" but from social activity in a faith that confronts evil and triumphs over it.

The preacher will note that religious faith may be either a flight from reality or a facing of reality, and that there is much to justify the psychologists' contention that it is often the former. Monasticism when it is due to despair of overcoming the evil in the world; certain metaphysical speculations of the Eastern church; the trust in magical efficacy of the sacraments, when divorced from ethical content; the individualism and subjectivism often found in Protestantism, are instances. They go far toward explaining anti-clericalism, and the Marxian charge that "religion is the opiate of the people."

This, however, is not the present tendency, and social activity is very generally characteristic of the church at the present time. What is needed is a call to a facing of reality which will take into account not only the social disorder and unrest in the world but also its spiritual causes in the sinfulness of the unredeemed human will. The Johannine doctrine of crisis is here of enormous importance: men face ultimate reality when confronted by Christ, and religion is the sum total of their response to the truth, beauty and goodness revealed in Him.

# THE SECOND SUNDAY AFTER EASTER

## LITURGICAL NOTES

GOSPEL: John 10:11–16. So the Sarum and Roman missals; seventh century. The reason for its choice is not clear; perhaps a remnant of continuous reading.

EPISTLE: I Peter 2:19–25. So (beginning with verse 21) the Sarum and Roman missals; the Reformation lengthening is a great improvement.

Apart from Whitsunday and Trinity the selections until Trinity 4 are all from the Catholic Epistles. As these writings are used at no other time and as the content of the Epistles chosen is in no way paschal, survival from primitive continuous reading is here the only explanation.

Both Gospel and Epistle present Christ as the Shepherd, and it is presumably to establish this agreement that the Epistles for this and the following Sunday were interchanged. And both Gospel and Epistle are centred around Christ's sufferings for us: what Christ did (Gospel) is the model for our conduct (Epistle).

## THE GOSPEL

For detailed exegesis see commentaries on the Fourth Gospel, especially G. H. C. Macgregor's. The allegory is composite: in verses 7–10 where we should expect Christ to be the Shepherd He becomes the Door, then Shepherd again in verses 11 ff. But it is the metaphor of the Shepherd, often applied to God in the Old Testament, e.g., Psalm 23, which captured the imagination of the early church and dominated its iconography, as in the catacombs in Rome, where representation of the crucifixion does not appear for several centuries. Divine and human associations are so mingled in the metaphor as to make it an ideal expression of the relation of Christ to His people.

Verse 12 is probably meant only to serve as a contrast to Christ's behavior, with no particular "hirelings" in mind: conceivably, however, the Evangelist thinks of specific pastors who fled when persecution threatened. For homiletical purposes it is quite warrantable to contrast the "hireling" who works only for his wage with the "shepherd" who works with a consciousness of his vocation, and to point out the social applications.

Attention should be directed to the intensity of the Christian experience voiced in verses 14–15. "For John 'knowledge' is not a purely intellectual process, but includes religious and moral elements by virtue of which it approached in content Paul's idea of 'faith.'"[1] Compare John 17.

The language in verse 16 is a bitter commentary on the present divided condition of Christianity. But the "one fold" of the King James Version is what Westcott called it, a "disastrous" mistranslation, and should read "one flock."

SERMON THEME: So far as believers are really devoted to Christ they are already "one flock" in their common relationship to the Good Shepherd, though divided into many folds.

The word church appears only twice in the Gospels. What is apparent there is not ecclesiastical organization but the establishment by Christ of a missionary fellowship among those whom He has brought into vital contact with Himself. This is the sole and sufficient ground of Christian unity. The fellowship is that of "the blessed company of all faithful people"; of "all those in whom the Holy Spirit dwells." Where two or three are gathered together in His name, Christ is in their midst. Where Christ is, there is His church.

This "one flock" does not elect its Shepherd, but is elected by Him. The divine initiative must be recognized in any adequate conception of the Christian church. "Ye have not chosen me, but I have chosen you." The life-principle of the new community is

[1] *Op. cit.*, p. 239.

love, based not upon men's love for Christ but upon His love for them, communicated to them by His Spirit and enabling them to love one another. Church membership does not create Christian unity but is the expression of it.

If this unity of Christians which exists already in virtue of their relationship to the Good Shepherd is to find outward and visible expression, provision must be made for unity in diversity represented by the different "folds." In the great ecumenical movements of the present time this principle is clearly recognized by the leaders. What is now necessary is that it be generally recognized by church members, in order that they may relinquish the conception of the Christian church as a club of those like-minded, and acquire instead the catholic conception of the church as God's family, coextensive in principle with a redeemed humanity, and therefore superracial and supernational as well as supernatural. For this, the conception must be Christ-centred. Our "unhappy divisions" would vanish could we but refrain from interposing other persons and other things between ourselves and Him.

## THE EPISTLE

The bulk of I Peter (1:3–4:11) is now generally recognized to be an address to the newly baptized. Within this, 2:18–3:7 is a section in "church order" style, detailing the duties of servants, wives and husbands, from the first part of which the present Epistle is taken. Before the Reformation the selection commenced with "Christ suffered for us," making a good opening but leaving the next clause much too vague; the Reformers consequently prefixed verses 19–20. Logically, no doubt, verse 18 is the beginning of the new paragraph, but this would restrict to "servants" teaching that is perfectly appropriate to all. In exposition, however, verse 18 may be used in the introduction: what Christians, who lived in the hard condition of servants, or rather slaves, in the ancient world, had to endure constantly makes most of our trials seem petty.

In verse 19, "grief" ("griefs" in the Revised Version) is better represented in modern English by "sorrow" or (in the context) "insults." In verse 21 "hereunto" equals "that we may patiently accept suffering for well-doing." The writer's insertion of "for us" (better "for you") here was unfortunate, since it makes the parallel between Christ and us imperfect (the slaves can scarcely be supposed to suffer "for" their masters) and it interrupts the argument; the expositor had best ignore it. Verse 22 resumes "when ye do well" and verse 23 "take it patiently" in verse 20.

The use of the familiar language of Isaiah 53 in verses 22-23 is continued into verse 24 and is responsible for the curious phrasing of the first clause, "who carried up our sins in his own body onto the tree." This has given rise to endless discussion, but there is no reason to think that the writer was endeavouring to set forth an individualistic theory of the Atonement; the unusual wording is merely due to his attempt to reproduce the language of Isaiah. Similarly the citation of Isaiah 53:5, "by whose stripes ye were healed," can hardly be meant to find atoning value in Christ's scourging; the language is not theological but devotional. In verse 25 (compare Isaiah 53:6) all parallel between Christ and ourselves is dropped. Here "bishop" is a synonym of "shepherd," a good translation would be "guardian."

SERMON THEME: Christ is our example in patience and gentleness; let us live accordingly when suffering wrongs that cannot be remedied.

To obtain a logically practical exposition the best method is to reverse the argument. Think what Christ did for us (verses 24-25). In so doing His patience and gentleness were absolute (verse 23), although He was treated with incredible injustice (verse 22). He is our example (verse 21); let us live accordingly (verses 19-20).

One of the reproaches directed by outsiders against the early church was that it contained few people of social prominence. The philosopher Celsus burlesqued it by representing it as saying, "Let no man come to us who is learned or wise or prudent." He declared that the converts the church cared to have (or indeed could get) were "the slaves, the women and the children." The early church contained a considerable number of slaves. In Roman society their condition was pitiable. They were protected by no humane restrictions, such as are to be found in the social legislation of the ancient Hebrews. Moreover the situation was irremediable: a servile insurrection was certain to be put down with merciless ferocity. All that the church could do was to point to Christ as an example in patient endurance of injustice, and assure them that although the body may be shackled, only sin can enslave the spirit. *Uncle Tom's Cabin* provides a modern illustration. Slaves could console themselves by emulating Christ's meekness.

Since slavery as a political institution has practically disappeared, the preacher's problem here is proper generalization. The Epistle was addressed to a definite class in a situation for which there was no remedy. "Door-mat psychology" is to be avoided; Christians are not to be urged to suffer social injustice if it is within their power to remedy the situation by legitimate means; patient endurance is the last resort when no other is legitimate. The practical application lies in the sphere of unavoidable suffering, *e.g.,* invalidism or other circumstances which cannot be bettered by valiant effort. Here the comfort of the message may be made plain and abundant: those "walking in the way of the cross may find it none other than the way of life and peace."

# THE THIRD SUNDAY AFTER EASTER

## LITURGICAL NOTES

GOSPEL: John 16:16–22. So the Sarum and Roman missals.

EPISTLE: I Peter 2:11–17. The Sarum and Roman missals continue to include "for this is acceptable" in verse 19, a most awkward ending.

Both Gospel and Epistle teach our citizenship in the heavenly world.

## THE GOSPEL

Apart from the textual problem discussed below in verse 16 the passage is free from difficulties. But the unexpected change in phrasing in verse 22 is of great importance to the preacher: it is not because we see Christ but because He sees us that our joy is eternal. And note that the disciples' joy begins here and now.

The King James Version, unlike the Revised Version, closes verse 16 as well as verse 17 with "because I go to the Father." This appears to be one of the very few cases where the older version is to be preferred. Usually the Revised Version is defended by arguing that the words in verse 17 really look back to verse 10 and that some copyist, not realizing this, made the phrasing of verse 16 correspond to that of verse 17. Moreover, in verse 16 the words appear illogical, interposing the Ascension (the going to the Father) between the resurrection and the appearances to the disciples.

Yet it was precisely this that Saint John held; compare 20:17. The appearance to Mary Magdalene was—so to speak—only in passing, hence the "Touch me not; for I am not yet ascended to my Father": and the other disciples were not permitted to see Him until He had actually gone to the Father. That is, He whom the apostles beheld was not in an as yet uncompleted stage of glory; He was the fully glorified Lord, endowed with all power in heaven and earth (Matthew 28:18). This expresses a vital religious conviction, although in language so unusual that the early church failed to understand it. And it may be that the obscurity of the phrase caused its omission from verse 16; as a matter of fact its early textual support is not bad. It is also quite possible, as Macgregor suggests,[1] that the larger reference of the words "a little while, and ye shall see me" is to the realization of the spiritual

[1] *Gospel of John*, p. 300.

presence of Christ in His Church as exemplified at Pentecost. "Christ has indeed returned, hints the Evangelist, and if the church still feels disappointment and perplexity, it is only because she has mistaken the nature of His coming." This is made definite in verse 22, so that those who today refuse to identify Christ's "second coming" with an apocalyptic manifestation but find it instead in the spiritual communion which believers have had with their Lord from Pentecost on, have support for their views in the Fourth Gospel.

SERMON THEME: It is not our love for Christ but His love for us which assures our salvation and constitutes our eternal joy.

This theme lies at the heart of Christianity. It could not have been made known except through a divine revelation, such as is recorded in the Gospels. Furthermore, it differentiates Christianity from the other great ethical religions with which it is in some respects comparable, for in them man seeks God, while in the Christian religion God seeks man.

The illustrations may be drawn at random from the literature of Christian experience, notably from the devotional literature of the Christian mystics who are without exception conscious of the "priority of God" in their communion with Him. "Our gospel speaks of a love that sought men, and still seeks them, just where they are and as they are: it is the love of Jesus, which is the love of God, and which finally pursued the hard and impenitent heart of man to the hill of Calvary. . . . There it is that the miracle takes place; the hardest thing in the world, the hard and impenitent heart of man, is softened and melted. Deep calls unto deep. Lover answers love; and the Atonement is accomplished."[1]

## THE EPISTLE

Two paragraphs on different themes are combined here. The first has as its subject the missionary power of a good life. It is

[1] R. S. Franks, *The Atonement*, p. 196.

perfectly straightforward, but "worldly desires" is much better than "fleshly lusts" (too narrow a phrase in modern English), while the Revised Version quite properly changes "conversation honest" to "behaviour seemly." In verse 11 "pilgrims" is an impossible rendition of a Greek noun meaning "settlers in a community to which they do not belong by birth and in which they have no citizenship." Psalm 39:12 is probably in mind, and "sojourners" is better than "pilgrims."

The second paragraph (verses 13–17) discusses relations to secular authority in the same spirit and partly in the same words as Romans 13:1–7 (Epiphany 4). If there is any connection with the preceding paragraph it may be, "Although you do not belong to this world, subject yourselves to its rulers." Compare verse 16 on the use of true freedom. In verse 17 "Honour all men" deserves attention. Recognition of the absolute worth of human personality is of the essence of the social message of the gospel and is the key to all genuine social reform. The homiletical bearings are obvious: as the honour due to all men has made an end of slavery so now it must determine the Christian attitude toward war.

SERMON THEME: The citizenship of Christians is already in the heavenly world: as they do not belong to this world they should not yield to its temptations.

Citizenship in the heavenly world does not mean an other-worldliness which renders Christians socially ineffective. It is one of the paradoxes of history that often the world has been moved upon most strongly and beneficently by the utterly unworldly and that society has been most influenced by men and women who, free from its temptations, were least trammelled by its traditions and conventions. Bernard of Clairvaux, Francis of Assisi, Raymund Lull, Johann Tauler, Joan of Arc, Saint Teresa are classic examples. Because they lived in the timeless and eternal world of mystical contemplation they saw human history in its true perspective. Because their citizenship was in heaven they touched human history with "the finger of God" and there manifested His creative will. Their heavenly citizenship freed them from prejudices, sharpened their intelligence, fortified their will, schooled them in patience, gave them the faith and hope which carried them through periods of depression, and enabled them to act upon their environment with saving power. The danger today is that with its growing absorption in the social objectives of religion Christianity will lose sight of that inwardness which is the very secret of its power.

# THE FOURTH SUNDAY AFTER EASTER

## LITURGICAL NOTES

GOSPEL: John 16:5-15. So the Sarum and Roman missals. The reversal of the order of the Gospels for Easter 3 and 4 was presumably to bring the promise of the Spirit in verse 7 nearer Whitsunday.

EPISTLE: James 1:17-21. So the Sarum and Roman missals.

There is no real relation between the Gospel and the Epistle, but liturgical unity can be gained by taking the Spirit as the supreme "good and perfect gift from above."

## THE GOSPEL

Verses 5-6 voice an emotion felt by all Christians as Ascension Day draws near. "Paraclete" in late Greek means simply "Helper"; expositors should carefully avoid all over-complicated explanations. "Comforter" having lost its Latin meaning does no justice to the Spirit as the source of strength. "Advocate," despite its one-time popularity, is out of the question.

The difficult verses 8-11 can be clarified by translating verse 8 as, "And he, when he is come, will teach the world the true meaning of these three words, 'sin,' 'righteousness,' 'judgment.'" Verse 9: Men have many definitions of "sin" but he whom the Spirit illumines knows its essence to be refusal to accept the standard mani-

fest in the teaching and Person of Christ. (In the Fourth Gospel
to "believe" in Christ is something very much more than to accept
a doctrine about Him.) Verse 10: The Spirit proves to us that
Christ is glorified; *therefore* the righteousness He taught and lived
reveals the moral meaning of God. Verse 11: To the "world" the
cross was the judgment inflicted on Christ, but through the Spirit's
light we see the self-same cross as the supreme condemnation of
evil.

The four verses can be summed up as "spiritual recognition of
eternal values."

Verses 12–15: Not only will the Spirit correct false vision; he will
give an ever-increasing range to true insight. In these four verses
Saint John makes his defence of his Gospel. He is perfectly aware
that much that he sets down as Christ's teaching was not actually
uttered in that form by the historic Jesus. But to limit Christianity
to the literal sayings of Jesus in their primary historical sense would
rob it of its endless possibilities; the Christian consciousness must be
free to adapt itself to problems undreamed of in earlier ages. And
when such problems are bravely faced in the spirit of Christ we
shall indeed find that Jesus has truly "yet many things to say unto
us." "Through Christ the Spirit had been vouchsafed to men; they
were no longer dependent on ancient forms and traditions but had
access to the living sources of power."[1]

Verses 13b–15 insist that in so meeting new conditions the enlightened Christian conscience is a safe guide, for its light is given
by God Himself. The earliest church, indeed, set practically no
limits to the knowledge that might be so learned, for through the
church's prophets the Spirit spoke directly. Long experience has
taught us to be more modest, and we realize that many false starts
and much groping are inevitable. But we know, too, that ultimate
truth is *one* and that, however costly may be the readjustments that
we may have to make, we need never fear the outcome if we follow the guiding of the "Spirit of truth."

[1]E. F. Scott, *Spirit in the New Testament*, p. 247.

SERMON THEME: The Holy Spirit is the Helper of Christians, illuminating the moral sense, heightening and deepening moral judgment, and giving them ability to meet new problems.

The opening verses of the section may be paraphrased, "Instead of asking me and getting comfort you are merely sorry." Too often we let ourselves become sorry about things instead of asking the reason. The reason for the "going away" of Christ was that even in His post-resurrection presence that presence was localized. Through the Spirit He can reach all men everywhere. Therefore the Ascension, instead of being really a "going away," meant the possibility of His coming infinitely near. "Thou wast taken into the heavens that we might receive thee into our hearts" (Saint Augustine).

Sin, righteousness and judgment are mysterious words which the Spirit enables Christians to understand. The essence of sin is failure to believe in Christ: this does not mean failure to accept a given theological formula about Christ, but failure to accept as a true revelation of ultimate values the nature of God as revealed in Christ. "Faith is the receiving faculty of the soul," and unbelief is non-reception of that which constitutes its very life.

The meaning of judgment is likewise interpreted by the Spirit. In the crucifixion the powers of this world, political and ecclesiastical, thought that they had judged Him. What they had really done was to write their own condemnation. The things that worked the crucifixion of Christ, easily discernible still in our modern world, are automatically "judged," *i.e.,* exposed in all their baseness by what they did.

John's apologia becomes that of New Testament scholars today. After two generations the significance of what Christ had said had become a great deal clearer. He believed that it was the function of the Spirit, not to pass down a letter ("the faith once delivered to the saints"), but to help knowledge grow from more to more ("progressive revelation"), to enable Christians to meet new problems as they arise. (*E.g.,* those presented by the principle of evolution, the most important idea of the nineteenth century.) As the sayings attributed by John to Jesus but received through the Spirit were just as authoritative as those reported in the Synoptic Gospels, so too all present revelations of God's truth are to be accepted as coming from the Spiritual Christ, whether or not they may be connected with sayings attributed to the historic or "documentary" Jesus. The Spiritual Christ is the Founder and the present Helper of the Christian religion.

### THE EPISTLE

This is a poorly selected passage, containing the end (verses 17-18) of one section and the beginning (verses 19–21) of another, which is only vaguely connected with the first. The subject of verses 12–18 is resistance to temptation, especially (verse 13) the temptation of pleading that one's sins were inevitable and so in some sense God-given. Such an excuse borders on blasphemy; God's moral nature is immutable (verse 17) and His purpose for us is wholly righteous. Verses 19–27 have as their theme self-control, which is to be gained by the study and following of the Bible. A unified exposition of the passage chosen for the present Epistle is consequently difficult. Verse 17 must be taken as an introductory general truth, which (verse 18) establishes our general duty, while verses 19–21 particularize it as that self-control taught in the Bible.

The first clause of verse 17 is an hexameter line—"Every gift that is good and every boon that is perfect"—which is possibly quoted from some source familiar to the readers. "The Father of lights" = "The Creator of the heavenly bodies." Yet even the most excellent of these, the sun, is inconstant to man, while God is ever the same. "Variableness" is an excellent rendering of a quite non-technical word. "Shadow of turning" is the best that can be done with a phrase that is obscure to the experts; apparently the writer has attempted to use an astronomical term that he does not quite understand. Verse 18: "As those whom God has created anew we must live according to His nature"; the writer probably thought that we were "begotten" in baptism.

The King James Version of verse 21 is wholly misleading and the Revised Version an insufficient improvement: "Putting away all the defilement that anger causes and the malice which is too common in men" gives the sense. Or perhaps "that omnipresent malice." The "word" is God's teaching in the Bible, which is "engrafted" because taken to heart ("inborn" in the Revised Version margin is quite wrong).

SERMON THEME: Anger is a defilement; Christians are to exercise self-control, which is to be gained by the close study and constant following of the word of God contained in the Bible.

Anger, as contrasted with just and controlled indignation which keeps itself in hand, never does any good. It is never true to say, "I was right in losing my temper," and to take pride, as many do, in having a quick or ungovernable temper, is a ludicrous example of infantilism. The best safeguard against the defilement of anger is the reception of the "engrafted word" found primarily in the Bible, especially when it warns us against anger, and specifically in the warnings contained in the Sermon on the Mount. See Matthew 5:22, where Christ in expounding the new and higher law quite definitely teaches that anger is included within the scope of the sixth commandment which prohibits murder (compare on Trinity 6). In Matthew 5:23–26 it is taught that the gift of one who has indulged in anger, scorn, and abusive language against his brother, is unacceptable to God and that the indulgence is a sin which incurs His judgment and condemnation.

This word of God, though "engrafted," has to be received constantly, but the preacher will find it helpful to emphasize the positive approach: the Christian fellowship implies mutual love which casts out anger as well as fear.

# THE FIFTH SUNDAY AFTER EASTER

## LITURGICAL NOTES

GOSPEL: John 16:23*b*–33. The Sarum and Roman missals end with verse 30, giving a better climax.

EPISTLE: James 1:22–27. So the Sarum and Roman missals.

The association of Gospel and Epistle is fortuitous, but they can be combined as prayer (Gospel) and action (Epistle).

It was in fifth-century Gaul that the three days before Ascension were set apart as a sort of vigil, dedicated to special supplications, and these days were not adopted in Rome until the time of Leo III (died 816). There they are known as the days of "Lesser Litanies," in contrast to the very ancient Roman day of prayer held on April 23rd or 25th. Their restriction to intercession for the harvest came later, and in the Roman missal is indicated only by their Epistle.

## THE GOSPEL

The Gospel for Easter 3 is continued, although the (confusing) first clause of verse 23 is omitted. An essential part of the joy no man taketh from us is our confident access to the Father; without this our joy would surely not be full.

To Saint John the essential words in verses 23–24 are "in my name." The precise historic force of this phrase is complicated, but excellent justice to its sense in the present passage can be done by paraphrasing it "in my service." An official summons a householder to open "in the name of the law," where the meaning of course is "to me who am in the law's service." Consequently to pray "in the name of Christ" is to pray as His servant for something needful for His service.

When the preacher wishes to observe Rogation Sunday specifically these two verses will afford him ample material. But too much time must not be spent on them if the whole Gospel is to be treated, and confidence in prayer must be handled briefly as only one of the joys of the matured Christian life. Verse 25 describes a second joy, that of understanding even more deeply the nature of the Father. This verse is a summary repetition of what was said in verses 12–13 (compare on Easter 4); here "in that day" corresponds to "when the Spirit of truth is come." "Proverbs" of course misses the point and the Revised Version's "dark sayings" should be adopted. The teaching of the historical Jesus when pondered leads to a knowledge at which the surface only hints. Verses 26–27, in part a continuation of verse 25, add still a third joy, the sense of immediate relation to the Father.

The "disciples" in verses 29–30 are really the ripened believers of a later day, who are learning constantly by experience more and more of what was involved in Jesus' historic message. And it is to these Christians—in expository terms, to *us*—that Christ speaks in verses 31–33. "Like my apostles of old you will have moments of doubt and panic in which you will be unfaithful to your trust. The tribulation you will have in the world will come from within as well as from without. Let not even this dismay you! I know you will have your failures; I tell you this in advance that even in their midst you may have peace. The world, outward or inward, cannot keep you from me, for I have overcome the world."

SERMON THEME: Among the joys of the matured Christian life are confident access to the Father, who will answer all prayers for things needed in Christ's service; deepening understanding of the nature of the Father; and the sense of immediate relation to the Father.

Only those who are "in Christ" are Christians, therefore the prayer of the Christian, conditioned by his status "in Christ," is as certain as Christ's own prayer of the answer of the Father. So the formula, "this we ask in the name of Jesus Christ our Lord"—or the briefer "for Christ's sake"—is neither a formality nor a magical incantation, but has a deep reality on which we reflect too little: to add these words is equivalent to saying, "We need this that we may serve Thy Son." If we are telling the truth God's response is certain; but much for which we make request under this formula has little relation to any such aim. The formula, consequently, should exercise a censorship over the contents of our petitions, and should be used only when we are sure that our needs are our needs as Christ's servants. This of course does not preclude petitions for material wants. Jesus Himself taught us to say, "Give us this day our daily bread." But it does preclude selfishness of any sort, and the preacher has here the opportunity to throw light upon perplexing problems of "unanswered prayer."

In speaking of deepening understanding of the nature of the Father, and the sense of immediate relation to the Father, the preacher need not be afraid to say that Christianity can actually be made too Christocentric. Super-orthodoxy may emphasize the deity of our Lord in a way that becomes unitarian. Nothing could have been further from the mind of Christ than that in His revelation the Son should eclipse the Father. In contemplating exclusively the revelation of God in Christ we can forget the words "spoken unto the Fathers by the prophets" (Hebrews 1:1), and forget also the infinity of divine nature that—so to speak—stretches back behind this manifestation; the overwhelming sense of God we feel on a starry night. The God revealed in the Old Testament belongs to our theology still. Yet it is our experience of Christ that enables us to interpret the wider vision. The purpose of verse 28 is not to state a bald theological dogma but to insist that, as far as a revelation of the infinite in human terms was possible, this revelation was given in Christ.

## THE EPISTLE

This is a direct continuation of the section for Easter 4, and the expositor will do well to start with 19b. Verses 22–25 depend on "receive (God's) word" at the end of verse 21. In the Bible we learn the ideal of human character and so realize our defects; it is like becoming familiar with the blemishes on our skin by gazing into a mirror. But unless we do something to remedy what is wrong the inspection is time wasted. Verse 26 returns to verses 19–20. The general word "religion" (see below) causes the writer to widen his outlook. Possibly this verse was a familiar proverb.

SERMON THEME: The proof of pure religion is gentleness and charity.

"Religion" in verse 26 is "religious activity," "attention to the externals of observance." Every one knows men and women who are persistent churchgoers but seem to gain only a spirit of faultfinding from their devotions. There are few congregations which do not need to be reminded that religion should mean control of the tongue and abstinence from uncharitable criticism, and that on the positive side it is exhibited in works of mercy. The church is the Body of Christ, the organ of His love, but it cannot teach the gospel of love unless it first practises it within the Christian brotherhood, and it cannot hope to draw the whole of mankind into fellowship unless by gentleness and charity fellowship is first established among its own members.

# ASCENSIONTIDE
# AND WHITSUNDAY

## THE SUNDAY AFTER ASCENSION DAY

### LITURGICAL NOTES

GOSPEL: John 15:26–16:4*a*. So the Sarum and Roman missals.

EPISTLE: I Peter 4:7–11. So the Sarum and Roman missals.

The English title for this day, "Expectation Sunday," describes accurately its liturgical character; the Ascension is forgotten in the tense looking forward to Whitsunday. Both Gospel and Epistle are devoted to "the Gift" and its missionary results: "ye shall bear witness," "even so minister." An inevitable consequence of this selection, however, is that an exposition which does justice to either Gospel or Epistle becomes an outright Whitsunday sermon. So the preacher is more or less obliged to make the exposition only introductory to a topical expansion of "expectancy."

### THE GOSPEL

Verses 26–27 are a perfect summary of the Christian doctrine of the Spirit. God gives us power from on high—but He gives it to us that this power may bear witness to the world through our changed lives, and that we may tell of what God has done for us and what He can do for all. "The witness of the Spirit must always be expressed through the witness of disciples; . . . the Evangelist's own 'Spiritual Gospel' is itself the best of all commentaries on the profound truths of verses 26–27."[1]

The world, to be sure, will not always listen to the "witness." For example, Christ's message of unselfishness is unwelcome to a so-

[1]G. H. C. Macgregor, *Gospel of John*, p. 294.

154

ciety founded on the principles of self-aggrandizement through ruthless competition, and every attempt to apply the principles of it to the reformation of our social life will be characterized as visionary, utopian, or even insane by the "practical" man of the world; in spite of the fact that his own policies have resulted in the paradox of starvation attributed to over-production and in the mad horrors of war. Special privilege everywhere, when it feels its power threatened, will fight back with no scruples about fair play, and with a rancour which often verges upon the pathological. We must expect this. But we must not be in the slightest degree dismayed by it: "these things have I told you."

SERMON THEME: In the life of the church and in the lives of individual Christians there are moments of expectant waiting, in which spiritual forces are gathering for a new manifestation of power.

The object of the preacher will be not only to vitalize the theme by historical and biographical illustrations, but also to induce the mood of expectant waiting by depicting the gift of the Holy Spirit as infinitely desirable, the one thing needful.

This will necessitate an excursion into Christian mysticism. The matter is the concern of personal religious experience, not of merely intellectual demonstration. In every allusion which Christ makes to the gift of the Holy Spirit and in every promise of it there is an element of mystery. There is a mystery of freedom in it and of origination (John 3:8). Those who have received the Spirit are free in a sense in which no other men are free. There is a mystery of authority in it and of creative power (Acts 1:8). History is molded and its destinies determined by those who have received the gift.

At the heart of all religion we find this element of mystery, the mystery of the self-giving of God in inspiration. Religion is a spiritual fourth dimension in which men and women, while not ceasing to be themselves, are conscious of union with the "Over-soul," that which is greater than themselves and yet not alien, a "Dweller in the innermost" who can express the vastness of His purpose through them.

## THE EPISTLE

This is the peroration of the baptismal address (compare on Easter 2), composed of short special exhortations and a closing doxology. In the liturgical use of the section the expositor should make verse 10 central. Then the highly effective apocalyptic appeal in verse 7 can be utilized in some such terms as "our treasure is not here but in heaven; let us live accordingly." "Brief life is here our portion," and for the individual Christian the end of all things is always "at hand"; the early church regarded the fact with calm confidence, and made no other preparation for it than prayer.

"Love covereth a multitude of sins" is from Proverbs 10:12. Here it means either "Love helps us to disregard the faults of others," or (more probably and better homiletically) "If a man really loves, God is quick to forgive him other faults." In the early church demands for hospitality (verse 9) were unceasing, since every journeying fellow-Christian expected to be cared for as a matter of course. Verse 10 is addressed to all, but verse 11 only to the leaders of worship: preachers must speak with such sincerity that the congregation hear the voice of God—not only the Pauline Epistles but all the Epistles bear witness to the ineffable dignity and responsibility of preaching,—while they who do the diaconal work of caring for the sick, needy, etc., must do it as partakers in the work of Christ's redemption, never wearying in well-doing. This exhortation passes with perfect naturalness into the doxology, an ideal expression of the highest Christian motive, to the glory of God through Christ.

SERMON THEME: As stewards of the grace of God Christians are to use their respective gifts from the highest Christian motive: that in all things God may be glorified.

Note the familiar theme of unity in variety: the first principle of moral action as of æsthetic perception. The gift of the Spirit imparts different and characteristic aptitudes, making each life individual and distinctive and enabling each to minister to others in the mutuality of Christian fellowship.

If the section is used for an ordination sermon, much may be made of the fact that the Christian ministry is in principle the most joyful of all callings because of its warm humanity. Nothing human is foreign to it: it touches human life, public and private, at a thousand different points of contact, and always with a beneficent purpose, always with the will to help, to guide, to redeem and to bless. It is also the most sacred of callings, because it is in closest association with the revealed will of God to uplift and to regenerate human life; it has no meaning except as it fulfills that will. The joy and the sacredness of the ministry may be kept alive through periods of routine, dullness and depressions by a constant maintenance of its sublime motivation, "that God may be glorified."

# WHITSUNDAY

## *A*

### LITURGICAL NOTES

GOSPEL: Luke 11:9–13.

EPISTLE: I Corinthians 12:4–14.

A new service, introduced in 1928. It has no relation to the traditional vigil use, in which both Sarum and Roman missals have as Gospel John 14:15–21 and as Epistle Acts 19:1–8; these lessons are baptismal.

## *B*

GOSPEL: John 14:15–31. The Sarum and Roman missals have John 14:23–31, a seventh-century Gospel. The Prayer Book selection, virtually a combination of the Sarum-Roman Gospels for the vigil and the Sunday, was first introduced in 1552; the 1549 Book had the Gospel for the vigil only.

EPISTLE: Acts 2:1–11. So the Sarum and Roman missals.

Pentecost, the second of the greater Jewish feasts, originally the festival of the wheat harvest, was in later times (compare John 5) observed by the Jews as commemorating the giving of the Law. That Jewish Christians kept it—naturally with the addition of special devotions of their own—was a matter of course (Acts 20:16), but its Christian significance brought it into early use among Gentile Christians as well. Its observance is first mentioned in the *Apostolic Tradition* of Hippolytus (*ca.* 217), but he takes it so for granted that its origin in Rome must lie far behind his time. In the third century the day seems to have been kept by orthodox Christians generally except perhaps in Spain.

When in the second century Easter was definitely detached from the Jewish Passover and observed always on a Sunday, Pentecost was naturally put "fifty" days later and therefore on a Sunday likewise.

The seven weeks after Easter—also known as "Pentecost"—were even in the second century a time of rejoicing in which fasting was forbidden. So Whitsunday originally had no vigil; the introduction of one came in the late fifth or early sixth century, in order to copy Easter. The corresponding addition of an octave, however, came more tentatively; a service for Thursday, for instance, was not instituted until the time of Gregory II (d. 731). And the development was complicated by the Ember Days, which were sometimes observed in Whit-week and sometimes later; different popes ruled differently on their date and their present position was not finally fixed until the time of Gregory VII (d. 1085). When placed here they broke the octave and left the following Sunday "vacant," and the present Roman Gospel for Pentecost 1 (Luke 6:32–42) is not Pentecostal but Embertide (compare on Trinity 4). Elsewhere in Europe, however, a full octave for Whitsunday was observed; compare on Trinity Sunday. And traces of a one-time Roman octave remain in the propers of the Whit-week Ember days, which are Pentecostal rather than penitential.

Pentecost, like Easter, was a solemn day for baptisms; our Epistles for Monday and Tuesday and both lessons in the missals for the vigil are baptismal; compare our Gospel for Trinity Sunday. And it is from the white garments of the newly baptized (compare on Easter 1) that the English "White-Sunday" is derived. The division "Whitsun-Day" was due to a misapprehension, which also created the (illegitimate) adjective "Whitsun." Attempts to connect this with the German "Pfingsten" (a corruption of "Pentecostes") are mistaken; so that "Whit-Monday," not "Whitsun-Monday," etc., is correct. The form "Whitsun-Week" has unfortunately made its way into the Prayer Book.

The purpose for Whitsunday exposition is to recover and apply the primitive conception of the Spirit as God's power, given to us to use for Christ's sake. Undoubtedly the early Christians thought of the Spirit in quasi-personal terms, but the dilemma "personal or impersonal," could not be propounded in the first century, for the category of personality was not yet developed in contemporary thinking.

## A

### THE GOSPEL

This section was chosen because of the mention of the Spirit in verse 13. The term, however, probably does not come from Jesus, since the parallel in Matthew 7:11 shows that the simple "good things" was the original form. But Saint Luke's alteration is perfectly legitimate, for the Spirit is the highest of all possible "good things," and embraces them all; if the Father is willing to give material gifts, how much more ready is He to bestow the perfect spiritual Gift! "Holy Spirit" is the source of every heavenly gift and contains the totality of them all.

Saint Luke's change makes the whole passage an exhortation to pray for spiritual blessings and, above all, for the blessing of social power.

On verse 9 see "The Strength of Wishes" in Canon Mozley's *University Sermons.* Verse 11: fish and bread formed the usual food of Galilean peasants, so the illustration is drawn from the commonest daily life.

SERMON THEME: Greatest of all the gifts of God is the Holy Spirit, through whom His power is given to us for Christ's sake, and by whom we are guided into all truth.

On the infinite desirability of the gift of the Spirit see on Ascension 1. We know that it is a gift more to be desired than any other, and that it is of the very essence of Christianity. There is a difference between morality and inspiration. To those who do not perceive the difference, who think that merely to live an upright, mannerly life without the seal of mystery upon it is enough, nothing more can be said. Like Nicodemus they are ignorant of the covenant truth that morality will not suffice, that men must be "born from above."

For instances of social power given through the Spirit, note the accompaniments of spiritual revivals in the church. The moral tone of Europe was purified and elevated by the influence of the Franciscan revival. The "Great Awakening" in New England was followed by a crusade against intemperance and by an extraordinary quickening of missionary zeal. What the Wesleyan and Oxford movements did for England and its colonies can be told in terms of heightened standards of public morals, a deepened sense of social responsibility, and a purifying of literature and speech.

On the Spirit's guidance into truth, see on Easter 4.

## THE EPISTLE

The same theme as in Romans 12—compare on Epiphany 1–3—although here treated more in detail. The list of gifts is slightly different, but there was of course no fixed scheme; writers set down whatever might come into their minds at the moment. How the Apostle distinguished "wisdom" and "knowledge" in verse 8 is uncertain—and wholly unimportant. "Faith" as a special gift (verse 9), distinct from the faith that all believers share, is explained in 13:2 as extraordinary power in prayer (compare on Quinquagesima). "Miracles," distinguished from "healings," are perhaps "exorcisms." "Discerning of spirits" is the ability to tell false prophecy from true. "Tongues," a religious ecstasy that causes its possessor to burst out into sounds incomprehensible to himself and others (14:2, 14). Yet certain Christians claimed the gift of "interpretation," which enabled them to explain the meaning of these utterances; whether truly or not, to be sure, there was no way of determining.

Compare for the whole on Epiphany 2. It is possible to find modern equivalents for the gifts described, but where this is difficult, as in the case of "tongues," it is wholly legitimate for the preacher frankly to substitute for them other activities of more immediate import today which are the gifts of the selfsame Spirit. The one thing needful is to keep constantly in mind the social implications of each endowment: they are bestowed "to profit withal," *i.e.,* "for the (common) profit."

SERMON THEME: All gifts of the Spirit are for the common profit; each several endowment has social implications; and in the church all individual aims are to be merged in desire for the common good, and so for the glorification of the common Lord.

The theme for Whitsunday is the giving of the Spirit and the preacher is warned against the common error of commemorating it as the birthday of the church. Jesus did not found a new church; He redeemed and reconstituted a church already in existence, the assembly of the people of Israel with whom God had entered into covenant relationship, narrowed as time passed by to the faithful remnant who were capable of responding to His claims. The whole destiny of this church of the old covenant was concentrated in

Jesus as Messiah: it found its fulfillment in His obedience, and then, reconstituted in Him, became the church universal. "Freed now from national limitations, the entry into it is no longer either by birth into a particular nation or by naturalization as a citizen of it, but by incorporation into the Body of the Messiah."[1]

On the *laissez-faire* attitude that because the church is the Body of Christ its life and purpose cannot fail, that it is "an affair of God to perpetuate it, and the privilege of man to enjoy what he wants of it," note the tragic failure of the church of the old covenant, and the warnings addressed in Revelation to its successor (Revelation 2:5, 3:3, 16). "The Christian life is a co-operative effort of man with God. God has given to men the high distinction and privilege of what seems to be equal share of responsibility for the Church of whose blessing we are chief beneficiaries."[2]

The merging of individual aims in desire for the common good is the essential principle of Christian unity. "Unity is not impaired because of diversity, but because of the failure to reckon with the fact that diversity is an essential concomitant of unity."[3]

## B

### THE GOSPEL

The Reformation lengthening of this Gospel was a mistake, since it is now too long for orderly exposition. Yet even the whole passage lacks missionary emphasis and is not as well adapted to Whitsunday as is the Gospel for Ascension 1.

"Truth" (verse 17) in the Fourth Gospel is not so much agreement with reality as it is reality itself. For a singularly helpful homiletic development of the thought compare Frederick W. Robertson's sermon, "The Scepticism of Pilate." There is a mystical touch in "seeth him not"; only the Divinely enlightened eye can

[1] William Temple, *The Church and Its Teaching Today*, p. 12 (Lecture I).
[2] T. D. Bratton, *An Apostle of Reality*, p. 113.
[3] *Ibid*, p. 162.

"behold" Divinity. Dante elaborates the thought in the third section of the *Divine Comedy*. In less mystical terms only the spiritual can comprehend spirituality. Verse 18: The Spirit, as the bond betwixt heaven and earth, re-establishes Christ's presence with His disciples. Verse 19: Macgregor notes[1] that while the primary reference may be to the Resurrection appearances, "the deeper intention is to point to that spiritual communion with Christ as an abiding presence which is the normal experience of the Christian and one more to be coveted than the enjoyment of special appearances granted, it may be, to confirm an unstable faith." Verse 22 voices Jewish expectation: The coming of the Messiah should be manifest to the whole world; what has happened that this is no longer true? The answer to this question of Judas (not Iscariot) is an answer to the questioner rather than to his question: love of Christ implies obedience, especially to His command of love, and only to those who so love and so obey Him will the revelation be made. Verse 28 corresponds to 16:7; the presence on earth of even the risen Christ was localized, but when raised to the Father He is available to all men everywhere. This while essentially an Ascension Day theme may be given a Whitsunday application by describing the Holy Spirit as Christ's "alter ego," one with Him as truly and as fully as He is one with the Father. Verses 30–31—not very appropriate to Whitsunday—look forward to the Passion: "so I do" in verse 31 means "I yield myself to those who will crucify me."

It is impossible to tell how much of this passage represents Jesus' original teaching, and how much John's interpretation of it; what is entirely certain is that it represents the profound experience of the church, guided into truth by the very Spirit whose work it describes. Consequently the expository preacher will do well to associate his doctrine of the Holy Spirit with the experience of the church, and especially with its sacramental life.

[1]*Gospel of John*, p. 30.

**THE EPISTLE**

Although according to Acts the experience of the Spirit was delayed until Pentecost the account in John 20:22 is historically preferable; compare on Easter 1. What gave this first Pentecost its infinite significance was something else, the fact that on this day the missionary work of the church began. Now for the first time since the Passover Jerusalem was once more thronged with pilgrims, "fields white to the harvest." In the power of the Spirit the apostles proclaimed their message to the multitudes, while the gift of tongues was prophetic of the time when Parthians, Medes, Elamites and all the rest would truly hear in their own languages the wonderful works of God, would hear and would believe.

It is of course on this aspect of the story that the expositor should dwell, not on the miracle that Luke so naïvely relates. Unquestionably the occurrence had a real basis in early Christian experience. A study of psychology reveals the fact that ecstatic speakers often interweave phrases from a foreign language into their utterances, thanks to a heightening of the memory that psychic excitement induces. And, as has often been observed, at Jerusalem pilgrims from all over the world loudly recited prayers in their own languages, so producing ideal conditions for the copying of these prayers by the Christian ecstatics. To the first century this was an evidential miracle of the first order, but it is not an occurrence that can or should impress us deeply today. In the American Prayer Book of 1928 the phrase "giving them the gift of divers languages," which was formerly part of the Proper Preface for Whitsunday, has happily been deleted. Expectation of this gift led some missionaries of an obscure sect to go to Japan with no other provision for learning the Japanese language; they returned in forlorn disappointment. It is significant, however, that the first believers cared enough about their religion to be carried away by it, in poignant contrast to the tepidity that too often satisfies us. Still more significant is the use that they made of their excitement; instead of prizing mystic ecstasies for their own sake, as is common in the history of mysticism everywhere, they turned the energy into constructive work that remade the world.

# LITURGICAL INTRODUCTION TO
## SUNDAYS AFTER TRINITY

The sequence from Advent to Trinity fills just about half the year, with no corresponding sequence for the Sundays that remain. The Prayer Book designation of these as "after Trinity" follows the pre-Reformation use in England and northern Europe. Somewhat earlier is the counting from "after Pentecost," a Gallican system that was eventually adopted by Rome as well. The earlier Roman use reckoned these Sundays "after Pentecost" until June 29, then "after the Apostles" (Saints Peter and Paul) until August 10, then "after Saint Lawrence" until September 26, and then "after Saint Cyprian." All these schemes—and there were others also—were merely for convenience of designation and are quite without liturgical significance.

The choice of the Trinitytide lections is at present equally without liturgical significance, both in the Prayer Book and in the Roman missal. In some instances, to be sure, a liturgical reason once existed for the selections, but this reason has now disappeared; for instance, the Epistle and Gospel for Trinity 4 were originally for Embertide, but these lessons are nowadays read a month after the Ember days are over, while in the Roman missal the Epistle and Gospel are read on different Sundays. But in most cases there never was any liturgical motive in the choice; the Epistles are a remnant of old continuous reading, represented only by a selection of passages (not always well chosen), but not even this much is true of the Gospels; compare the table on page 311. And in nearly every instance the association of Epistle and Gospel is wholly haphazard.

# TRINITY SEASON

## TRINITY SUNDAY

### LITURGICAL NOTES

GOSPEL: John 3:1-15. So the Sarum missal, following an English tradition that can be traced back to Bede and which was well represented also on the continent of Europe. This was selected originally as the Gospel for the octave of Pentecost, for which it is admirably adapted, especially with its reference to baptism. But it was so appropriate for the Trinity festival likewise that no change was necessary when this Sunday received its new dedication. The Roman missal has the purely Trinitarian passage Matthew 28:18-20.

EPISTLE: Revelation 4:1-11. So (without verses 10-11) the Sarum missal. Presumably also originally for the octave of Pentecost (verse 5). The Roman missal has Romans 11:33-36.

The observance of a special feast in honour of the Trinity began at Liège in the tenth century and became general in northern Europe before it made its way southward to Rome. It was established officially for the West in 1334 by John XXIV, who also fixed it on the first Sunday after Pentecost; up to this time there had been considerable divergence, with Pentecost 14 and Next Advent popular days in various uses. But in Rome the festival never attained the dignity given it in the north; it was limited to a single day, while in England and elsewhere it was provided with a vigil and a full octave. The introduction of this octave necessitated moving the services for the following Sundays each forward a week and in numbering them "After Trinity" instead of "After Pentecost."

The Prayer Book contains a reminiscence of the former Trinity octave in directing that the Collect, Epistle and Gospel, although not the proper Preface, are to be used until the following Sunday.

## THE GOSPEL

In this section Nicodemus represents many Jews at the close of the first century, who were genuinely impressed by Christianity (verse 2) but were unable to grasp its radical departure from Jewish ideals. They recognized that Judaism was inadequate, but were afraid of offending their coreligionists (Nicodemus came "at night"), and the fact that a new religion demanded a wholly fresh set of values—a "new birth"—bewildered and repelled them. The Evangelist writes in the name of the community to whom these fresh values were its very life, who put every would-be convert to a drastic test and accepted him only when he proved his willingness to transform his ideals. They would administer baptism only to those who subjected themselves to the rigorous discipline of the Christians' existence; under these conditions the sacrament actually did mean a birth into a life that was all-in-all to the believers but which outsiders could not understand. Naturally these rigid conditions entailed the loss of many converts—such as Nicodemus—but it also meant that those who were accepted had a genuine resolve to live as Christ would have them live.

It was this difference between Christians and non-Christians that explains the dualism of verse 6; compare II Corinthians 5:17. Verse 8: The outsider can no more appreciate what the believer finds precious than he can explain the wind; compare I Corinthians 2:14. (The Greek word-play on "wind" and "Spirit" is not very important to the sense.) In verse 11 the community speaks frankly in the first person plural: "If we Christians show you how men's lives are changed and you do not understand, what use would there be in trying to explain the deeper mysteries of the faith?" Verse 13: "Yet we Christians know these mysteries, for the heavenly Christ has revealed them to us." This verse also contains in passing a polemic against Jewish boasts based on Moses' ascent into heaven as described in Exodus 24. Verses 14–15: The descent of Christ from heaven was followed by His return to His place on high, from whence He gives believers the heavenly life that enables them to understand. Here, as always in the Fourth Gospel, the "lifting up" of Christ on the Cross is taken as the first step in his Ascension. Note the mystical language by which "eternal life" is the source of heavenly knowledge.

The passage is ideally Trinitarian, for even though the Father is not named explicitly, His presence is assumed throughout behind the work of the Son and the Spirit.

Or it is perfectly adapted to treating the doctrine of the Trinity as a "heavenly thing" whose value only believers can appreciate. The essence of Christianity is love. Then, to those who have a truly Christian experience, it is inevitable that in the Godhead love must have its infinite fulfillment, that divine love to be perfectly divine must have a divine object. So within the unity of God there must somehow be a plurality, within which such love can be interchanged.

Liturgically a Trinitarian sermon is called for, but for the expositor the passage is so significant a record of the spiritual experience of the early church that he will feel the need of returning to it at another time to appraise its sacramental and evangelical values, and especially its emphasis upon the "new birth" or "birth from above" as essential in Christianity.

SERMON THEME: The Father through the Spirit creates the new life of those who believe in the Son of God.

## THE EPISTLE

A vision of God rather than a vision of the Trinity. To analyze the flaming imagery in detail destroys its effect, which is symphonic; the apocalyptist himself would probably be unable to decide, for instance, whether the "elders" of verse 4 are human or angelic. His art consists in heaping up a multitude of touches, largely taken from tradition and so appealing to the memory, but shot through with the unique colouring of his own genius. So pulpit use of the passage is extremely hazardous; if attempted at all, the section should be used as the setting for a devotional meditation on God's majesty. As an antidote to the so-called humanism of the age which has made man the measure of all things, the teaching which makes God the measure of all things is essential; but the imagery of Revelation is so alien to modern thought that it is better to substitute for it symbols of God's glory chosen from the field of modern sciences, especially the science of astronomy. Or the passage may be used as the background for a sermon on the Divine Unity. Trinity Sunday is the festival of the Trinity in Unity, and nothing in Christian theology contradicts the stern monotheism of the Hebrew prophets.

SERMON THEME: The majesty of God revealed in the works of creation calls for a response of awe, wonder and worship.

# THE FIRST SUNDAY AFTER TRINITY

## LITURGICAL NOTES

GOSPEL: Luke 16:19-31; so the Sarum missal. This is not a Sunday Gospel in the Roman missal but it is assigned for the third Thursday in Lent.

EPISTLE: I John 4:7-21. So (without verse 7) the Sarum missal and (for Pentecost 1) the Roman missal.

The theme common to Gospel and Epistle is selfishness as a barrier between man and God.

## THE GOSPEL

Recent research has shown that the true emphasis in this story is in verses 27-31. What precedes is an oft-told tale, frequently used by Jewish teachers to illustrate God's reversal of man's judgments, and employed in similar fashion by Jesus to introduce a special warning of his own. God gives us sufficient light to follow His will; it is a matter of indifference whether we describe this light as our conscience or as "Moses and the prophets." And when a conscience has become so dulled that it is content with selfishness, its condition is well-nigh hopeless. Such a man will not be "persuaded if one rise from the dead"; religious zeal based on panic is worthless. Men cannot be terrified into a realization of their duty to their fellows; the change must come from within. In other words, the passage belongs to Christ's replies to the Jews' demand for a sign. That miracles would not bring true repentance was a matter of experience.

In the preface verses 19–26 Jesus' only significant contribution to the familiar tale is to make the sin of the rich man indifference to misery at his doorstep: Lazarus sought food, *but* (not "moreover" or "yea") all he received was pollution by the dogs. (To Orientals dogs are utterly unclean.) The scene in Hades is purely conventional and no stress should be laid on its details; it may be noted, however, that in most of the other versions of the story the sinner's sufferings are only for a set time; here the issues are inexorable? Jesus constitutes himself the champion of the neglected poor, and by implication a critic of the social order which permits such neglect. But the application here is direct and personal and is in accordance with the teaching in Matthew 25:31–46.

SERMON THEME: If a soul habitually resists its better impulses ("Moses and the prophets") and becomes content with selfishness that is indifferent to the misery of others, it will lose the power to live, and fear of impending judgment will not restore it.

## THE EPISTLE

For the purpose of I John compare on Epiphany 6 and Easter 1. Cerinthus' disciples were taught to regard themselves as supermen, who had no duties toward the rest of humanity (verse 20); the God Cerinthus preached consequently concerned Himself only with a tiny fraction of mankind. Saint John's reply is in essence an amplification of the theme of Matthew 5:45; God is concerned with all men (verse 14) and the dualism of Cerinthus is viciously false. And from the character of God Saint John deduces human duty exactly as is done in Matthew 5:43-48; God is Love, and His children must resemble Him. Whoever has this love for man is God's son; whoever lacks it—no matter what his religious pretensions—knows nothing of God. Here and nowhere else is the final test of any religion. And this test does not involve unverifiable theorizings; it simply asks whether an obvious and unmistakable duty (verse 20) is fulfilled. Behind it, for the Christian, lies the authority of Jesus, who associated love of the neighbour with love of God, and made love the criterion of Christian discipleship.

Here, as always in the Johannine writings, the intensely mystical concepts in "begotten of God and knoweth God" (verse 7) represent a mysticism that can be developed only through social relations.

The mention of scrupulosity in verses 17-18 resumes the more explicit treatment in 3:19-20 (Trinity 2).

SERMON THEME: Since true sonship involves likeness of nature, the children of God and of the light must resemble their Father in their unlimited love for men.

# THE SECOND SUNDAY AFTER TRINITY

## LITURGICAL NOTES

GOSPEL: Luke 14:16-24. So the Sarum and (for Pentecost 2) the Roman missals.

EPISTLE: I John 3:13-24. So, but ending with verse 18, the Sarum and (for Pentecost 2) the Roman missals.

In both Gospel and Epistle the choice is offered between following the world or Christ.

## THE GOSPEL

Historically this parable explains why Christ's disciples were so largely recruited from the lower classes; the "wise and prudent" had been deaf to His call so their places were taken by the "babes."

Note how in the story God's recompense overshadows everything else; in other passages Christ has indicated the sacrifices and self-denial required by the heavenly calling, but here its joy swallows up these considerations: the guests are bidden to a banquet.

In verse 21 the poor, etc., of the "city" are the unprivileged classes of the Jews, while those "out" of the city in verse 23 are the Gentiles (compare in Simeon's *Nunc Dimittis* "a light to lighten the Gentiles"). Verses 22–23 are Luke's addition, for when the parable was spoken this wider part of the servant's commission was not yet in view.

SERMON THEME: God's work will always go on, whether or not we choose to co-operate with Him. If we respond our reward will be rich, but if we disobey He will summon others. And what is true of individuals is true of classes, of nations—and even of churches.

### THE EPISTLE

The Reformation lengthening of this section has made it rather cumbersome, but at least public reading is secured for the important verses 19–22. They treat of the very important and common problem of scrupulosity, which tortures countless souls and keeps them from the enjoyment of their Christian heritage of freedom as God's children. (Compare T. Puller: "Others, by their weakness and fear and *scrupulousness,* cannot fully satisfy their own thoughts with that real benignity which the laws do exhibit."[1]) Saint John attacks the evil in verse 20 with a startling declaration: God judges us less harshly than we judge ourselves! But this of course is contingent upon verse 18, "let us love . . . in deed and in truth." Saint John knows the injury that worries about his spiritual condition can inflict upon a scrupulous person. He knows, in particular, that Cerinthus played on these worries to gain converts: "Are you

[1] *Moderation of the Church of England*, p. 10.

troubled with the burden of your sins? Come to us and we will make you free; we Gnostics have no sin" (1:8). Just so today there cannot be the slightest doubt that much of the modern indifference to Christianity is the result of the exaggerated emphasis laid in the past on "penitence" (as contrasted with all-important "change of mind" or "conversion"), until men finally have rebelled.

Saint John returns to the theme in 4:17-18 (Trinity 1): the joyous activity that faith in Christ should produce is clogged and damaged by fear. This statement can be turned immediately into the terminology of modern psychology, an acquaintance with which is well-nigh indispensable in present-day preaching.

To avoid repeating the treatment of Trinity 1's Epistle it is probably advisable to centre on this theme of over-scrupulousness. The corrective to overemphasis is supplied in verses 14-18 and 23-24. This must be given full value—we must have real grounds in our conduct if we are to assure our heart—but must not be pressed so hard as to destroy the point of verses 19-22; Saint John is not writing to great saints but to ordinarily earnest men and women. His teaching is summarized in Saint Augustine's *Dilige et quod vis fac:* if we love "in deed and in truth" we have "passed from death unto life"—the life of liberty.

Verses 13-14 express the usual Johannine church-world dualism. It is to be remembered that the "world" which Saint John found so intolerably evil was not modern Christendom—still bad enough after nineteen centuries of Christian leavening—but the contemporary paganism of which the vices are described with terrible candour by Saint Paul in Romans 1; the contrast between this world and the infant church could hardly be exaggerated. Verse 15 is a succinct citation of Matthew 5:21-22. Verses 16-18 voice the experience of the early Christian communities, when to be called to lay down one's life for the "brethren" was always a very real possibility. Note how verse 24b returns to the scrupulosity theme.

SERMON THEME: The joyous activity that faith in Christ should produce is hampered by fear; when a Christian with a loving will is trying to do his best for those about him, he should dismiss worries about his spiritual state as morbid and harmful.

# THE THIRD SUNDAY AFTER TRINITY

## LITURGICAL NOTES

GOSPEL: Luke 15:1–10. So the Sarum and (for Pentecost 3) the Roman missals.

EPISTLE: I Peter 5:5–11. So (without verse 5) the Sarum and (for Pentecost 3) the Roman missals.

God's care for His children, whether erring (Gospel) or afflicted (Epistle), is the common theme.

## THE GOSPEL

The Rabbinic literature abounds with descriptions of God's willingness to welcome repentant sinners. But the picture in these parables of God seeking for sinners *before* they repent has no Rabbinic parallel.

Luke's introduction (verses 1–3) expresses the thought adequately enough but is conventional. "Joy in heaven" and (more boldly) "joy in the presence of the angels of God" are periphrases for "rejoicing by God"; the parallels in verses 5–6 and 9 do not hesitate to make the human counterpart of this joy robust to the point of boisterousness. Every human personality is infinitely precious and no pains can be too great to rescue a soul from evil.

"The ninety and nine" in verses 4 and 7 are incidental only and no time should be spent in discussing them. "Just persons" is not sarcastic and there is certainly no allusion to the Pharisees, but who these persons are has nothing to do with the moral; the whole phrase may be a gloss. Verse 7 is psychologically exact; an enduring possession may give happy satisfaction, but not "joy."

God deems every soul worth searching for; the Pharisees erred in thinking a publican beneath attention: that is the moral of the story. This moral is personified in Jesus, whose teaching attracted the ostracized (verse 1) in spite of the austere idealism which made no terms with sin, and is the mainspring of the missionary effort of His church. For an extraordinarily daring poetical description of the persistence of the Divine love see Francis Thompson's *The Hound of Heaven*.

SERMON THEME: The love of God for His erring children even before they have repented, and the initiative of His questing love strike the new note in religion which makes Christianity a gospel.

### THE EPISTLE

The aphorism (from Proverbs 3:34) at the end of verse 5 led the Reformers to prefix most of this verse to the pre-Reformation section, but the result is unfortunate; verses 1–5 (on church duties) and verses 6–11 (conduct under persecution) have nothing to do with each other. Moreover "humility" in verse 5 is manward, in verse 6 Godward, so that the opening sentences of our Epistle are confusing. Verse 5 should therefore be disregarded.

The setting of verses 6–11 is a great persecution in which every Christian stood in real peril of death; probably the Domitian persecution of A.D. 93 is implied, but for homiletic purposes this is immaterial; by strange and unlooked-for developments a nearer setting may be provided from contemporary history; in countries where the State is in conflict with the Church, Christians are again being persecuted for their faith. According to the Epistle the situation is to be accepted humbly (verse 6), fearlessly (verse 7) and steadfastly (verse 9). No one should think of his distress as unique and exceptional (verse 9). Since through God victory is certain (verse 10), to Him be all praise for ever (verse 11)!

SERMON THEME: Under persecution Christians are to conduct themselves without complaint, without anxiety and without wavering, since through God the victory of their faith is assured.

# THE FOURTH SUNDAY AFTER TRINITY

## LITURGICAL NOTES

GOSPEL: Luke 6:36–42. So the Sarum and (for Pentecost 1) the Roman missals.

EPISTLE: Romans 8:18–23. So the Sarum and (for Pentecost 4) the Roman missals.

The liturgical unity lies in the fact that these lections were originally for Embertide: the duties of Christian teachers (Gospel) and their hope (Epistle). But disassociation from the Ember days makes this unity impractical for the expositor.

## THE GOSPEL

The passage as Luke has arranged it is a close-knit whole with the opening verse as its theme. In verse 39 the "blind leader" and in verse 40 the "master" are those who try to lead or teach arrogantly and harshly. Such a leader will lead those who follow him into the ditch; such a teacher will make his pupils loveless copies of himself. Just so in verse 42 the "mote" represents the ordinary faults of mankind but the "beam" is the spirit of proud and carping criticism, an infinitely greater evil from Christ's standpoint. The expositor, in fact, can well add verses 43–45, which carry the development of the theme to its conclusion. The danger in such an exposition is lest the expositor denounce lovelessness in a loveless manner; this must be guarded against by keeping the Father's mercy (verse 36) constantly to the fore. God's mercy is shown in patience with the undeserving; His love goes forth even to the loveless, and it is to this ideal, exemplified in Christ, that His followers are called.

"Shall they give" in verse 38 represents an Aramaic impersonal plural, used in place of the passive. The real subject is of course "God."

Homiletically it is to be noted that Christ's warnings against cen-

soriousness were directed to the religious people of His day, and that
this is as much as ever their besetting sin. "The faults which religious people ignore in themselves, while criticizing the failings of
their neighbours, are like planks of wood compared to tiny specks."[1]
According to Jesus, not love but lovelessness is "blind."

SERMON THEME: Censoriousness is a greater evil than the ordinary faults of mankind which it condemns in a loveless manner;
love like that of God alone gives true perception and enables men
to judge justly.

## THE EPISTLE

This Epistle carries on the thought of the Epistle for Trinity 3
so perfectly that it may actually have been selected for this reason.
Its ending is a little abrupt, but the continuous flow of Romans 8
does not make for good stopping points; to have included verses
24–25 would have been a mistake.

In verse 18 the "sufferings" have nothing to do with formal persecutions, as in I Peter, for these had not yet begun when Romans
was written. Hardships incidental to the Christian life are meant.
The argument in verses 19–21 is difficult for moderns to follow,
since it is written in terms essentially of the first century. What
Saint Paul has in mind is Genesis 3:17, "Cursed is the ground for
thy sake." Not through any fault of their own, but by reason of
God's sentence passed on Adam, even the inanimate and the brute
creations have been made subject to corruption ("vanity"). And so
creation "groaneth and travaileth," storms and earthquakes work
havoc, fields are sterile, poisonous plants flourish, beasts of prey destroy their victims. Yet this subjection is not without hope. It will
cease when men regain their nature (are "manifested") as true "sons
of God": then everything will be restored to Edenic peace and glory.
(Compare Isaiah 11:6–9.)

The expositor should make no attempt to rationalize these verses;

[1] W. Manson, *The Gospel of Luke*, p. 72.

# THE FOURTH SUNDAY AFTER TRINITY

179

the passage must be treated as what it is, naïve Jewish Messianism.
Its value lies in its firm acceptance of God's work; "God saw everything he had made, and behold, it was very good." Christianity re-
jects dualism without compromise. The world itself is an object for
God's redemption. To turn apocalyptic into evolutionary terms: as
men are more and more manifested as sons of God, cruelty, waste
and destruction grow less and less. It is even possible to separate
what is essential in Saint Paul's thought, his hope in God, from the
first-century concepts in which it is expressed, and to substitute for
his peaceful Eden the actual beginnings of our world, in a process
of painful travail, with "nature red in tooth and claw." If this is
done, the homiletic interpretation becomes most fruitful. Quite as
truly as the most modern of scientists, Saint Paul perceives that the
relation between man and nature is vital and organic; that together
they are subjected to a law of development, to a discipline pro-
tracted through immense stretches of time. The pain involved in it
is productive. A travailing creation is a world, not in the process of
dissolution, but in the process of becoming.

Verse 23 stands outside the influence of the Genesis passage and
can be used directly. Above all, man's physical nature will be redeemed; the "body," now a constant impediment to our free development, will be transformed into a perfect instrument for the soul.
In this connection the preacher may well pay his tribute of recognition and gratitude to those who, often quite unconsciously, are
working with God to effect this end: physicians and research workers who have already been instrumental in eradicating many of the
ancient plagues and in lengthening materially the span of human
life.

SERMON THEME: Although there is evil in the world, the world
itself is not evil; it too is an object for God's redemption, and in
this redeeming work man has his share.

# THE FIFTH SUNDAY AFTER TRINITY

## LITURGICAL NOTES

GOSPEL: Luke 5:1–11. So the Sarum and (for Pentecost 4) the Roman missals. Originally appointed for the Sunday before Saint Peter's Day.

EPISTLE: I Peter 3:8–15a. So the Sarum and (for Pentecost 5) the Roman missals.

Christ's appeal to the unconverted, whether through those formally engaged as "fishers of men" (Gospel) or through the lives of all believers (Epistle), is a theme common to these sections.

## THE GOSPEL

Historically this paragraph belongs to a secondary Synoptic strain, and its development is somewhat complicated. Basic is the fact that Simon, Andrew, James and John were called "fishers of men" by Jesus, in allusion to their former occupation. From this developed the picturesque tradition of Mark 1:16–20, which made the title vivid by depicting Jesus' call to these four when actually engaged in their tasks. From one standpoint the present section is a further enlargement of the same tradition by including the account of the miraculous draught. This, however, appears to be derived from what was originally a resurrection story, better preserved in John 21 and perhaps referred to in Matthew 14:28–31, in which Peter poured out his contrition to the risen Lord, received forgiveness and was sent out to preach.

In any case there can be little doubt that Saint Luke understood the story allegorically, seeing in the draught of fishes by the apostles a figure of the overwhelming success of the apostolic preaching. And this allegory should be followed frankly by the expositor. Jesus chose as His messengers persons who often seemed quite unadapted to their task, such as fishermen. They were conscious of their own inadequacy, but none the less obeyed Christ's command (verse 5). And through Christ's power they wrought a miracle compared to which the physical draught of fishes sinks into insignificance; their missionary work met with such extraordinary success that they were overwhelmed by the number of converts who flocked in (verses 6–7). It is in the presence of this response to the Gospel message that we realize our own faults and weaknesses; which would abash us utterly were it not for Jesus' gracious "Fear not!" (verses 8–10). "Depart from me" (verse 8) need express no more than simple terror at the presence of the supernatural, and is not to be analyzed too closely.

In John 21 the allegory is even more patent. The fish number "one hundred and fifty three" because according to the scientists of the day such was the number of all the kinds of fish in the world; *i.e.,* the converts come from every nation under heaven.

SERMON THEME: As Christ on earth attracted disciples by His transcendent personality, creating in them a sense of the "numinous" (verse 8) and then made them apostles, "fishers of men," so now the risen Christ awes His church with the same sense of the supernatural, reassures by His love, and gives the great commission, world-wide evangelization.

## THE EPISTLE

For the setting compare on Easter 2–3. The "church order" ends with 3:7, and with verse 8 the writer begins his general appeal. It is coloured by the impending persecution, and the motive given in verses 10–12 (from Psalm 34:12–16) is the desire for self-preservation: he who is respected for his goodness is unlikely to be attacked. But this somewhat sub-Christian argument is raised to a higher plane by the context, especially 2:19–25 (Easter 2), which is recalled here by verse 15 (in which "Christ," not "God," is the correct reading). The expositor, consequently, should summarize 2:19–25 briefly —particularly 2:24—to give the exhortation its proper colouring.

The archaisms of the King James Version are satisfactorily enough corrected in the Revised Version. But "courteous" in verse 8 translates a corrupt reading in the Greek text; "humble-minded" is correct.

SERMON THEME: The conduct of Christians is to be determined by a heart anxious in all things to acknowledge Christ as Lord.

# THE SIXTH SUNDAY AFTER TRINITY

## LITURGICAL NOTES

GOSPEL: Matthew 5:20-26. So (without verses 25-26) the Sarum and (for Pentecost 5) the Roman missals.

EPISTLE: Romans 6:3-11. So the Sarum and (for Pentecost 6) the Roman missals.

The righteousness which exceeds that of the scribes and Pharisees (Gospel) is the righteousness of the Christians' walk in newness of life through the resurrection of Christ (Epistle).

## THE GOSPEL

Verse 20 is really the theme for the whole body of the Sermon on the Mount, but it is of course wholly appropriate as an introduction to the treatment of hatred in verses 21-26; the section, therefore, can be used as a unit. There are four divisions: the extent of righteousness (verse 20), the evil of hatred (verses 21-22), the care that should be taken to correct it (verses 23-24) and the peril of delay (verses 25-26).

The "righteousness of the scribes" was the outgrowth of a literalistic legalism (changed in later Rabbinism) that measured guilt quantitatively by the punishments laid down in the Law. The Law that forbade murder provided the death penalty for murder; hence the sin in murder is defined by this penalty. The guilt in lesser offences is consequently proportionately less, while offences too slight to have a legal penalty affixed—such as mere anger—are

negligibly sinful, if sinful at all. Jesus replies that this whole scale
of guilt is wrong: God's judgment on anger may be as severe as
the Law's judgment on murder, and His judgment on angry words
may be as rigid as the Law's judgment on the graver crimes reserved to the "council" (the Great Sanhedrin) or even the abhorrent offences punished by the direst penalty known to Judaism,
burning in the Valley of Hinnom ("hell-fire" is hopelessly wrong;
in all the second clauses human, not divine, punishments are meant).
Verses 23–24 are self-evident, but Jesus' insistence that the "merely
moral" takes unhesitating precedence of the "merely religious"
should be noted: the gravest moral defects of ecclesiasticism are due
to reversing this order of precedence. Verses 25–26 (compare Luke
12:58–59) = "Worldly prudence teaches men to adjust hopeless
suits at law before judgment is rendered; how much more should
men repent before God judges!" This little parable must not be
allegorized by asking who is the adversary or the officer; as in all
parables the moral lies solely in the central teaching, not in the details. In Matthew's context this moral is narrowed slightly to repentance for offences against the neighbour; Luke's general exhortation is more original.

The moral ideal set forth in the Sermon on the Mount is sometimes spoken of as "impracticably high." It is meant to be so. The
ideal of the scribes and Pharisees, while difficult, was attainable and
men could boast that they had reached it (Trinity 11). But the
righteousness that Christ sets forth as the Christian ideal is nothing
less than the righteousness of God Himself, and once this ideal is
accepted no man can profess to be satisfied with his attainments;
we hope for salvation not because we have earned it but because
God is our Father. Whatever righteousness we may acquire is not
our work but God's work, the gift of His grace and love. Here,
despite differences of terminology and emphasis, Catholic and Protestant theology are at one.

SERMON THEME: The righteousness which "exceeds" that of the

scribes and Pharisees differs from legalistic righteousness not in degree but in kind; it is the righteousness of the new life which comes from receiving Christ as an animating motive and desire.

## THE EPISTLE

A more extended form of the teaching of the Epistle for Easter Day, with the accent thrown more directly on moral conduct. The first five chapters of Romans show that justification comes not through works but through faith. The sixth chapter then raises the question, "If this be so, why need we be good?" And the answer given here is: "No believer will ask 'How much sin may I safely commit?'; to any one realizing his union with Christ any ideal but goodness is unthinkable; he has 'died unto sin.'"

The intensely realistic mysticism of the section must be thoroughly understood by the expositor, although for most congregations translation into moral terms is needed to make the passage intelligible. As regards details, the vivid sacramentalism of verse 3 voices Saint Paul's own baptismal experience; it was at baptism that he felt the inrush of the Spirit that raised him to ecstasy (I Corinthians 12:13, etc.). Since, however, the experiences of other Christians were different (Acts 8:15-16, etc.), the Pauline baptismal teaching should not be hardened into a dogma: it is the experience of the Spirit that is essential, not the means by which in individual cases the experience is given. The Friends, who do not practise baptism, yet have given so abundant evidence of the possession of the Spirit, are a case in point. The imagery of the baptismal ceremony (by immersion) in verse 4 is self-evident. The Father's "glory" is a Jewish paraphrase for His power, which is also our strength for a life of holiness. Note at the end of the sentence how the indicatives are replaced by a subjunctive, "we should walk," not "we shall walk"; the transformation is not mechanical but depends on our co-operation. In terms of their union with Christ the Corinthians are already "dead unto sin," but in terms of their behaviour they are still far from the realization of this ideal. "The paradox runs through Paul, as it runs through Christian experience, peace and struggle, victory and temptation, hope and questioning. The Christian is one who is becoming what he is."[1]

The beginning of the next sentence (verse 5) should be rendered: "For if we have been united to him by the likeness of his death (baptism), the union will be perfected by the likeness of his resurrection (righteousness)." The "body of sin" is human nature in its lowest aspect; this has lost its power finally to direct the conduct of believers, even though they may succumb to it from time to time. "He that is dead is free" is a popular proverb, used here with perhaps not entire relevance, but the context shows its meaning. In the rest of the passage "to die" is "to sin," and "to live" is "to live righteously"; physical death and future resurrection are here not in point.

SERMON THEME: The Christian's consciousness of a heavenly life already begun, a life in which there is both a vision of righteousness and a sense of power to achieve it, strips unworthy pursuits and pleasure of all their lure.

# THE SEVENTH SUNDAY AFTER TRINITY

## LITURGICAL NOTES

GOSPEL: Mark 8:1-9. So the Sarum and (for Pentecost 6) the Roman missals. This Gospel at or about this point is practically invariable in the mediæval lists but the reason for its choice is wholly unknown.

EPISTLE: Romans 6:19-23. So the Sarum and (for Pentecost 7) the Roman missals.

The common theme is Christ's gift of grace.

[1] C. A. Anderson Scott, *Foot-notes to St. Paul,* p. 40.

### THE GOSPEL

Compare on Lent 4. In Mark this second feeding of a multitude takes place on non-Jewish soil and is used by the Evangelist as predicting the Gentile mission. A missionary use of the section would therefore be legitimate. Or verses 2–3—the only characteristic feature in the section, which is historically a doublet of the earlier feeding—can be employed as teaching Christ's response to urgent faith. But the former use is preferable; and the expositor will be following the lead of the Evangelist if he allegorizes by taking the first feeding of the multitude as a parable of the Jewish people finding in Christ the satisfaction of their spiritual need, and this second feeding as a parable of the Gentile world.

SERMON THEME: Christ's compassion on the multitude becomes the incentive for those who share His spirit to engage in missionary effort, while His sensitiveness to their hunger justifies the social service associated with modern missions.

### THE EPISTLE

The section unfortunately begins in the middle of a sentence and the expositor will have to go back to verse 15 to gain clarity. This verse restates the question asked in verse 1 and answered in the Epistle for Trinity 6: "Does God's ready forgiveness make it safe for us to continue sinning?" The answer, however, here takes a different line. Character is formed by habit (verse 16). In the past Saint Paul's readers had been slaves of their bad habits, but now they are becoming the slaves of good habits (verses 17–18; for homiletic illustration compare the chapter on Habit in William James's *Psychology*). "Slaves," to be sure, is a very inexact term (compare the Collect, "whose service is perfect freedom"), but the figure at least makes the idea clear to persons not yet accustomed to mature spiritual thinking (verse 19); Christians are not really "slaves," for their "service" is that of sons and as such is also their hearts' desire and their joy.

There was a time when the readers were not troubled by their consciences and could indulge themselves in selfishness (verses 19–20).
"What good did such conduct do you? Now you are ashamed of
it!" (verse 21; literally translated). No one who has experienced any
progress in holiness will think of surrendering this "fruit" of good
habits, even apart from the infinite future of life with God (verse
22). Verse 23 summarizes the argument. On "eternal life" as the
gift of God, Anderson Scott calls attention to a characteristic sentence of Baron von Hugel: "The noblest root and flower of the
Jewish-Christian religion and of European civilization is this sense
of givenness, of grace, of dependence upon a Reality other and
higher than ourselves."[1]

SERMON THEME: Unrestrained indulgence in evil results in complete degradation of character and slavery to sin; the good habits of
the Christian have as their fruit freedom from sin, and this freedom
is God's gift to those who persistently seek righteousness.

# THE EIGHTH SUNDAY AFTER TRINITY

## LITURGICAL NOTES

GOSPEL: Matthew 7:15–21. So the Sarum and (for Pentecost 7)
the Roman missals.

EPISTLE: Romans 8:12–17. So the Sarum and (for Pentecost 8)
the Roman missals.

The Gospel sets forth the test of religious experience, the Epistle
the fruit of an experience that stands the test.

## THE GOSPEL

This is a familiar but often misused passage; the "false prophets"
attacked were in no sense what we call heretics but were teachers
of a false morality; primarily the "scribes and Pharisees" of Matthew
5:20 (see on Trinity 6), whose "righteousness" was legalistic and

[1]*Foot-notes to St. Paul*, p. 41.

not the fruit of a transformed nature—the "good tree" of verse 17. The proper application, consequently, is a stern warning against all who teach contentment with a morality that does not "exceed" legalism, or who compromise with evil by casuistry (compare Hermann's *Faith and Morals*). The "sheep's clothing" historically was Pharisaic devotion to the externals of religion; the "ravening wolves" describes those who "devour widows' houses and for a pretence make long prayers." In the charge to a newly consecrated bishop the Prayer Book echoes the warning in "Be to the flock of Christ a shepherd, not a wolf; feed them, devour them not." Such devotion to externals was a danger which neither the Protestant Reformation nor the Catholic Counter Reformation has wholly overcome. But nowadays greater danger is to be found in the ethical teachers who profess to show their love for mankind by condoning or even approving free indulgence of the baser instincts: against these modern "false prophets" the flock of Christ needs constantly to be warned.

Verse 19, which breaks the context, is an intrusion from the preaching of John the Baptist (3:10) and should be relegated by the expositor to its proper context. Verse 21 properly belongs to the following section (verses 21–23); if used here it should be combined with verse 15 in defining the characteristics of the "false prophets." Christ's indignation with those who call Him "Lord, Lord," and do not the things which He says finds repeated expression.

SERMON THEME: The worst enemy of Christianity is not the hostile critic from outside, but the church member whose conduct belies the ideals to which he renders lip service.

## THE EPISTLE

The thought of the Epistles for Trinity 6 and 7 is continued, but with the emphasis now almost entirely on our possession of strength to avoid evil and to live righteously. "We are not debtors to the flesh" = "our lower nature no longer fetters us," "we *can* overcome bad habits by good." In modern English "mortify" may be rendered "break the force of," "discontinue obeying." The words "die" and "live" (verse 13) are used not in their physical sense but in terms of fellowship with God; the true life of the soul. Verse 15 has a play on "spirit" and "Spirit" that is very difficult to reproduce: "When you used to think of God as a taskmaster, your spirit was filled with fear, but now His Spirit teaches you that He loves you as His children." This is the sense of "spirit of adoption."

Verse 15 refers historically to a baptismal custom of early Christianity. Converts were not allowed to use—perhaps were not even taught—the Lord's Prayer until the time of their baptism, uttering it for the first time as they stepped forth from the water. Then it was shouted aloud ("cried") in an ecstasy that proved the inrush of the Spirit. Modern attempts to restore the custom in certain circles have usually proved somewhat mechanical, and certainly afford an insufficient basis for any such plea as is here made by Saint Paul. And the excesses of revivalists have, in fact, led most Christians nowadays to deprecate fixing on any single emotional moment as proof of conversion. But full justice can be done to the thought by appeals to the presence of the inward stirrings of ideals and valiant attempts to realize them; he who strives to live as God would have him can unhesitatingly call on God as Father.

In verse 17 "suffer" has no reference to persecutions; it describes the sacrifices that must be made in the pursuit of goodness (see on Trinity 4). To "suffer with" Christ is to share His sympathies which extend to the "least" of His brethren (Matthew 25:40), in other words, so lovingly to identify oneself with one's fellow men as to bear their sorrows as did Christ. And the result of this is to be "glorified together"; "together" at the end is "together with Christ," not "with one another."

SERMON THEME: All our yearning and struggle toward good is

a proof of a power in us that assures certain victory; the very desire of our hearts to address God as "Father" proves that we are His children.

# THE NINTH SUNDAY AFTER TRINITY

### LITURGICAL NOTES

GOSPEL: Luke 15:11–32 (American) and Luke 16:1–9 (English). The American section is a 1928 innovation, to avoid the somewhat enigmatic character of the older section, which is that of the Sarum and (for Pentecost 8) the Roman missals.

EPISTLE: I Corinthians 10:1–13. A Reformation lengthening of the Sarum and (for Pentecost 9) Roman sections, which began with verse 6.

With either Gospel liturgical unity is not easy to establish. Perhaps, while in the American Gospel God's eagerness to welcome penitents receives its classic expression, yet (Epistle) we must not use His mercy as an excuse for putting ourselves in the way of temptation. With the English Gospel the steward's cleverness in worldly matters should (Epistle) be used in avoiding occasions of sin.

### THE GOSPEL

(American.) Grotius expressed the common mind of the church when he described this as the most beautiful and affecting of all the parables of Christ. In no other is the love of God for man, the misery of man's life apart from God, the readiness of God's forgiving mercy and the joy of reconciliation set forth in terms so moving: the parable is evangelical in the deepest sense.

It is not, however, "evangelical" in the narrow and party sense of the word, for it contains no reference at all to the Atonement —an omission that sorely perplexed many of the older commentators; indeed, to those who held the rigid doctrine that Christ's death alone made forgiveness possible the difficulties of the parable were almost insuperable. But if it be held that the primary purpose of the Atonement was to "reconcile us to God," these difficulties vanish; and we can do better justice to Christ's revelation of God as One who by His very nature is Father. And we need no theological devices to convince us that He everywhere accepts His children when they turn to Him, even though they have never heard of Christ.

The expositor should also note that the parable is not an allegory in which a very wise and good father is used to represent God. On the contrary the reproach in verse 29 indicates that the father's treatment of the elder brother has been niggardly and selfish, and that the youth has good reason to complain. Similarly, moderns often point out that fathers were warned against disposing of their property prematurely (Ecclesiasticus 33:19), and that to turn the younger son loose, with his pockets full of money and no one to guide him, was most injudicious. Then the moral is: If so negligent a father can be awakened to a sense of his responsibility by the recovery of a lost son, *how much more* will God be ready to care for a returning soul? This reasoning from the best in faulty and fallible human fatherhood to the infinitely better of the Divine fatherhood is a familiar course of argument with Jesus (compare Matthew 7:9-11). On the theological implications compare B. H. Streeter: "To think of the Infinite in abstract or impersonal terms is unconsciously to liken Him to forces lower, poorer and less full of vitality than ourselves, such as electric current, or the life principle in a tree. To say that God is 'personal but something more' is to say that the Creative Principle must be higher than the highest, richer than the richest, more full of life than the alivest of all things that it has produced,—and that is surely common sense."[1]

Verse 17, "when he came to himself," may be allegorized slightly as "words of deepest significance, saying as they do that to come to one's self, and to come to God, are one and the same thing; that

[1]*Reality*, p. 141.

when we truly find ourselves we find Him; or rather having found Him, find also ourselves."[1]

Traditional exposition of the parable is usually highly unfavourable to the older brother, although there are exceptions, especially since Cajetan espoused his cause. But to paint him in too dark a color goes beyond legitimate interpretation and cannot be reconciled with his having remained ever with his father in dutiful obedience, or with the assurance of favour which he receives in verse 31. In fact, a fresh treatment of the familiar material can be gained by centring on the older brother, taking him as the type of those who do their duty faithfully, although ploddingly and at times impatiently. If this earthly father could be so awakened to the value of his obedient son, how much more does God always prize those who persevere?

SERMON THEME: The fatherly love of God for man is shown in His eagerness to welcome penitents, while the misery of man's life apart from God indicates that sonship is his true and natural condition.

## THE GOSPEL

(English.) This is a confused passage as it stands, for Saint Luke extracted verses 1–8 from an earlier source, in which "the Lord" (not "*his* lord") meant Christ; Luke, however, thought of the steward's "lord" (verse 3) and distinguishes him sharply from Christ by making the latter speak in the first person in the moralizing addition of verse 9. The result is to make the steward's master praise the steward for defrauding him!

The expositor, accordingly, should limit himself at first to verses 1–8. Verses 1–7 are in no sense a parable but a story, very possibly of an actual recent happening. The tone is pure comedy; people were chuckling over the ingenuity of a clever scamp. Verse 8:

---

[1] R. C. Trench, *Notes on the Parables of Our Lord*, p. 398. *Cf.* also St. Augustine, *Serm.* 96:2.

"Jesus himself was amused at the device; he wished that the children of light would devote as much trouble to their vocation as worldlings do to devious ways of making money." The moral is obvious. Saint Luke, however,—whose sense of humour was small —appends verse 9 to prevent any possible misunderstanding: "This steward won a temporal home by a wrong use of money; you should try to win eternal homes by its right use" (primarily by alms-giving). But this unduly limits the moral, which teaches the right use of opportunity in general. And Saint Luke's attempt to copy the wording of the story has produced confusion; not only is the "I" here impossible (compare above), but nothing comprehensible can be made of these "friends" who "receive" men into heaven. This verse consequently should be omitted by the expositor. If he wishes, however, to follow Saint Luke's narrowing, he will find a far-reaching application in advocating the use of wealth to effect a reconstruction of the social order upon principles consistent with the gospel of Christ.

"Mammon of unrighteousness" means "the wealth that unrighteous men count supreme."

SERMON THEME: Men will exercise infinite patience and ingenuity in order to win earthly success; should not those whose ideals are higher devote even greater diligence and forethought in fulfilling their aim?

## THE EPISTLE

The Epistle sequence for Trinity 6–8 is continued by a warning against needless exposure to temptation in an over-reliance on spiritual privilege.

The passage is part of Saint Paul's answer to the Corinthians' question: "What shall we do about food dedicated to heathen deities?" (8:1). In general the Apostle regards eating such food as a matter of indifference, but in the present passage a specialized form of the problem is discussed: "Should Christians attend banquets

given in honour of such deities?" Feasts of this kind were very
common in the Hellenistic world, chiefly in connection with meetings of social clubs, trade-guilds, etc., nearly all of which were under
the patronage of some god. Some of these meetings were actually
held in the deity's temple (8:10), and at all of them the deity was
invoked and libations, etc., were made in his honour. Refusal to
attend banquets of this kind meant cutting one's self off from most
of the social and business life of the day, and so entailed real hardship. And the Corinthians argued that, since the deities in question
were non-existent, attendance could do no harm; while in any case
the Christians were protected by their own sacraments from any
contamination that might be present.

Saint Paul agreed (verse 19) that the deities had no existence.
But their worship created an atmosphere of evil in which all kinds
of immorality were encouraged; at such gatherings Christians had
no place. The present passage is concerned with refuting the theory
of "sacramental immunity" by an argument from history: the Jews
of the Exodus had "sacraments," too, but these proved no safeguard
against their recipients' folly. Using Rabbinic traditions—for the
details of which commentaries must be consulted—Saint Paul takes
the passage through the Red Sea as a "baptism," and the water from
the rock as a "eucharist," in which they really partook of Christ.
But look at their fate. Only Joshua and Caleb survived to enter
the promised land! And the sins of the rest were precisely those to
which the Corinthians would expose themselves in these banquets
—lusting after evil—idolatry—licentiousness—discontent—rebellion.
(The Old Testament passages cited by Saint Paul should be consulted for the precise meaning in each case.) Verse 11 applies the
lesson to the Corinthians; this application is assisted by a theory
of history according to which all the contents of the Old Testament
were to find their fulfilment in the Apostolic age. Presumption is
a grave danger! Undoubtedly real self-sacrifice was called for and
the readers had the Apostle's sympathy. But, after all, this particular

trial was not overwhelming—and God will more than make up to His servants all they surrender for His sake.

The meaning of the word translated "common to man" in verse 12 is dubious; perhaps "arising out of purely human conditions" comes nearest to the sense.

The section is rather long and complicated for pulpit exposition but there is no way of abbreviating it; the pre-Reformation opening with verse 6 omits the hearts of the passage. But under less formal conditions it can be treated most happily, and it yields an ideally practical moral: moral foolhardiness may prove disastrous. The sacraments of baptism and the eucharist are potent safeguards but they are not talismans whose magical properties relieve the Christian from the need of sober precaution and avoidance of occasions of sin.

SERMON THEME: Spiritual privileges do not confer immunity, therefore the Christian must avoid needless temptations.

# THE TENTH SUNDAY AFTER TRINITY

### LITURGICAL NOTES
GOSPEL: Luke 19:41-47a. So the Sarum and (for Pentecost 9) the Roman missals.

EPISTLE: I Corinthians 12:1-11. So (without verse 1) the Sarum and (for Pentecost 10) the Roman missals.

There is no liturgical unity.

### THE GOSPEL
Two Lukan sections (verses 41-44 and 45 ff.) are conjoined here, making the second give the reason for the first: God's chosen city was doomed, for its worship of money blinded it to the presence of its Redeemer. Compare on Advent 1 and Lent 6.

Historically verses 41-44 are largely a dramatization of Christ's (undoubtedly historic) prediction of the destruction of the Temple. The place Luke has chosen for the little paragraph is highly effective although it may have been transported from another context.

SERMON THEME: Groups and nations which through pride, exclusiveness, or selfish retention of special privilege reject the humane principles of the Christian religion are doomed to destruction.

## THE EPISTLE

Compare on Whitsunday A, with verses 1–3 as the only new material. The opening sentence takes up a question asked by the Corinthians: "Which is the most desirable spiritual gift? In particular, how highly should we appraise the ecstatic 'speaking with tongues'?" Their letter then went on: "A man in our assembly shocked us by calling out in an ecstasy 'Jesus is accursed!' But he was so clearly possessed by a supernatural power that we are afraid to discipline him; what ought we to do?" Saint Paul's reply is that what seems supernatural is not necessarily good. The sense of verse 2 is: "You remember in your pre-Christian days orgiastic ecstacies that were abominable." The greatest of all spiritual gifts is the Holy Spirit who imparts wisdom and understanding that make possible just evaluations of religious experience. It is interesting to note that while the "Great Awakening" was in progress in New England, similar ecstatic phenomena were in evidence, and that Jonathan Edwards judged them with Pauline sobriety and intelligence.

SERMON THEME: By the illumination of the Holy Spirit Christians obtain a right judgment in all things, and are able to discriminate not only between the true and the false but also between the best and the second best.

# THE ELEVENTH SUNDAY AFTER TRINITY

## LITURGICAL NOTES

GOSPEL: Luke 18:9–14. So the Sarum and (for Pentecost 10) the Roman missals.

EPISTLE: I Corinthians 15:1–11. So (without verses 10b–11) the Sarum and (for Pentecost 11) the Roman missals.

The contrast between the Pharisee's boast of merit and Saint Paul's acknowledgment that all he has done is God's work gives a genuine unity.

## THE GOSPEL

The point of this story lies in the fact that the Pharisee is supposed to be speaking the exact truth, and the moral is ruined by making him out a hypocrite, full of secret vices. His fault lay in treating God's righteousness as so small a thing that he could congratulate himself on having attained it; in this way he, so to speak, brought God down to his own level and turned devotion to a Father into satisfaction in having fulfilled a contract. His self-superiority, irritating though it is, is but one symptom of an evil that lies far deeper. He was of those who "trusted in themselves that they were righteous, and despised others." He was so unaware of the terrible righteousness of God, of the awfulness of the Divine requirements, that he swaggered into the presence of his Judge. His prayer is no prayer, but becomes unconscious blasphemy through his presumption. And this man dared to "despise others," adding to his sin against God a sin against his neighbour. The homiletic bearings of the parable are evident; and the expositor can find an all too painful modern instance in the self-satisfied member of the church who, having complied with its formal rules and ritual requirements, shows scorn and intolerance of his fellow Christians of other denominations. On the positive side the prayer of the publican is to be taken as a perfect illustration of what is meant by the New Testament doctrine of "justification." God gives, we do not earn, salvation; it is our part to accept with childlike trust. Where bargaining enters into religion all savour evaporates.

SERMON THEME: Those whose compliance with the formal rules and ritual requirements of "respectable" religion makes them self-satisfied and scornful receive condemnation; while those who, distrustful of self, throw themselves upon the Divine mercy, receive in overflowing measure God's forgiving and redeeming grace.

## THE EPISTLE

This section is only the preface to the elaborate argument that fills the whole of I Corinthians 15; Saint Paul begins by rapidly recalling an elementary Christian truth before he attacks the real problem at stake. The basic fact of Christianity is that Jesus Christ is no mere great figure of the past; He is a living and immediate source of spiritual life to all who call upon Him.

The Apostle is not for a moment trying to prove Christ's resurrection, however. He is simply reminding his readers of a formula, taught by all Christian missionaries ("whether it be I or they"), which listed as follows the most important appearances:

> To Peter;
> To the Twelve;
> To more than five hundred brethren;
> To James;
> To all the apostles.

And this list he expands with comments, especially at the end, where he recognizes that his addition of

## To Paul

is not accepted by all Christians. And it is only in dire necessity that he is obliged to include the egotistic-sounding clause in verse 10 (compare on Sexagesima), doing his best to avoid the appearance of boasting by the clauses that precede and follow it.

It is this same verse 10 that is really the heart of the passage; it gives the palmary argument for Christ's resurrection as the power that enables us to "labour abundantly." Paul's own experience of redemption, together with the power to "labour abundantly," are

proof of the authenticity of the revelation to him of the heavenly
Christ, seen of him "as of one born out of due time." For all
Christians of a later day the ultimate proof of the resurrection lies
in their experience of a living Christ, and that proof is unshakable.

> Yea, with one voice, O world, though thou deniest,
> Stand thou on that side, for on this am I.[1]

SERMON THEME: The historic Jesus whose resurrection was attested by many witnesses is identical with the heavenly Christ whose
gifts of redemption and of power prove His resurrection in the personal experience of believers.

# THE TWELFTH SUNDAY AFTER TRINITY

## LITURGICAL NOTES

GOSPEL: Mark 7:31–37. So the Sarum and (for Pentecost 11) the
Roman missals.

EPISTLE: II Corinthians 3:4–11. So the Sarum and (for Pentecost
12) the Roman missals.

The ministration of life is the common theme.

## THE GOSPEL

Mark uses the healing miracle as a preface to his account of
Christ's work on Gentile soil; this is the point of the geographical
notice in verse 31. While the cure is meant to be taken quite literally, it has the added symbolical sense of opening the ears of the
(spiritually) deaf (= the Gentiles), and it is from this standpoint
that it can be made most profitable. Now as then, the power of
Christ to heal physical disorders, which is a blessed illustration of
the Divine benignity, is of secondary importance; His primary task
is to be the "caster out of demons," to contend against sin in its

---

[1]F. W. H. Myers, *Saint Paul.*

every form of unbelief and selfishness and to bring in the kingdom of God.

SERMON THEME: Christ's ministration of life is shown in His healing of spiritual disorders.

## THE EPISTLE

The ministers of Christ have the glorious commission to impart life. They are to be "competent ministers of the new covenant." The abruptness of the opening—"such" is left unexplained—is due to disregard of the context, but the rest of the passage is excellently unified. Verse 6b, the key to the whole, is perhaps the most frequently misquoted verse in the New Testament. It is usually cited as if it meant, "the letter of a law should be disregarded in favour of its spirit," but Saint Paul's sense is something wholly different. The antithesis is between salvation by obeying a legal code and salvation by the inner working of the Holy Ghost. Saint Paul speaks from the depths of his own experience. He believed, with all Jews, that the Law of Moses set before him a perfect ethical code, and promised him salvation if he could live up to it. But this promise was delusory. Sinlessness, which the Law demands, is beyond human reach and the struggle to attain it breeds scrupulosity and despair that lead to rebellion and collapse: "the letter killeth." Preaching and teaching too exclusively centred about ethical imperatives defeat their own object. None the less, the ethical ideal is indispensable, and there is real truth in the story of the glory that shone from Moses' face as he proclaimed it (Exodus 34:29-35). But, if men are to have hope, this ideal must be taught as the expression of the nature of the Father, who works within His children that they may grow more and more into His image. For "You must!" is thus substituted "Some day you will!"

SERMON THEME: "Contract religion" kills; life comes through the Holy Spirit.

## THE THIRTEENTH SUNDAY AFTER TRINITY

### LITURGICAL NOTES

GOSPEL: Luke 10:23–37. So the Sarum and (for Pentecost 12) the Roman missals.

EPISTLE: Galatians 3:16–22. So the Sarum and (for Pentecost 13) the Roman missals.

Perhaps some sort of unity can be established between the Epistle and the opening verse of the Gospel, but the attempt is scarcely to be recommended.

### THE GOSPEL

Verses 23–24 are the impressive close of the wonderful section Luke 10:1–24 and were certainly never intended by the Evangelist to serve as an introduction to the story of the Good Samaritan. Nevertheless, this story, which breaks down all racial prejudices, fully merits the most solemn preface possible. But the expositor may do well to reserve these verses to heighten the effect of his final summary.

It is highly important to note that the "summary of the Law" in verse 27 is given not by Jesus but by the "lawyer" (= "scribe"). Jews were fond of formulas that purported to condense the whole Pentateuch into a single sentence, and this combination of Deuteronomy 6:5 and Leviticus 19:18 was very natural; its disappearance from later Judaism is almost certainly due to its adoption in Christianity. But, whatever the origin of this combination, it is forever associated with Jesus and not with any pre-Christian Rabbis; the reason being that He took it seriously and they did not. They might hold academically that every legalistic act somehow expressed love to God or to the neighbour; but for practical purposes each precept was a precept, rigidly binding because "written," and

whose eventual meaning was only a matter of speculation. But to
Jesus the "summary" was a practical means for determining duty,
the only basis for a true system of ethics. If in any given case a
conflict of duties arose, it was to be settled by deciding which course
of action most directly contributed to love of God or the neighbour.
And in case of an apparent conflict between these two loves, love of
neighbour was to be taken as expressing love of God. Compare,
e.g., Matthew 5:23–24 (Trinity 6).

Furthermore Jesus insists that the demands of the Law must not
be restricted by legalistic interpretation of a precept's wording.
Verse 29: "To justify himself"; "to show there was real reason for
his question." The lawyer—typically—argues that Leviticus 19:18
commands only love of *neighbours,* not of non-neighbours, with the
result that "Who is my neighbour?" is a crucial question. To which
Jesus replies in a story that needs no explanation at all; in particular, allegorizing of any sort is unpardonable.

It is well to remember, however, that in the time of Christ Sa-
maritans, while despised heartily by Jews, were not yet regarded
with the intense hatred that the war with Rome produced; John 4:9
reflects the later conditions. The contempt felt for them by the
Jews had its parallel in the contempt felt by the Greeks for the
"barbarians," and has its modern (often more extreme) counterparts in all sorts of racial antagonisms, such as that of the Nazi for
"non-Aryans." The expositor has in this section an ideal base from
which to attack the most dangerous and disintegrating prejudices
which threaten the peace and safety of modern civilization. If in
this connection he reverts to verses 23–24, their solemn joy will be
associated with the "salvation from unneighbourliness" which the
Bringer in of God's Kingdom has for those who truly see and hear
Him.

SERMON THEME: To be a good neighbour is to show mercy wherever there is need.

## THE EPISTLE

The theme of the Law's impotence is continued from Trinity 12, the question now being, "If the Law was so useless, why was it given at all?" And the answer is, "It served a genuine purpose in training humanity." The development of the thesis, however, is carried out in terms of a Rabbinic scholasticism so eminently of the first century that real understanding of it has been regained only in very recent years; most commentaries in English still miss essential points.

Verse 15 is essential to the argument and should not have been omitted; "once a contract has been solemnly closed, it cannot be changed." Verse 17: "God, who is completely immutable, made such a contract with Abraham, to hold in his day and to hold again when Christ came, but not to hold in the intervening time." This is the sense of the use of Genesis 13:15, which is explained in so scribal a fashion as to be unconvincing to modern readers—for whom, however, Saint Paul was not writing. Verses 17–18: "Since nothing can change a contract, the Law certainly could not. Hence at the present time it is the promise (salvation by faith), not the Law that holds."

The Law, consequently, could have only an interim value. What was this? Verse 19 explains, "it was added because of transgressions," a cryptic expression that is explained in Romans 7:11-25 as meaning actually "to create transgressions"—*i.e.,* to bring evil to light and to identify it as evil; "it was given to teach men what evil is."

Verses 19*b*–20, once considered hopelessly obscure, are nowadays clear enough, although their declaration is rather startling: "The purely interim character of the Law is proved by the fact that it was not given by God at all, but by the angels!" Here Saint Paul takes for granted a Jewish tradition (Acts 7:53, Hebrews 2:2) which avoided the anthropomorphism of (*e.g.*) Exodus 31:18 by explaining that God gave the Law to angels, who carried it down to Moses. "The hands of a mediator" is a reference to Moses. Saint Paul also takes "mediator" in the sense of "spokesman," for which there is Greek authority. The argument then runs: "A group of persons wishing to convey a message need a spokesman, for they cannot all speak at once, while a single person has no such need. But God is a single person. Consequently the Law is not from God; it was not only transmitted but actually 'ordained' by the angels."

Yet (verse 21) this does not make the Law useless; far from it! It set before men a perfect ideal of righteousness (compare on Trinity 12), and this was good for them to have, even though their attempts to reach it made them despair. This very despair (verse 22) was precious, as it enabled men really to appreciate the life brought to them by Christ.

Scholastic and strange though this argument may seem to us, it is a valiant attempt with inadequate means to state a profound truth: while only Christianity can finally satisfy the heart, lesser glimpses of God have a genuine value of their own. The contrast between Christianity and other religions, then, is not the contrast between "true" and "false," but between "complete" and "imperfect." The ethics of Confucius, the compassion of Buddha and the monotheism of Mohammed, like the Jewish Law, prepare the way for Christ. As the Apostle possessed no critical tools, he had to have recourse to what are to us very strange devices, but underneath the complexities of the discussion is the realization that the Old Testament revelation is not all on the same plane and, in particular, that the legalism lies on a lower level. He can explain this only as by coming from a lesser source of revelation; but the fact that a Jew of the first century could see the distinction at all is a miracle, and a lesson to Christians of the twentieth century who do not yet read the Old Testament as a progressive revelation. (Compare Jesus' dictum in Mark 10:5 that certain commandments were written only because men were unwilling to do their best.)

The section is not easy to treat in the pulpit, but it has wide possibilities of application: the justification of Biblical criticism, the proper standpoint in studying other religions than ours, the utility (and dangers!) in the less spiritual types of Christianity, etc. It can even be used very properly in discussing the training of children, especially where modern interest in "self expression" finds all discipline abhorrent. The disciplines of commandment and prohibition cannot of themselves impart a right spirit but are a necessary preparation for its impartation by a more vital source. So in the wider educational context, the training of mankind: the Law is temporary, but it serves its purposes, bridging the interval until the gift of the Spirit who makes legalism superfluous, writing "not in tables of stone, but in fleshly tables of the heart" (II Corinthians 3:3).

SERMON THEME: Law is temporary, but it serves its purpose, bridging the interval until the gift of the Holy Spirit makes legalism superfluous by making love the principle of life.

# THE FOURTEENTH SUNDAY AFTER TRINITY

## LITURGICAL NOTES

GOSPEL: Luke 17:11–19. So the Sarum and (for Pentecost 13) the Roman missals.

EPISTLE: Galatians 5:16–24. So the Sarum and (for Pentecost 14) the Roman missals.

The thankfulness of the Samaritan can be connected with the list of fruits of the Spirit in the Epistle.

## THE GOSPEL

Historically this section appears to be a moralizing expansion of some such cleansing of lepers as that recorded in Mark 1:40–45. The composition is not very skillful; were not all the lepers healed by faith (verse 14b), and not only the Samaritan? And—it might well be argued—were not the nine others restrained from turning back because of Jesus' explicit command to show themselves to the priests? These considerations, however, did not occur to the editor; the story to him conveys the general lesson of thankfulness, with a secondary reflection on the ingratitude of the Jews. So the expositor had best treat it broadly, as teaching the lessons which the Evangelist undoubtedly wishes to convey: that it is the mission of Christ to heal both body and soul (leprosy, regarded as the most terrible of diseases, a veritable "sacrament of death," has its counterpart in sin); that thankfulness for God's mercies assures the continuance of them by establishing communion with Him; and that unexpected response to the gospel of redemption is to be found in unpromising circles (the Jews, "children of the covenant," are represented by the ungrateful "nine," and the Gentiles by "this stranger," verse 18). Incidentally, the gratitude of the Samaritan shows him in so favourable a light as to disarm national antipathy (compare on Trinity 13).

SERMON THEME: Thankfulness for God's mercies assures the continuance of them by establishing communion with Him.

### THE EPISTLE

The theological discussion in Galatians is turned into practical terms at the close of the Epistle, beginning with 5:13; this section, consequently, can be used as continuing directly the discussion of Trinity 13. Since we are not "under the law," but "under grace," let us use our freedom in gracious and fruitful living. No believer will desire anything else. Compare on Trinity 6–8.

The list of vices in verse 19–21 is conventional and might well have enumerated other sins; probably no attempt should be made to analyze it closely. Anderson Scott renders[1] "emulations" as "fanaticism," "strife" as "party spirit" and "heresies" as "factious

[1]*Foot-notes to St. Paul*, p. 169.

cliques"—the word has no theological reference. But the virtues in verses 22–23 are chosen with more deliberation for their immediate social value and may be studied in detail. Note that "faith" here = "fidelity" (between man and man; as we say, "good faith") and that "meekness" is better rendered "gentleness." Note also that although these virtues are described as "fruits of the Spirit," none of them is ecstatic; they all belong to "routine" life. Compare on Quinquagesima.

For a nobly adequate homiletic treatment of verse 16 see Phillips Brooks' sermon from the text.[1]

SERMON THEME: Since Christians are freed from the hampering scrupulosity of legalism, and since they are endowed with the power of the Spirit, let them manifest the fruits of the Spirit by devoting all their energies to abundant living.

# THE FIFTEENTH SUNDAY AFTER TRINITY

## LITURGICAL NOTES

GOSPEL: Matthew 6:24–34. So (without verse 34) the Sarum and (for Pentecost 14) the Roman missals.

EPISTLE: Galatians 6:11–18. A Reformation section, replacing the Sarum and (for Pentecost 15) Roman Galatians 5:25–6:10.

Both Gospel and Epistle teach that believers must view this world, as it were, from heaven; only then can the interests and cares of life be seen in true proportion.

## THE GOSPEL

The connection established by the Evangelist between verse 24 and what follows is probably not original (compare Luke 12:22–31 and 16:13) and gives to "anxiety" a more evil colouring than Christ intended; the folly, rather than the sin, of worry was meant. Still,

[1]*The Purpose and Use of Comfort*, p. 353.

needless worry is so common among believers who ought to know
better, and is so generally due to immoderate care for possessions,
that Matthew's arrangement has real expository value. Note the
ease with which our "belongings" can become our "masters." "Mammon" means simply "money." No man can be both a servant of
God and a slave of his possessions.

In the American Prayer Book of 1928 the Revised Version was
very properly substituted for the King James. "Take no thought"
sounds today like an injunction to be thoughtless and is no longer
comprehensible English for "be not anxious"; while in verse 27
"stature" was always a bad translation: life is viewed as a journey
along a road, "life's way," so that a cubit added to that long way
would prolong existence only a tiny instant: anxiety will not even
do that. The "lilies" (really "anemones") of Palestine are not
white but gorgeous in purple and scarlet, genuinely suggestive of an
Oriental potentate's robes. In Palestine grass is literally "cast into
the oven," to preheat it before the oven is used for baking.

The accent is in verse 33, "seek ye his kingdom." ("Kingdom"
does not mean "church," for Christians do not "seek" the church.)
God will give what is needed for His service; compare Easter 5.
But more than this is not promised, least of all is promised immunity from trials and hardships, and the passage must not be used
to teach a facile—and often disappointing—worldly optimism.

On verse 34 may be compared *Sanhedrin* 100*b:* "Trouble thyself
not about the trouble of the morrow, for thou knowest not what
a day brings forth. Perhaps on the morrow thou wilt not exist, and
so wilt have troubled about that which does not exist for thee."
This verse has been described as a "secular" saying of Christ's. It
is not despondent or pessimistic but gently humorous: "There is
so much real trouble right now: why add to it unnecessarily?"
But Christ was never merely "secular."

SERMON THEME: They who work for God may be sure of all

they need for the tasks He entrusts to them, and may work without anxiety, for His purposes cannot fail.

## THE EPISTLE

In Galatians the Epistle proper ends with 6:10. After an amanuensis had made a fair copy of this, the Apostle added a postscript in his own handwriting, emphasizing by the size of the characters —"see how large letters I am making"—the importance of what he had to say. Hence the Revised Version, not the King James should be used.

The heart of the section is verse 15; compare II Corinthians 5:17 "if any man be in Christ, he is a new creature." And it is this separation of the earthly from the heavenly that gives the "cross of Christ" its significance in verse 14 (the Atonement is not in point). With ceremonial (or the reverse), when adopted as merely helpful to an individual, Saint Paul had no quarrel (Romans 14). In fact, if a Christian preferred to live as a Jew and wished to have himself circumcised, the Apostle had no objections in principle, even though he advised against it (I Corinthians 7:18-19). But when an observance was put forward as important for salvation— as was the case in Galatia—he attacked with all the vigour of which he was capable.

The point in verses 12-13 seems to be that certain Jewish Christians argued for circumcision because to make—at least nominal— Jews of Gentiles would curry favour with the Jerusalem authorities. The "marks of the Lord Jesus" in verse 17 are probably scars left by scourging (II Corinthians 11:25, compare Mark 15:15).

The circumcision controversy is long since obsolete, but there are myriads of other practices which men have confused—and still confuse—with Christ's religion: ritualism, anti-ritualism, fasting laws, Sabbatarianism, total abstinence, and countless others. To detach men's hearts from such concrete observances and to induce them to view Christianity as centred "in heavenly things in Christ" and concerned with the "new creature" is a most difficult task. But it is vitally necessary, and in attempting it the expositor has behind him the full weight of the authority and moral passion of Saint Paul.

SERMON THEME: Neither the use nor the non-use of ceremonial observance has anything to do with Christianity, whose ideal is wholly elsewhere; Christianity is centred in heavenly things in Christ and concerned with a new creation.

# THE SIXTEENTH SUNDAY AFTER TRINITY

## LITURGICAL NOTES

GOSPEL: Luke 7:11-17. So (without verse 17) the Sarum and (for Pentecost 15) the Roman missals.

EPISTLE: Ephesians 3:13-21. So the Sarum and (for Pentecost 16) the Roman missals.

God's power, protecting His own through Christ's love, is the common theme.

## THE GOSPEL

The Christian motive in this section is that the miracle was wrought through sheer compassion; otherwise it has the form of typical ancient "wonder" stories. Note especially the initial insistence on the very large number of witnesses, as in John 11:31; contrast Mark 5:40. The youth's death is proved by the fact that the body is being carried out for burial. Christ's wholly supernatural power revives him by a mere touch, terrifying the onlookers. (But the last clause of verse 16 does not attest Christ's divinity; "God has sent a marvellous messenger" is a fair paraphrase.) For the whole compare Epiphany 3. But here no allegory is apparent and attempts to find one are impossibly artificial.

The expositor, consequently, must frankly admit that the section has been drastically redacted, the original probably being something like Mark 5:35-43. But this very redaction makes the moral clearer. God is "not the God of the dead, but of the living" (Mark 12:27). Only, we shall be raised not to resume this life but to enjoy a life in which this mortal shall have put on immortality, the life of the world to come. "There is no death; what seems so is transition." That loving human relationships will persist, that the widow of Nain will receive her son again, and Martha and Mary their brother, is the sublime reality which underlies this Gospel. Those who are "in Christ" have experienced in God's gift of eternal life a greater and more blessed miracle than the mere prolongation of their earthly existence.

SERMON THEME: God's love for His children extends so far that death is no obstacle at all to His infinite power, which will preserve all loving human relationships through the great change.

## THE EPISTLE

A sequence from Ephesians begins here and continues for five Sundays, apart from the interruption on Trinity 18. The expositor consequently should keep in mind the general structure of Ephesians as a whole. Chapters 1-3 describe the reconciliation in a higher unity of the warring Jews and Gentiles, while chapters 4-6 outline the duties that follow from the privilege of membership in this new society. The social note, accordingly, must be emphasized at every point.

The inclusion of verse 13 was unfortunate, and gives an entirely wrong force to "for this cause" in verse 14. This last phrase looks back over all written thus far, and the argument for a moment pauses in rapt contemplation and thanksgiving: such is our wondrous privilege; "for *this* cause I bow my knees!" All that we know of "family" goes back to God as the primal Father, so that in His family—of which we are now members—all family ideals find their realization. And the writer prays that we, the whole body of believers, knit together by the Spirit and the indwelling Christ, may learn constantly more fully the Father's marvellous plan for us. From this vision comes the strength for the corporate work that we have to do. Endless praise be unto Him!

The theme of the section, then, is realization of destiny as the source of action, a destiny to be won corporately by all who work for Christ. Social revolutionaries find courage in the hope of a better material world; Christians have this hope as well, but they look beyond it to an infinitely more glorious future. So their zeal should be endlessly more intense!

In verse 15 "the whole family" should be "every family." The Greek has an untranslatable word-play between "Father" and "family," but the paraphrase above gives the sense. "Glory" in verse 16 means "power," as often. In verses 17–18 being "rooted and grounded in love" (for one another) is the indispensable basis for advance in spiritual knowledge. "Breadth, length, height and depth" in verse 18 must not be connected with "the love of Christ" in verse 19; it is an independent (originally astrological) phrase, meaning here "the secrets of God's plan." At the end the social emphasis appears once more in "in the church." Naturally the worst possible exposition would be to take this last phrase in a merely ecclesiastical sense: the church here means "the blessed company of all faithful people," or "all those in whom the Holy Spirit dwells."

The section may be treated homiletically as an ideal form of intercessory prayer (compare John 17). Note that to be "in Christ" means to have fellowship one with another, that this fellowship, intensified by common worship, is a condition of spiritual insight into the Father's plan, and is reflected in moral conduct which makes the believers workers together with God (II Corinthians 6:1) in carrying out the divine "plan."

SERMON THEME: God's universal fatherhood constitutes the entire human race one family, of which Christians are conscious members, and in which all family ideals find their realization.

# THE SEVENTEENTH SUNDAY AFTER TRINITY

## LITURGICAL NOTES

GOSPEL: Luke 14:1–11. So the Sarum and (for Pentecost 16) the Roman missals.

EPISTLE: Ephesians 4:1–6. So the Sarum and (for Pentecost 17) the Roman missals.

Both Gospel and Epistle commend lowliness.

## THE GOSPEL

Verses 1–6 and 7–11 are independent sections, having in common only their anti-Pharisaic bias and the very external circumstances that have to do with a dinner. For the Sabbath healing compare Jesus' attitude on ceremonial matters as discussed on Trinity 6. Verse 5 is His passionate protest at all the countless inhumanities that have been practised in the name of religion.

Verses 8–10 are not much more than a paraphrase of Proverbs 25:6–7, and, as they stand, are open to the objection that they inculcate worldly rather than heavenly wisdom; there is, in fact, hypocrisy in the ostentatiously humble act performed with the expectation of public praise, than which nothing could be more foreign to the spirit and teaching of Jesus. What has happened is that an isolated saying of Jesus (verse 11), which has to do with heavenly things, has been supplemented from the Old Testament (verses 8–10) and the result has been furnished with an introduction (verse 7) by the Evangelist. So the expositor should confine himself to verse 11, as an objective law of the spiritual world.

If the whole section is to be treated together, the only possibility is a criticism of the spirit of ecclesiasticism that leads to cruelty (verses 1–6) and pride (verses 7–11).

SERMON THEME: Self-exaltation leads to downfall; self-forgetful-
ness in the service of others alone confers true greatness.

## THE EPISTLE

The "therefore" in verse 1 parallels the "for this cause" in 3:14,
and like it resumes the whole Epistle up to the end of 3:13; after
the digression in 3:14-21 (Trinity 16) the argument is resumed.
The social privileges given to believers result in the social duties
now summarized. More specifically, while all Christian ethic is
social, the responsibilities of Christians toward one another are
heightened by the unique closeness of the relationship in the church.

"Meekness" in verse 2 should, as always, be "gentleness." Verse
3: Peace is the bond whereby the Spirit-given unity is preserved.
The exquisite sentence in verses 4-6 can be translated immediately
into practical terms; it is an inimitable expression of common interests. "Faith" in verse 5 is not "creed" but "spirit of devotion,"
since the early believers—in accord with their Jewish background—
laid very little stress on intellectual agreement; it was not until the
extreme vagaries of gnosticism that any attempt was made to for-
mulate creedal statements. The end of verse 6 is "in all (things),"
not "in you all."

The section is especially adapted to a sermon on church unity.
The differences between Catholics and Protestants today are no
greater than those which existed between Jewish and Gentile Christians in Saint Paul's day, yet these two branches of the early church
were triumphantly unified by the doctrine set forth in the Epistle
to the Ephesians. Now as then the reconciliation must be effected
by the indwelling of the Holy Spirit.

SERMON THEME: No differences between believers are comparable
to what they have in common, therefore let them realize their
essential fellowship and keep the unity of the Spirit in the bond of
peace.

# THE EIGHTEENTH SUNDAY AFTER TRINITY

## LITURGICAL NOTES

GOSPEL: Matthew 22:34–46. So the Sarum and (for Pentecost 17) the Roman missals.

EPISTLE: I Corinthians 1:4–8. So the Sarum and (for Pentecost 18) the Roman missals.

The break in the Ephesian sequence is due to the fact that at this point in the series there stood originally the "vacant" Sunday after the September Ember days, and the gap was filled by these Embertide sections: the Two Great Commandments and the confession of Christ as Lord (Gospel) are the basis of all advance in Christian knowledge (Epistle).

## THE GOSPEL

Again the Gospel is formed of two paragraphs (verses 30–40 and 41–46) without inner unity. After a long series of questions addressed to Jesus (beginning with 21:23), of which verses 34–40 record the last, He turns suddenly on His inquisitors and silences them: verse 46 looks back to 21:23. The paragraphs here, however, can be unified by showing that it is *because* Jesus so reduced conduct to its ultimate basis that we can accept Him as Lord.

On verses 34–40 compare on Trinity 13.

The saying in verses 43–45 is rightly placed at the very close of the ministry. Jesus' faith in His Messianic vocation was absolute, but He had long known that His death was inevitable. On the usual Jewish premises the two convictions were incompatible: a "son of David" Messiah could not be slain. Hence His Messiahship—which was the *only* Messiahship—must be of a very different character from that taught by the scribes; His reign would come after death, and would be not earthly but heavenly. Hence the Messiah is not David's "son" but David's "Lord."

This conclusion is corroborated by the 110th Psalm, which is of course used as any one would use it in the first century. It may be noted, however, that it could be used equally effectively without attributing it to David: "Does not God in the Scripture say to the Messiah, 'Sit thou on my right hand'? How could this be said to a Davidic prince?" The Messiah is descended from David but is immeasurably exalted above him.

There is no reason to question the general authenticity of this section. Jesus could have reached no other conclusion about His own destiny than this; the early church may have made what He said slightly more explicit, but even this much revision is very doubtful. And He frequently refuted His enemies by propounding unanswerable questions to them; this one was eminently appropriate to the time when He knew they had resolved upon His death. For us today it is a key to the understanding of Old Testament prophecy, much of which, based upon belief in a national God, looks forward to a national hero to bring in His Kingdom. In a sense the expectation was verified—Jesus was a Jew—but beyond this He was Son of the universal Father and Redeemer of the world, and all "Old Testaments" whether of the Jewish religion or of others which foretell the coming of the Deliverer, must be read and interpreted through the Jesus of history, the Redeemer who actually came.

SERMON THEME: As Christ's reign came after His death, and is not earthly but heavenly, Christians, however much they may and should strive to better the conditions of earthly life, can never be satisfied with a merely earthly goal.

THE EPISTLE

The break in the Ephesians sequence serves at least to summarize God's gifts in general before passing on to the special gifts detailed on Trinity 19. "Utterance" and "knowledge" (verse 5) formed the large substance of Greek education as "rhetoric" and "philosophy." But the appearance of these terms in the Christian vocabulary was momentous, as they foreshadowed nothing less than a revolution in the conception of the faith. On Jewish soil worship and practice were primary, so much so that, as long as these were preserved, individuals might speculate much as they pleased; Judaism accepted a few fundamental dogmas but knew nothing of any system of dogmatics. But to the Greeks speculation was all important. To them a religion was inadequate until it could be analyzed as a philosophy ("knowledge") and expressed in terms acceptable to cultured taste ("utterance"). It was this task the Corinthians were undertaking: at Corinth Christianity was making its first appearance as a *theology*.

The greater part of I Corinthians 1–4 is occupied with warnings against the evils that the new method was already producing, evils to be infinitely intensified as church history went on, and as men substituted for the Gospel their conceptions of the speculative truths underlying it. But the Apostle's warnings are prefaced by the warm praise in the present section: when not abused, both "utterance" and "knowledge" are precious gifts of God. And in these days when dogma is so greatly undervalued, it is well to remember that the "first and great commandment" contains the injunction to love God with all one's "mind." There is great need that the church of the twentieth century be enriched in the "utterance" and "knowledge" which the Apostle praises before he warns against the abuse of them.

SERMON THEME: Although speculative theology can never be a substitute for the Gospel, the formulation of Christian truths and the expression of them in terms acceptable to cultured minds are warranted undertakings, to which the church is called afresh in every age.

# THE NINETEENTH SUNDAY AFTER TRINITY

## LITURGICAL NOTES

GOSPEL: Matthew 9:1–8. So the Sarum and (for Pentecost 18) the Roman missals.

EPISTLE: Ephesians 4:17–32. A (very pronounced) Reformation lengthening of the Sarum and (for Pentecost 19) Roman section 4:23–28. The result is rather overloaded; the older section, despite the fact that it began in the middle of a sentence, was vastly more concentrated.

Both Epistle and Gospel deal with Christ's power to relieve men from sin, by absolution (Gospel) and by infusing new life (Epistle).

## THE GOSPEL

This passage (even in its earlier Markan form) has undergone drastic editing; it makes Jesus at the beginning of His ministry speak of Himself in public as "Son of man," and it makes Him use His healing power as a "sign" of His spiritual commission. But such a "sign" was something that He refused on principle to give, as in Mark 8:12, Luke 11:29; compare on Advent 3. As the section stands it is early Christian apologetic; the gifts of healing proved that believers enjoyed the favour of the celestial Son of man, and were therefore freed from their sins. This argument, however, proved too much, for even the most debased cults can boast of cures wrought among them. The expositor, consequently, had best take the whole as a half-allegory, with the emphasis on verse 2. Christ's absolution frees us to arise and walk spiritually; in this way the passage appeals to all, and not merely to those who are physically afflicted. But this absolution is no light thing; the declaration of it is unique in connection with Christ's healings, and a whole Gospel may be read in the "Be of good cheer" of verse 2. Moreover, we now know body and soul to be so intimately related that wonders of physical healing may still be looked for in those who have heard and appropriated the spiritually emancipating word.

SERMON THEME: The forgiveness of sins is the creative act of God, enabling those who accept Christ's absolution to walk in newness of life.

## THE EPISTLE

"Natural" desires (verses 17–19) are to be transformed by believers (verses 20–24). In Christianity falsehood is wrong (verse 25) not only abstractly but because it is a sin against social relations; how can a body function if its parts deceive each other? Anger is always grave (verse 26). In theft selfishness violates the rights of others; the Christian's ideal is the exact opposite, readiness to give, even when this involves physical labour to win the wherewithal (verse 28). Verse 30 recalls the supernatural strength that is always present, and verses 31–32 summarize the anti-social vices and the social virtues. In an exposition of the whole section its length debars much dwelling on details; but it is so straightforward that the expositor can follow it exactly as it stands, reserving for the future fuller analysis of the separate parts.

Behind it all is the invariable Pauline teaching. *Because* you have the Spirit (verse 30), you are able to avoid walking as do the Gentiles (verse 17).

In verse 18 Jewish precedent is followed in making the fundamental sin of the Gentiles (wilful) ignorance, which results in alienation from God and hardening of the heart; compare Romans 1:18–32. Verse 19 likewise follows the same precedent in reducing Gentile sins to sexual license and covetousness as the root evils. "If so be" in verse 21 is perhaps slightly sarcastic; "if any believer does not imitate Christ, presumably he has never learned about him!" To have "heard" Christ does not mean to have heard Him speak, but to have heard Him proclaimed. In verses 22–24 "put off" and "put on" describe changing characters in terms of changing garments; the picture is of God offering the soul a better nature, to put on if it only will. The citation of Psalm 4:4 in verse 26 produces a somewhat curious wording, but the meaning is simply "do not let yourselves commit the sin of anger"; the angry man serves the devil (verse 27). (For occasions when anger is not a sin compare Mark 3:5.) Verse 32 summarizes the teachings of Jesus concerning brotherly love and forgiveness and adds a new warrant, "even as God for Christ's sake hath forgiven you." As always, Christian ethic is deduced from Christian doctrine. For the central place of forgiveness in Christian ethic see H. S. Nash, *The Atoning Life*.

SERMON THEME: In the new life of the Christian his selfish desires are transformed into unselfishness; his good conduct is not the cause but the result of his salvation in Christ.

# THE TWENTIETH SUNDAY AFTER TRINITY

## LITURGICAL NOTES

GOSPEL: Matthew 22:1–14. So the Sarum and (for Pentecost 19) the Roman missals.

EPISTLE: Ephesians 5:15–21. So the Sarum and (for Pentecost 20) the Roman missals.

The opening verse of the Epistle can be connected with the last section of the Gospel; those who accept the King's invitation should conduct themselves accordingly.

## THE GOSPEL

Compare Trinity 2. Verses 1–10 are a later version of the parable as it stands in Luke, with allegorical additions that are all self-evident. But "bad and good" in verse 10 prepares for the addition in verses 11–13, which voices early post-apostolic experience. The Apostles went out into the highways and hedges and compelled them to come in—but the result was sometimes unfortunate. The allegory is not skillful; how could a man pressed into the palace under such conditions be expected to appear in proper clothing? (That Oriental potentates were accustomed to present robes to their guests is wholly mythical.) But, no more than the very awkward addition in verse 7, does this trouble the Evangelist; every one knows that converts are expected to amend their lives, and this man did not try to do so. The last clause of verse 13 ignores the setting. Verse 14 is an isolated saying of Jesus, which fits very badly in this place. In the Evangelist's mind, however, the one man in verse 11–13 typifies a large part of the church. Many are bidden, who refuse to come, and many of those who come will be rejected at the end; so it is true that "few are chosen." But the original sense that Jesus gave the saying is irrecoverable.

The expositor, then, must use the passage in the sense the Evangelist meant it to bear, without concerning himself with attempting to make the allegory smooth. Those who profess genuine interest in Christianity are in a minority, and those whose lives correspond to their professions are only a part of the minority. From this the Evangelist deduces that the vast majority of mankind are bound straight for hell. But in some respects the church of the twentieth century knows the mind of Christ far better than did the church of the first century: we cannot draw so cruel a conclusion and for the hell which is indicated in verse 13 we must substitute missing the higher destiny. Yet we must not miss the positive sternness of the warning.

SERMON THEME: God is merciful—but those who with full opportunity to do good choose to do wrong must expect to reap as they have sown; and to miss the destiny of being children of the light is a loss so tragic that the Son of God died to save men from it.

THE EPISTLE

Although in liturgical use the "therefore" in verse 15 has been omitted, the connection with 5:1–14 (Lent 3) is intimate; "you are children of light, therefore walk not like the fools (of verse 6), but with the wisdom that befits you, exercising care, making good use of the present evil days." The exact force of "redeeming the time" perplexed even the Greek Fathers; the literal sense is "buying up the season," "things are bad, but they can be turned to good account." The mention of "folly" suggests drunkenness and so leads to verses 18–21. "If you need exhilaration, find it not in wine but in the Spirit"; note that Christianity does not suppress natural instincts but turns them into wholesome channels. (For a classic exposition of this passage see Frederick Robertson's sermon, "Sensual and Spiritual Excitement."[1]) "Excess" should be "riot," as in the Revised Version. "Speaking to yourselves," not to "one another," is right; personal, not congregational, devotion is meant, and antiphonal singing is quite beside the mark—the melody is made "in the heart" (compare Jonathan Edwards' account of his personal religious experience, "walking alone in the woods, and solitary places, for meditation, soliloquy and prayer and converse with God; and it was always my manner at such times to *sing forth my contemplation*"). The "psalms" here may be those of the Old Testament or Christian compositions of similar form. Probably "hymns" and "spiritual songs" were indistinguishable. The climax is in verse 20, and verse 21—a transition verse to lead into verses 22 ff.—is best disregarded. If used, read "Christ" at the end, not "God."

SERMON THEME: Christians are never to be gloomy; when times are bad let them give close attention to conduct and through thanksgiving to God preserve their serenity.

[1] In *Sermons Preached at Brighton,* no. ix.

# THE TWENTY-FIRST SUNDAY AFTER TRINITY

## LITURGICAL NOTES

GOSPEL: John 4:46–54. So (without verse 54) the Sarum and (for Pentecost 20) the Roman missals.

This sudden appearance of a Johannine section in the midst of a Matthean sequence is practically universal in the Middle Ages, but its reason is wholly unknown.

EPISTLE: Ephesians 6:10–20. So (without verses 18–20) the Sarum and (for Pentecost 21) the Roman missals.

Our war against the powers of evil (Epistle) is supported by an omnipotent Leader (Gospel).

## THE GOSPEL

The Johannine version of the healing of the centurion's servant (Epiphany 4 [3]); "nobleman" should be "officer." In John, as in the Synoptists, the story prefigures the extension of the Gospel to the Gentiles, but in the Fourth Gospel the comparison with the Jews is dropped and the emphasis thrown more on the value of insistent faith. To be sure the faith is defective and the hunger for miracles is properly rebuked. Yet Christ realizes the desperate seriousness of the man's need, and overlooks the surface weakness; compare Mark 9:23–24.

It is this aspect of the section that is the most profitable for exposition. In any case the Johannine editing should be disregarded; in the desire to heighten the miracle the actual distance from Cana to Capernaum—fifteen miles—is extended until it becomes two days' journey. Verse 48: the apparent harshness may be relieved by the explanation that the reply of Jesus is not an answer to the request but a warning to curious spectators—"except ye see" is plural. "Signs and wonders," the combination occurs only here in the Fourth Gospel. The "wonder" of a miracle is its strangeness; the "sign" is its correspondence to some hidden reality of the spiritual world of which it is the symbol: all the miracles of Jesus are "signs," the significance of which it is the expositor's business to discover. But here the sense is unfavourable: "what you call signs"; the true signs are something different.

SERMON THEME: Christ's works on earth corresponded to hidden and everlasting realities of the spiritual world where He now lives and where His word, independent of time and space, has still its ancient power; faith makes it available for healing.

## THE EPISTLE

To avoid too hackneyed a treatment of this familiar passage, the expositor should remember—compare on Advent 1 and Lent 1—that "armour" is a defective rendition for "arms," offensive as well as defensive. Bunyan's description of Christian's fight against Apollyon represents a too-prevalent individualistic conception of the passage. Our warfare is very much more than personal resistance to temptation; as Christ's soldiers we are to share His conflict "against principalities, against powers, against the rulers of the darkness of this world, against spiritual wickedness in high places" in magnificent aggression. Disbelief in a personal devil in no wise minimizes the stark and grim reality of the spiritual conflict; under any Christian concept of it the heavenly Lord arrays His followers against the powers of evil. But God is might, and in the power of that might the outcome is certain. *Deus nobis, quis contra?*

It is inadvisable to analyze too closely the correspondence between the virtues' names and their functions in the panoply. They are really distributed somewhat at random and can be interchanged with equal appropriateness, *e.g.,* "sword of truth," "girdle of faith," "breastplate of the Spirit." Verse 15 is influenced by Isaiah 52:7; the meaning is "always prepared to spread the gospel of peace" (note the intentional paradox, "peace" while in battle-array).

The expositor should close with verse 18 and its impressive final exhortation to intercessory prayer. The pre-Reformation section ended too abruptly, but the Reformers went to the opposite extreme.

SERMON THEME: Fortified by prayer the Christian is called upon to engage in offensive as well as defensive warfare against the powers of darkness.

# THE TWENTY-SECOND SUNDAY AFTER TRINITY

## LITURGICAL NOTES

GOSPEL: Matthew 18:21-35. So (beginning with verse 23) the Sarum and (for Pentecost 21) the Roman missals.

EPISTLE: Philippians 1:3-11. So (beginning with verse 6) the Sarum and (for Pentecost 22) the Roman missals.

The contrast of the anti-social and social attitudes gives liturgical unity.

## THE GOSPEL

The less exegetical arts are practised on this section, the better. Its meaning is perfectly obvious and the expositor should confine himself to illustration and application. The Unmerciful Servant could not have it both ways: he was either "under the law" or "under grace." If he would receive grace, he must show it to his fellow servant; if he would revert to law and the insistence upon rights, then that reversal would bring him again into the realm of law and legal rights and legal definitions, and by that law he would be judged and condemned.

SERMON THEME: If we would receive grace from God we must show mercy to our fellowmen.

## THE EPISTLE

This is another perfectly straightforward passage, which pictures "the fellowship that follows from accepting the Gospel." And the picture is the more striking because it is not idealized. The Philippians have by no means achieved what *we* call "sainthood" and are in real need of the apostle's warnings; but their sincerity and their affection for their leader more than make up for many deficiencies. The passage may be summarized as "the consecration of natural affections."

Verse 7: "Your zeal for me and for my missionary work justify my confidence in you." Note the stress on intellectual progress in verses 9–11. Growth in intelligence helps them to "approve things that are excellent" ("understand where duty lies"), and so to be filled with the fruits of righteousness.

SERMON THEME: In the fellowship that follows from accepting the Gospel all natural affections are consecrated.

# THE TWENTY-THIRD SUNDAY AFTER TRINITY

## LITURGICAL NOTES

GOSPEL: Matthew 22:15–22. So (without verse 22) the Sarum and (for Pentecost 22) the Roman missals.

EPISTLE: Philippians 3:17–21. So the Sarum missal. The Roman section for Pentecost 23 is continued to include 4:3.

Our citizenship is in heaven (Epistle); render to God the things that are God's (Gospel).

## THE GOSPEL

Pharisees and Herodians do not, as is sometimes said, represent contrasted points of view on the tribute question, for both agreed that its payment was lawful. The Herodians, to be sure, went farther and, as upholders of the Roman supremacy, urged that such payment was a legal duty. But even the Pharisees as a party—although not always as individuals—accepted conditions as they were; as long as they were permitted to observe the Law in their own way, they did not deeply concern themselves with civil problems. The "temp-tation" in the question, accordingly, must have been due to a sus-picion that Jesus might share the opinions of the extreme national-ists; the elaborate praise of His sincerity is designed to catch Him off His guard, and provoke a declaration that God's people should pay tribute to God alone. This would arouse Pilate to instant action, and save the Jewish authorities from troubling further.

Jesus gives the only answer He can give. The ultra-nationalistic spirit is not from God; there is nothing in the Law that supports the desire for rebellion against Rome. And so payment of tribute is in no wise forbidden. But, as always, He does not content Him-self with the immediate question at issue, but probes to the bottom of the principle involved. The form of His reply, however, uses a concept that belongs to the thought of the day. Roman tribute must be paid in imperial coinage, which by virtue of the legend and portrait was regarded as the Emperor's personal property; the Law cannot possibly forbid returning to a man what is already his own. In modern terms this might amount to saying: Since your com-merce owes its very existence to Rome's protection, Rome can claim tribute as a just debt. With such matters God's Law is not con-cerned—but God has other claims on you!

For the application to present-day conditions compare the Epistle for Epiphany 4. In countries where democratic principles are estab-lished the question may be asked: "What duty does Cæsar owe to God?"

SERMON THEME: God's Law does not conflict with the duties of earthly citizenship, but it has other and greater requirements of obedience.

## THE EPISTLE

The American Prayer Book has substituted the Revised Version for the King James in this passage; a great improvement, for the Elizabethan phrasing is not only archaic but misleading. Not "conversation" but "citizenship" or "domicile" is the right translation in verse 20; and in verse 21 "vile" is an impossible modern rendering for a word which in Luke 1:48 is properly rendered "low estate." Our earthly body is of "low estate" because it is subject to death and its corruption: compare I Corinthians 15:53.

The persons denounced were incipient Gnostics, of the type discussed in I John (Epiphany 6, etc.). They went so far as to take a perverted pride in their debaucheries, literally "glorying in their shame"; boasting of their freedom to do what less "enlightened" mortals shrank from in horror. The expositor will not be at a loss to find modern counterparts in present-day literature. "They are enemies of the cross of Christ" because the cross is the token of utter rejection of lower values for heavenly.

SERMON THEME: As it is of heaven, not of earth, that we are primarily citizens, let us live as becomes that high estate.

# THE TWENTY-FOURTH SUNDAY AFTER TRINITY

## LITURGICAL NOTES

GOSPEL: Matthew 9:18–26. So the Sarum missal, but concluding with verse 22. The Roman missal (for Pentecost 23) continues through verse 26.

EPISTLE: Colossians 1:3–12. The Sarum missal has 1:9–11; the Roman missal (for Pentecost 24) has 1:9–14.

No liturgical unity is apparent.

## THE GOSPEL

In their Markan form (Mark 5:25–43) these two cures belong to a very early stratum of Synoptic tradition; they may originally have been independent and were associated because of the mention of "twelve years" in each (Mark 5:25, 42). The expositor should notice the absence in them of the "wonder" features of the later miracle-

stories. The woman is told explicitly that her cure is due to her own
faith, while Jesus' recognition of her as the one who touched Him
is not ascribed to supernatural knowledge (contrast the later revision in Luke 8:43-48). So in the raising of Jairus' daughter pub-
licity is not sought but avoided, the death of the girl has taken
place only a few minutes previously (stronger in Mark than Matthew), and we have Jesus' explicit declaration—whatever it may
mean—"she is not dead, but sleepeth." All of this, of course, does
not guarantee detailed accuracy in even so early a tradition; in fact,
even if we could be certain that we have reports by eyewitnesses
—as is really probable—we should not yet be in a position to recon-
struct exactly what happened; *e.g.,* was the girl dead, or was she
*in articulo mortis,* or in a stupor from which Jesus roused her?

We do not know. But we do know that whatever took place was
the result of trust in Jesus. "Thy faith hath made thee whole";
"Fear not, only believe" (Mark 5:36; Matthew's omission of these
crucial words is unfortunate). Past doubt, invincible faith can and
does work miracles such as these, heal diseases where human skill
has been in vain, bring back to life even those who seem to have
passed over the boundary of death. This is marvellous, but its
greater consequence lies in the "inward and spiritual grace" of
which it is the "outward and visible sign." There are other infinitely greater and more permanent miracles that Jesus can perform
on us if our faith in Him is steadfast.

SERMON THEME: The healing of physical maladies by faith is a
sign of greater things which may be expected in answer to steadfast faith in Christ: the healing of ravages wrought by sin; the
awakening of the sleeping soul to a new day of life eternal.

## THE EPISTLE

This opening of Colossians is not unlike the corresponding part
of Philippians (Trinity 22). Here, however, the thought of fellowship plays a smaller part—Saint Paul had never been in Colosse—

and, as befits more immature Christians, the normal process of spiritual growth is analyzed more in detail. "Spiritual growth" is, in fact, the theme for the expositor, who will find that the section can be followed closely.

Note the "faith, love, hope" triad in verse 4–5, the foundation of what follows. The mention of "all the world" in verse 6 warns the Colossians against forming too individualistic a type of belief (the main theme of the Epistle as a whole). "Also" in verse 7 is a gloss, to associate Saint Paul with Epaphras; the latter being in fact their sole teacher thus far. As in the Philippians passage the exhortation culminates in an appeal to enrich spiritual qualities with intellectual; "knowledge" is also a spiritual gift.

To be noted throughout is the exclusive stress on positive attainments; there is not a negative note in the entire passage. Verse 12, "the inheritance of the saints in light" is "the content of the 'hope' in verse 5."[1]

SERMON THEME: Spiritual growth should be enriched by intellectual qualities and by social sympathies as well; no man's problems are unique, and the broad stream of Christian experience must never be ignored.

# THE SUNDAY NEXT BEFORE ADVENT

## LITURGICAL NOTES

GOSPEL: John 6:5–14. This section was very widely used in Europe and formed part of the Roman sequence in the seventh century (for Cyprian 7). It was afterward replaced (for Pentecost 24, the Roman "Next Advent") by Matthew 24:15–35, properly an Advent Gospel, found in some minor uses for the fifth Sunday before Christmas.

The reason for the choice of this Johannine section here is unknown; the only plausible explanation yet suggested being that its

[1]C. A. Anderson Scott, *Foot-notes to St. Paul,* p. 200.

mention of Andrew connected it with the (near) festival of this saint (November 30). Compare on Trinity 5.

EPISTLE: Jeremiah 23:5–8. So the Sarum missal. There is no parallel in the Roman missal, which has no service for Pentecost 25.

Presumably this was originally chosen as an "advent" section, looking forward to Christmas.

However Gospel and Epistle came to be associated, they form together an admirable close for the Church Year, the Gospel looking back over Christ's care for His people and the Epistle looking forward to His reign.

## THE GOSPEL

Compare on Lent 4. As suggested above, on this Sunday the section is best used generally to resume all that Christ has done for us, with perhaps especial attention to "Gather up the fragments that remain, that nothing be lost."

SERMON THEME: Christ's care for His people extends even to the fragmentary things of their lives.

## THE EPISTLE

The expositor should extend his study of this passage back to the beginning of the chapter, where in verse 1 the "shepherds" are the kings of Israel, who in Jeremiah's day seemed to have gone from bad to worse. In particular, about B.C. 597, the King of Babylon (Nebuchadrezzar) set up a puppet king of his own, whom he named "Zedekiah," or "Righteousness of the Lord" (II Kings 24: 17). Verse 5 contains a contemptuous reference to this princeling by giving to the ideal king of the prophecy a name almost exactly the same; in this case the monarch *really* will be one who establishes the rule of "The Lord our Righteousness." Under such a one truly Judah shall be saved and Israel shall dwell safely. As is conventional in Jewish thinking the coming ruler will be of David's line, a "branch of David" (Zechariah 6:12), who shall reign as gloriously as David did. But in verses 7–8 the vision broadens; this king shall do what David never did; he will bring back to Palestine all God's people, no matter how far they may be scattered.

The critical assumptions in the above are that verses 5–6 are Jeremiah's and verses 7–8 later apocalyptic editing. As regards verses 7–8 Old Testament specialists are generally agreed, but it is only right to note that some very capable scholars think that even verses 5–6 are later than Jeremiah. But for expository purposes the result is much the same, even though the telling reference to Zedekiah is lost; in contrast to corrupt worldly rulers God will send a righteous king, whose work will excel all that human beings can do (or in whose day God will intervene with a superhuman miracle).

"Branch" in verse 5 is more properly "shoot" or "sprout"; the figure is fresh life sprouting from an apparently dead stump. "In the earth" originally meant (in all probability) "in the Land" (= "Palestine"). In verse 8 "I" should be "he." In the very hour of national disaster the prophet's faith enables him to foresee a restoration greater than was the Exodus itself.

SERMON THEME: Hebrew prophecy, which looked forward to the coming of a righteous King, found its fulfilment in Christ and is now continued in Christian anticipation of His universal reign.

# PART THREE

# EPISTLES AND GOSPELS
# FOR HOLY DAYS

# EPISTLES AND GOSPELS
# FOR HOLY DAYS

## SAINT ANDREW

### *November 30*

GOSPEL: Matthew 4:18–22. So the Sarum and the Roman missals.
EPISTLE: Romans 10:9–21. A Reformation lengthening of the Sarum (and Roman) Romans 10:10–18.

Liturgical unity, of course, is found in the missionary concept.

Andrew was one of the earliest disciples closely associated with Jesus, and with Peter, James and John he belonged to the inner group of the Twelve. In the Fourth Gospel he appears as the proto-missionary.

November 30 as the day of his death is found in the apocryphal Acts of Andrew and appears to go back into the third century. The feast was adopted in Rome in the sixth century after earlier Eastern observance.

### THE GOSPEL

The two brief scenes are possibly concrete embodiments of the call of the four Apostles from their work as fishers, dramatized by making the "Follow me" come to them in the very midst of their task. But this is unimportant. All that is essential is Andrew's abandonment of his livelihood for love of Jesus and in order to become a "fisher of men."

### THE EPISTLE

This section was chosen for this day as a picture of the work of the apostolate. But its real purpose is rather different; it is a rebuke to the Jews for rejecting Christianity, and the missionary activity serves as a contrast. If the argument in this Epistle is to be followed, the expositor must go back to the beginning of the chapter, emphasizing verse 3 as Saint Paul's thesis: God revealed salvation to the Jews but they rejected it in favour of their own preferences. Then verse 9 means: If the Jews had been confronted with an obscure and intricate message, they might have some excuse, but the Gospel is simplicity itself. Verses 10–11 confirm this and verses 12–13 repeat it in an enriched and beautiful form.

The logic in verses 14–21 is not easy to grasp, because the main theme is complicated with the contrasting theme. When Saint Paul speaks of Jewish unbelief there is constantly present in his mind the fact of Gentile belief, so that he writes on both subjects simultaneously. Verses 14–15 ask a series of questions that are (in the context) rhetorical or ironical: "Can Israel plead ignorance?" The answer—"of course she cannot"—is taken for granted, and verse 17 draws the conclusion, "The fault is unbelief." Verse 17 prepares in verse 18 for the emphatic repetition of one of the questions in verse 14, and then the Apostle replies: "Why, the whole world has heard!" In verses 19–21 another repeated question is answered with three Old Testament quotations; to any one in the first century the climax of the argument. "Provoke to jealousy" in verse 19 prepares for the new theme in chapter 11.

A real exposition of this section, consequently, would be possible only to a group highly trained in Paulinism. Under such circumstances it could be made fruitful; with the emphasis laid on men's ingratitude, both to God whose offer is so overwhelmingly generous and to His ministers who burn themselves out in their work. But the passage is so complex that the task is beyond the preacher to the average congregation. Yet the passage contains some of Saint Paul's finest single verses for textual analysis, while on Saint Andrew's Day the missionary sayings may be treated as a whole, the anti-Jewish polemic being subordinated or ignored.

# SAINT THOMAS

*December 21*

GOSPEL: John 20:24-31. So (without verses 30-31) the Sarum and the Roman missals.

EPISTLE: Hebrews 10:35-11:1 (American; first introduced in 1928) and Ephesians 2:19-22 (English and the earlier American Prayer Books). The latter is in the Sarum and the Roman missals; it was an earlier "common."

In the Synoptists Thomas is merely a name in the lists of the Twelve, where he is coupled with Matthew. In the Fourth Gospel he is the only Apostle who is really individualized; his despondent fidelity in 11:16 (compare 14:4) is quite in keeping with his doubt at the Christ's resurrection. The Evangelist's description of him— a fertile theme for preachers—may embody genuine reminiscence. But "Didymus" (John 11:16, etc.) is simply the Greek form of the same (Aramaic) name, not a title describing his character.

Thomas in later story is one of the five "Apostles of the East," the others being Bartholomew, Matthew, Simon and Jude; these were deemed to have pursued their mission beyond the limits of the Roman Empire. It would, in fact, have been natural enough for Jewish Christians to work among the populous Jewish communities of Parthia, but the basis of the tradition is incapable of verification. At all events local commemoration of these five saints spread very slowly in the West; at Rome it was adopted in the ninth century.

Origen speaks of Thomas as having laboured in Parthia, while legend extends his journeyings into India, and the apocryphal Acts of Thomas make him the hero of extraordinary adventures. At Edessa his cult is attested early in the sixth century. The Greek church commemorates him on October 6.

It is a pity that this feast is not placed in the Easter season.

### THE GOSPEL

An invariable feature in the Johannine miracles is attestation of the marvel by witnesses other than believers; here Thomas occupies the place of, *e.g.,* the servants at the Cana marriage (2:9). Critically, then, there is no reason to regard this particular attestation as more historic than the others. But the real point of the section lies in the Evangelist's comments at the end. To him Christ's miracles were, above all, "signs," and to regard Christ primarily as a wonder-worker is nothing—or less than nothing (2:23-25, etc.). All the accounts are so framed as to point to deeper values underlying the outward manifestations, and the reader is always meant to look beneath the surface. In other words, our faith in Christ's resurrection must not rest on any record of what Thomas did with his hands; it must come from our knowledge of the ever-living Christ.

### THE EPISTLE

(American.) This definition of "faith" falls a little short of the Pauline-Johannine conception—which is that of Jesus—by putting the accent so strongly on the future. The writer has not an intense sense of immediate and present relationship to the heavenly world; but perhaps this very fact makes his definition of greater practical value to earnest but unmystical souls like himself.

The Revised Version rendition of 11:1 is excellent.

### THE EPISTLE

(English.) This section has no special reference to Thomas but, in accord with its origin as a "common," describes apostolic fellowship generally. The comparison of the development of the community to the erection of a temple may be drawn ultimately from some non-Semitic source, but to know this hardly helps in appreciating the perfectly lucid figure. The "prophets" are not Old Testament but Christian; with the apostles primary sources of the revelation that makes Christian life possible. There are minor exegetical problems in verses 21–22 but they do not affect the general sense.

# CHRISTMAS DAY

## December 25

The Western adoption of an Epiphania-Nativity feast began in Gaul and Spain, countries so strongly under Eastern influence that they followed the then Eastern custom of dignifying greater feasts with more than one eucharist. And as observance of this festival spread throughout the West, this Eastern custom spread with it, making Christmas noteworthy as a day on which several masses were said, each with its own propers.

By the time of Gregory the number was established as three and so remains in the Roman missal. The Prayer Book of 1549 omitted provision for the second celebration and the later English Prayer Books omitted the first as well; the latter was restored in the American Prayer Book of 1892.

For the second Christmas mass the Sarum and Roman missals have as Epistle Titus 3:4–7, as Gospel Luke 2:15–20.

## A

GOSPEL: Luke 2:1–14. So the 1549 Prayer Book, the Sarum and the Roman missals.

EPISTLE: Titus 2:11–15. So the 1549 Prayer Book, the Sarum and the Roman missals.

In the Gospel the Incarnation is presented as conferring salvation; in the Epistle as conferring responsibility.

### THE GOSPEL

This perfect story is from the expositor's standpoint beyond the reach of criticism; it tells the Christian message incomparably. All that it says about earth is utterly commonplace; the birth of a child in poverty-stricken surroundings, the religious excitement of a few ignorant shepherds. Yet it is echoed by the multitude of the heavenly host as eternal tidings of great joy.

### THE EPISTLE

"Hath appeared" in the opening verse is "hath made its epiphany," and "appearing" in verse 13 is "epiphany": for the Incarnation and the Second Advent the same term is used. This parallels the contrast between earth and heaven in the Gospel. God's gift to us—which is both past and future—makes us utterly responsible for our response.

### B

GOSPEL: John 1:1-14. So the Sarum and the Roman missals.
EPISTLE: Hebrews 1:1-12. So the Sarum and the Roman missals.
This Gospel and Epistle are related like those above, with the conception of the Logos as an additional common theme.

### THE GOSPEL

The teaching about the Logos as it is used in the Fourth Gospel is adopted and modified from a late and popularized form of Platonism admixed with Oriental elements. According to this philosophy, God in His essence is wholly beyond the reach of human thought; above not only the phenomenal world but the noumenal world as well. All we can reach at the very summit of the noumenal world is the Idea-of-God, which is the Logos. From this Idea all lower ideas are derived, forming, as it were, a pyramid, increasing in number as they become more concrete, while from the lowest Ideas in turn are derived their physical embodiments in the phenomenal world. Hence through the Logos "all things were made, and apart from him was not anything made." And since it is in the Logos alone that men can conceive God, the Logos is the only "Light" of men. This is the background of the prologue, to which Christianity has added the teaching—impossible in true Platonism—that "the Word was made flesh and dwelt among us."

Understanding of the passage has been vastly aided by the discovery—now generally accepted—that in John 1:1–18 a quasi-hymn in honour of the Logos has been interpolated with statements in relative depreciation of the Baptist, together with some intense anti-Jewish polemic.

The hymn may be disentangled:

1. In the beginning was the Word,
   And the Word was with God,
   And the Word was God.

2. The same was
   In the beginning
   With God.

3. All things were made through him,
   And apart from him was not anything made,
   That was made.

4. In him was life;
   And the life was the light of men.

5. And the light shines in the darkness;
   And the darkness has not understood it.

10. He was in the world,
    And the world was made through him,
    And the world knew him not.

11. He came into his own,
    And his own received him not.

12. But as many as received him,
    To them gave he power to become the sons of God.

14. And the Word was made flesh,
    And dwelt among us.

And we beheld his glory,
Glory as of the only-begotten of the Father,
Full of grace and truth.

16. For of his fulness we all received;
And grace upon grace.

18. No man hath seen God at any time;
God only-begotten, who is in the bosom of the Father,
He hath revealed him.

Here verses 1–3 are the Logos philosophy of the day, taken over unaltered and with little thought of the theological implications that were later to perplex students. "In the beginning"—perhaps a reminiscence of Genesis 1:1—is as far back as human thought can go. In that "beginning" the Logos "was"; verse 2 emphasizes this with its three brief clauses.

In verse 4 the philosophy is suffused with religion. The equation of "life" with "light" is technical mysticism; only he who shares in God's life can "know" Him (and vice versa). Verse 5 elaborates this by its converse: "darkness" cannot understand "light" since there is no community of nature. The (ethical) dualism thus introduced is sharpened in verse 10: the Logos and the "world" (unredeemed humanity) are in utter opposition. In verse 11 the first "his own" is neuter (the physical world; here the specifically Christian element begins); the second masculine (men as the Logos' creatures; perhaps more definitely the Jews). Verbally verse 12 could be used by a philosopher, apart from the final clause which appears to belong with the polemic in verse 13. This sharing in the Logos' "life" gives the "light" to recognize him despite the lowliness of the Incarnation (verse 14). The perfection of the gifts is re-emphasized in verse 16, while verse 18 resummarizes the teaching as a whole, now completely Christianized.

Verses 6–9 and 15 are polemic against belated followers of the Baptist, who were exalting their master at the expense of Christ;

it is probably no accident that disciples of John are found at Ephesus (Acts 18:24-19:7), the home of the Gospel. The best translation of verse 9 is: "The true light, which lighteth every man, was coming into the world."

Verses 12c-13 are a savage attack on the Jewish confidence that sonship to God is attained through physical descent from Abraham; this makes spiritual character dependent on the processes of procreation. Verse 17 is equally anti-Jewish and is couched in explicit Pauline terms. Quite possibly this verse may give anti-Jewish colouring to the opening clause of verse 18: the Jews boast that Moses saw God face to face (Exodus 33:11), but this boast is false.

With these disparate elements any homiletic treatment of John 1:1-18—or 1:1-14—as a whole is out of the question, and even the "hymn" contains far too much material for any single exposition. Even historical treatment limited to the central concept of the Logos is impracticable in the pulpit, for the thought-world in which the Evangelist moved is beyond the reach of a modern congregation. But we are faithful enough to his purpose if we translate into modern terms somewhat as follows:—"Words" are the mediums through which knowledge is conveyed. So Christ is God's "Word" because in Him we have knowledge of God; to the question "What is God like?" the perfect answer is "Look at Jesus Christ and see!" And not only at Christ risen and ascended, not only at Christ the worker of miracles, not only at Christ the perfect Teacher, but even at Christ the babe in the manger of Bethlehem.

## THE EPISTLE

While the Old Testament revelation within its limits was genuinely and wholly divine, the perfect revelation of God is found in Jesus Christ. Verses 2-3 use the Logos concept, even though the term does not appear. God's "glory" and His "substance" (not "person") are beyond thought, but they are brought into the noumenal realm by His Son; in this way the glory is "bright" to the eyes of faith, and the substance is "expressed" to our thought. This Logos became Man for our redemption, but now sits at the Right Hand of the Majesty and there controls the destiny of the universe. Hence we are bound to obey Him absolutely.

This necessity of obedience is the theme of Hebrews, variously elaborated in the successive sections that make up the writing. The first of these begins with verse 4 and reaches its application in 2:1-4, verses unfortunately omitted in the section chosen, for all the remainder of chapter 1 simply leads up to them: if the Law given through angels was so stringently binding, how utterly compelling is the revelation given through the Son! The preacher consequently should on no account omit these four verses and should make them the basis of his appeal.

On the other hand 1:4-14 may be passed over rapidly. No one questions that Christ is more important to us than the angels, while the use of proof-texts is taken from the methods of first-century Hellenistic scholasticism. Yet something real lies behind it all. We may pity a savage's blind obedience to tribal taboos; we may be irritated at the Puritan's acceptance of a dour legalism. Our standards, we know, are infinitely higher and purer. But do we live up to them better than the savage and the Puritan lived up to theirs?

# THE POST-CHRISTMAS DAYS

The adoption of Christmas as in a special sense the Festival of Christ led very rapidly to associating with it the names of the greatest disciples. Here Stephen, the proto-martyr, was an almost inevitable choice, and to him were added in pairs James and John, Peter and Paul. The calendars, however, show considerable discrepancy in the order of the days and more serious discrepancy as to which "James" and which "John" are meant; there is reason to think that originally the Lord's "brother" and the Baptist were intended. At any rate at Rome December 26 was assigned to Stephen, while "John" was identified as the Evangelist. James—if he ever was really accepted in Rome—was soon dropped, while Peter and Paul naturally had their long-established day in June. The place of the latter saints was supplied by the Innocents, whose feast was of Western—apparently Carthaginian—origin, although in earlier times (fifth century?) these infants were commemorated at Epiphany.

The familiar symmetry of the three days—martyrs in-will-and-deed, in-will, in-deed—is an afterthought, although perfectly legitimate.

## SAINT STEPHEN

### December 26

GOSPEL: Matthew 23:34-39. So the Sarum and the Roman missals.
EPISTLE: Acts 7:55-60. A Reformation modification of the Sarum (and Roman) Acts 6:8-10, 7:54-60.

The liturgical unity is obvious.

The account of Stephen's office in Acts 6 is contradictory: appointed to "minister tables" in order to free the Apostles for the ministry of the word, he appears immediately as himself a minister of the word—and an extraordinarily successful one. This confusion is due to Luke, who has edited the tradition about Stephen in terms of the church order of his own day. Picturing as he does the apostolic college as the "bishops" of Jerusalem, he conceives that the (subordinate) heptad in his source must have been "deacons," and so describes them. Their original status cannot now be defined, but since they all bear Greek names it is probable that they were the leaders of Jerusalem's Greek-speaking Christians.

The speech ascribed to Stephen in Acts 7 begins by asserting the absolute Jewish "orthodoxy" of the new faith, magnifying to the utmost God's promises to the patriarchs and the wholly divine mission of Moses. A parallel is then set up between Moses and Christ. As the Jews rejected the one, so they now reject the other; it is the Christians, not the Jews, who truly obey this Moses who predicted Christ. Verses 44–50 are an excursus. It is true that the Christians prophesy the destruction of the Temple, but in so doing they do not contravene the Law. The Temple has no connection with the Law, for it was not built until the time of Solomon.

In other words, of the two charges brought in 6:14 the first is admitted but argued to be no offence, while the second is indignantly rejected in a passionate counter-attack. Consequently the speech has nothing to do with the future extension of the Gospel to the Gentile; it moves within rigidly Jewish lines, and is a summary of Jewish Christian polemic against the unconverted Jews. To take the speech as in any way prefiguring Paulinism is to misread it completely. And it would have been just such arguments as these that Stephen must have used in his defence; whether or not the speech be regarded as an accurate report.

In any event the fact that he was singled out for martyrdom in a community that had thus far enjoyed comparative toleration shows that his preaching must have been unusually bitter. And verses 44–50 give an adequate explanation of this: he had threatened his recalcitrant countrymen with destruction and the near return of Jesus, when the Temple in which they trusted would be destroyed.

We are to think of Stephen, consequently, as one in whom outspoken courage led him to proclaim the truth with an utter disregard for consequences.

How his martyrdom was permitted by the Romans we do not know, although the fact is not to be called in question. From the Roman standpoint the proceedings may have been a lynching which the authorities may not have thought worth while to punish. Or there may have been a vacancy in the procuratorship. Or the Jews may have been permitted (at times?) a larger liberty of action than is assumed in most of the textbooks on Palestine.

## THE GOSPEL

The section is made up of two paragraphs, originally disassociated (verses 34–36 = Luke 11:49–51 and verses 37–39 = Luke 13: 34–35). In Luke the former section is introduced by "Therefore said the Wisdom of God," a phrase almost certainly characterizing the following words as a quotation from some (lost) source. These words, accordingly, are hardly to be taken as an original saying of Jesus, although they may very possibly be a citation that He used with approval. In their source, which was obviously apocalyptic, they form a prediction of one of the coming "woes of the end," a lament that all God can do for His people will only serve to harden them.

"Abel" (Genesis 4:8) and "Zechariah" (II Chronicles 24:21) are the first and last martyrs in the Hebrew Old Testament, which closes with II Chronicles. The sense is: "The guilt of this generation equals that of all former generations combined."

In verse 35 "son of Barachiah" (not in Luke 11:51) is an unfortunate addition of the Evangelist's, due to confusion with the prophet (Zechariah 1:1). A Zechariah mentioned in Josephus (*BJ* IV, v, 4) is sometimes thought to be referred to here, but no Christian writer would pick a non-Christian assassinated *ca.* A.D. 70 as the climax in the Jews' sins.

The lament in verses 37–38 must belong to the extreme end of Jesus' ministry. The "house" is probably the Temple. "Desolate" is perhaps an addition to the text, but if omitted the sense is unchanged: "God has abandoned your house." Verse 39 is apocalyptic: "The Jews will not see their Messiah until they accept Christianity"; it is quite conceivably an early gloss.

Despite the heterogeneous origin of its parts this Gospel does not lack unity. For those who give themselves to evil God's best efforts can do nothing; a terrible consequence of sin is that it leads to ever greater sin until gross crimes are committed without remorse. Yet even under such conditions brave souls, like Stephen, will still try to do what they can, even if the attempt leads certainly to martyrdom.

## THE EPISTLE

The story illustrates the Gospel passage poignantly. The contrast between verse 60 and II Chronicles 24:22 may be noted.

# SAINT JOHN EVANGELIST

### December 27

GOSPEL: John 21:19–25. So (without verse 25) the Sarum and the Roman missals.

EPISTLE: I John 1:1–10. A Reformation substitute for the Sarum (and Roman) Ecclesiasticus 15:1–6.

These sections were obviously chosen for their personal allusions.

## THE GOSPEL

Despite the interest of this story it is as a whole hardly fruitful for exposition on Saint John's Day. The preacher, consequently, may do well to centre on verse 24. Nor is there any occasion to enter into the intricacies of the Johannine problem; the "John" honoured by the church is he who has given us the Gospel (even though perhaps not quite in its present form) and the three Epistles. And this seer can be considered apart from any questions of precise historic identification.

The Fourth Evangelist's supreme achievement was to face fearlessly the problems of his own day. His thought-world and the thought-world of his people were no longer those of two generations earlier, and he wasted no time in attempting to set the clock back. He put his trust in the Spirit of Jesus and proclaimed Christ in language that His people could understand and in terms that met their needs. For pedantic historical accuracy he cared little; the church was already provided with records where the curious could learn what they pleased. To him the sole interest was to answer the question "What does Jesus Christ mean to me?" And it is because his answer to that question is eternally satisfying that his disciples could close the Gospel with the confident assertion, "We know that his testimony is true."

His "modern" phraseology has naturally in some measure become archaic to us. But what seems to us overwhelming truth will appear equally outworn 2000 years from now. Yet if we are as faithful to truth as John was, we—and the future generations—can do what John did: strengthen and comfort our people with the knowledge of the eternally living Christ.

## THE EPISTLE

For I John compare on Epiphany 6, Easter 1, Trinity 1 and 2.

Verses 1–4 are the general introduction to the Epistle as a whole; verses 5–10 the first section in its anti-Cerinthian polemic. But even the very first verse is an attack on docetism. The Incarnation was real. Jesus Christ incarnate could be seen with physical eyes, could be handled with physical hands. So from the start the Christian philosophy is asserted uncompromisingly: this world is God's creation; any dualism that treats matter as evil is un-Christian through and through. Compare the Gospel for Epiphany 3 (2).

It is not easy to see in verse 1 anything but an assertion that the writer—whatever his identity—belonged to the dwindling group of actual eyewitnesses described by the "we." (Scholars unable to accept this hold that the chain of tradition connecting him with these witnesses was so strong that he could include himself among them. This really comes to much the same thing.) "Our" experience has taught "us" that the world we live in is God's world. "We" have the joy of salvation in the world, not by flight from it; compare John 17:15. So "you" may firmly believe the same. The gnostic dualism is false. But (verse 5) there is a different dualism that is true, the dualism of right and wrong. Here God is wholly "light," wholly on the side of the good; wherever there is any acquiescence in evil no "religious" achievements mean anything.

The phrases introduced by "if we say" in verses 6, 8 and 10 are Cerinthian formulas: the gnostic by his cult, ascetic practices and "knowledge" is beyond good and evil, "having fellowship with God," "free from present sin," "free from past sin." All such boasting is vain. The only way to salvation is to walk in the light by a life of love (4:16), to confess our shortcomings and to trust in God, through Christ, for their pardon.

# HOLY INNOCENTS

## December 28

GOSPEL: Matthew 2:13-18. So the Sarum and the Roman missals.
EPISTLE: Revelation 14:1-5. So the Sarum and the Roman missals.
The poor victims of Herod's wrath were martyrs at least in "deed," even though not in "will," and so glorified God by their deaths. This is the traditional theme of Innocents' Day. But neither the Gospel nor Epistle has any but the vaguest connection with this conception, and the preacher using it should choose a topical, not an expository, approach.

## THE GOSPEL

This Gospel is an integral part of the Epiphany story; for the critical problems compare on Epiphany. The purpose of the section is to relate how God delivered the wondrous Child from the counsels of Herod (Psalm 2:2; compare Acts 4:25 ff.). To the writer the slaughter of the infants was only another among Herod's traditional acts of senseless cruelty and not a very significant one; he was quite unconscious of any further problem and was not at all concerned with the after-fate of the little ones.

The two Old Testament passages cited have helped determine the form of the story.

## THE EPISTLE

In one of his flaming interludes the Apocalyptist pauses to depict a class of particularly exalted saints, who will accompany the Lamb at the final victory. Their identification depends on the meaning found in verse 4a. Taken literally, it makes them ascetics, who had preserved their physical virginity. For this interpretation—undoubtedly the source of the choice of the section for this day—precedent can be found in I Corinthians 7, with ample attestation in later church history. Against it, however, stand (1) the impossibly large number, after making all allowance for apocalyptic exaggeration; (2) the fact that opposition to gnosticism—in which Revelation shares—gave anti-asceticism a powerful impulse at the close of the first century; (3) the Jewish outlook of the writer, which would not regard abstinence from marriage as a virtue at all; (4) the fact that this point of view leaves the passage disconnected from the rest of the work. Not much better is the theory—perhaps present in the Reformers' minds—that sees here Christian children who die before reaching the age of sin; in an age of constant martyrdoms the death of children would hardly receive such explicit attention, while in this case the symbolism would be needlessly obscure.

So it is preferable to take verse 4a in the familiar Old Testament sense that equates "fornication" with "idolatry." It would be possible then to understand these saints as the martyrs generally, who died rather than break their covenant with God; this is the basic theme of Revelation. But against it can be urged that 6:9 ff. gives a different picture of these martyrs' place in heaven. So the best explanation—although, unfortunately, the least useful to the expositor—is that which identifies these 144,000 with those of 7:3–8; they are the Jewish Christians who have never had to repent of idolatry. And this gives an immediate explanation of "firstfruits" in verse 4b and accords perfectly with the Apocalyptists' deeper sympathies (11:13; compare Romans 3:1).

Expository treatment of the passage will therefore probably be most helpful when not too close to the text. An innocency never lost is really different from the innocency regained through repentance.

# THE CIRCUMCISION

## January 1

GOSPEL: Luke 2:15–21. The Sarum and the Roman missals have only the single verse Luke 2:21; compare below.

EPISTLE: Philippians 2:9–13 (American; first introduced in 1928) and Romans 4:8–14 (English and the earlier American Prayer Books). The Romans section was introduced at the Reformation to replace the Sarum (and Roman) Titus 2:11–15; compare below.

This day was originally the octave of Christmas—hence the pre-Reformation Epistle—and was specially dedicated to the Virgin Mary; it was her earliest festival in the West. The Gospel was Luke 2:21–32, all but the first verse of which was transferred to the Purification when the latter feast was instituted. Special observance in honour of Christ's circumcision began in Gaul in the sixth century and spread slowly, reaching Rome at an uncertain but much later date. In fact, apart from the Gospel none of the "propers" in the Roman missal mention the event but are concerned either with the Christmas message or with Mary's intercession.

In the Pauline theology the fact that Christ was born under the Law is utilized for certain incidental arguments but is no vital part of the Apostle's thinking. Reformation hyper-Paulinism endeavoured to go further and to make Christ's circumcision essential to soteriology; an attempt not to be commended. But a certain practical end can be served by pointing out how Christ identified Himself with Judaism and so was able to preserve and transform its finest values.

## THE GOSPEL

The single verse of the earlier rites seemed too brief to the Reformers and they prefixed verses 15-20; this gives better length but introduces matter not relevant to the festival. If however the Circumcision be treated as the feast of "the Name of Jesus"—as is the case in the American Prayer Book with its new Epistle—the humble manifestation to the shepherds can be utilized; compare Christmas *A*.

## THE EPISTLE

(American.) Compare on Palm Sunday.

## THE EPISTLE

(English.) Verses 8 and 14 should not have been included, since they belong to the Apostle's wider argument about justification in general. They should be omitted in exposition.

Saint Paul's palmary contention here is the obvious fact that God's acceptance of Abraham through faith (Genesis 15:6) stands earlier in the Bible than the description of his circumcision (Genesis 17: 9-14). Hence the rite cannot be essential but must be only a "seal," something confirmatory added to a condition already existing. And what was true in Abraham's case must be true for mankind generally. It is their faith, not any "seal," that is crucial; it is those who believe, not those who are circumcised, who have the true right to address Abraham as "father." And by widening the meaning of "circumcision" all this can be made useful today. In every religion there are two parts, the inner relation to God and the outer observance, and of these the latter has worth in so far—but only in so far—as it is the "seal" of the former.

## THE EPIPHANY

### January 6

GOSPEL: Matthew 2:1–12. So the Sarum and the Roman missals; seventh century. The use of this section created a tradition that has identified "Epiphany" with the visit of the Magi. But this is an undue specialization; for this day the Gospel in the Greek Church is Mark 1:9 ff., while its Matthæan parallel appears as an optional alternative to Matthew 2:1 ff. in more than one mediæval Western list.

EPISTLE: Ephesians 3:1–12. The traditional Western section was Isaiah 60:1–6 (so the Sarum and the Roman missals) but at the Reformation a selection from the New Testament was preferred.

Liturgical unity is of course to be sought in the "epiphania" theme.

#### THE GOSPEL

Considered as factual history the section teems with difficulties; stars, *e.g.,* that lead travellers in a fixed direction and then come and stand over houses cannot be identified astronomically. And, speaking critically, there can be little doubt that the section assumed its form under the influence of Isaiah 60. All this should be admitted frankly. But it has nothing to do with the purpose of the exquisite story, which reads Matthew 28:19–20 back into the Infancy; from the very beginning this Christ made His appeal to all the world.

The editor of the First Gospel was a Jew, whose Christianity never freed him from believing that God is best pleased when Jewish practices are maintained. Yet at the opening of his Gospel he sets this account of the divine guidance given to men who were not Jews at all and who never became Jews. In Christ they acknowledged God's Chosen One, and to Him they offered their gifts. But, this done, they did not remain in Palestine but departed into their own country. So the Evangelist endorses Saint Peter's words: "God is no respecter of persons, but in every nation he who feareth him and worketh righteousness is acceptable to him."

It is useless to speculate about the nationality of the Magi or their religion; the Evangelist himself probably did not think beyond what Isaiah 60:6 sets forth. From this verse the "gold and frankincense" are taken, but there is no hint that they have any symbolism, while in the addition of "myrrh" a royal perfume (Psalm 45:8) was far more probably in the Evangelist's mind than an embalming medium. *I.e.,* the Magi brought gifts befitting a king.

## THE EPISTLE

An ideal summary of the Epiphany message. To be sure, it is no longer novel or striking that the Gentiles have been admitted to the heritage of the Jews, but much of the original force can be regained by applying the passage to class, race or national enmities. The first Christians discarded their Jewish pride and welcomed the Gentiles they had so persistently despised. Can we do less?

In verse 3 "as I wrote afore" looks back to chapters 1–2; "as I have just written" would be clearer. The "prophets" in verse 5 are those of early Christianity, not of the Old Testament. The Authorized Version's "fellowship of the mystery" in verse 9 is cryptic; the meaning is practically "the working-out of God's plan, whose meaning was hitherto unsuspected." For the "principalities and powers" in verse 10 compare on Trinity 13. But here these beings are definitely evil (6:12) and are said to be "in heavenly places" because Jews usually thought of Satan's throne as in the sky (Luke 10:18; Revelation 12:7–9). "The hosts of wickedness have now revealed to them the destruction of their own power."

# CONVERSION OF SAINT PAUL

## January 25

GOSPEL: Matthew 19:27–30. So (without verse 30) the Sarum and the Roman missals. Somewhat curiously in the latter this is also the Gospel in the "common of an abbot."

EPISTLE: Acts 9:1–22. So the Sarum and the Roman missals.

The older Roman festival of Saint Paul was on June 29, which was dedicated to him with Saint Peter as the joint apostolic founders of the local church. But as the Roman shrines of the two apostles were a long distance apart, this double observance proved irksome, and Gregory transferred the commemoration of Saint Paul to June 30: this is still his primary festival in the Roman missal. A special feast in honour of his conversion is of eighth century Gallican origin, which made its way at some undetermined later date to Rome. Why this particular day was chosen is not known.

### THE GOSPEL

An unfortunate choice as the section stands, since the "twelve" before "thrones" in verse 28 was explicitly meant to subordinate Saint Paul to the original Twelve. But in Luke's parallel (22:30) "twelve" does not appear at this point; and I Corinthians 6:3 shows that this was the original form—and incidentally gives the saying unusual attestation as an actual utterance of Jesus. It is perfectly in accord with His teaching as a whole. In the heavenly kingdom will be found all who in their lives have recognized God as their Father. But they who have been in close and personal contact with Christ, who even while on earth by sharing His power, can be said to be "in" the kingdom, will be the natural leaders. And (obviously) the closer their spiritual relationship to Christ here on earth, the greater their authority hereafter. So, if the expositor omits the mistaken "twelve" in verse 28, the passage lends itself admirably to the theme of the day. No one whose name we know has done the work of the Master like the great Apostle to the Gentiles.

In verse 28 "judge" is used in the Old Testament sense of "rule." Verse 30 is best omitted on Saint Paul's day, as in the pre-Reformation sections. It is a warning that any pride, even in achievements for Christ, may prove disastrous.

## THE EPISTLE

Little comment is called for. 9:1–30 is from a special source used in Acts. The account of the conversion itself has perhaps been somewhat externalized, but its character as an inward experience remains unmistakable. Naturally the conversion would have been impossible if even the unconverted Saul of Tarsus had not felt the attraction of the message of Christ; Acts 26:14c—which the King James Version prints as part of Acts 9:5—may really express the contest between the old and the new in his heart.

The story of Ananias is told in a form quite unaffected by later ecclesiastical developments, and the Jewish elements in the Apostle's earliest Christian preaching are fully recognized (verse 20; compare II Corinthians 5:16).

The last verse of the section, with Paul as the object of Jewish persecution, gives an admirable climax.

## THE PURIFICATION

### February 2

GOSPEL: Luke 2:22–40. The Sarum and the Roman missals had Luke 2:22–32 (compare on the Circumcision). The 1549 and 1552

Prayer Books shortened this to Luke 2:22–27a but it was extended to include verse 40 in 1661.

EPISTLE: Malachi 3:1–5. The Sarum and the Roman missals had Malachi 3:1–4. The 1549 and 1552 Prayer Books omitted an Epistle for this day altogether and directed the use of that for whatever Sunday preceded. The present selection was adopted in 1661.

Compare Leviticus 12. The festival is apparently of late fourth-century Palestinian origin and appears at Constantinople around the year 500. It was adopted in Rome perhaps a century later. In the East the forty days were at first reckoned from January 6, but in Rome of course from December 25, giving the present date.

Liturgically this festival is distinctly awkward. The Epiphany season presents Christ's manifestations in an orderly sequence, beginning with the Nativity and leading on to the final Advent. So to be recalled suddenly to the Infancy is a blunder, which is particularly grave in those years when the Purification follows Septuagesima.

The rite of purification was in Judaism a remnant of archaic taboos connected with childbirth. But in New Testament times it had entirely lost its primitive meaning and was observed only because commanded in the Old Testament; when later Rabbis undertake to explain the ceremony their arguments are merely fanciful. An entirely separate rite was the presentation of a woman's first-born son (Exodus 13:2, etc.). Here the conception was that all that is first-born belongs to God and therefore must be redeemed by a payment. No sacrificial offerings were connected with this payment, and it could be made to any priest anywhere; but parents living in the neighbourhood of Jerusalem presumably made it in the Temple and in conjunction with the mother's purification, as here. According to Numbers 18:16, to be sure, the amount (five shekels) was due a month after birth, but there is evidence that rigorous observance of this interval was not required.

As to the ritual in force in Christ's day we have no certain knowledge, but even in later tradition little ceremony was involved. The mother presented her offering to an official at the entrance to the Court of the Women and was then and there pronounced clean. The father took the child to a priest, who received the money and asked certain set questions, to which the father gave prescribed answers. This was all. With the actual offering of the sacrifices neither parent had anything to do and—despite traditional Christian pictures—no part whatever was played by the high priest.

In the liturgies for this festival the presentation overshadows the purification almost completely, justifying the lengthy title used in the Prayer Book. The Greek term for the day is "The Meeting" (with Simeon), while in the propers of the Roman missal Mary is mentioned only at the post-communion. On this day the Lord came to his Temple, as in Malachi; the liturgical theme is therefore the confrontation of religion with its Object: "who shall stand when he appeareth?" Compare Advent 1.

When the Roman church instituted the festival on February 2, the day was already occupied by a much older observance, a penitential procession that was a Christianized form of the pagan "Amburbale." This was continued and is still maintained in the Roman use, and from the fact that the officiants carry lights the day is known as "Candlemas." But although some features of each ceremony have found their way into the other, "Purification" and "Candlemas" are wholly unrelated. Indeed, when a pre-Lent Sunday falls on February 2, Purification (as a feast) is transferred to Monday, but the procession (a penitential exercise) is never transferred with it.

## THE GOSPEL

To all intents and purposes this is an Advent section: the Messiah brings salvation but only after judgment (verses 34–35).

In verse 22 before "purification" nearly all the evidence reads "their," and the "her" of the King James Version is a late correction based on the Old Testament. This "their" includes both Mary and the child; the former must be purified according to the Law, while the latter was still under legal disprivilege until the presentation had been performed. Joseph and Mary were certainly poor, but verse 24 calls no special attention to the fact; later Jewish tradition takes for granted that the regular offering was two birds, not a bird and a lamb (Leviticus 12:8). "The consolation of Israel" (verse 25) is the final redemption, or (less likely) "The Consolation of Israel" is the Messiah. Simeon's identification of the child comes from immediate divine revelation. In verse 29 "lettest thou" is an indicative: "now thou lettest." Verse 32 is strictly Jewish, the Gentiles receive "light" but Israel receives "glory." In verses 34-35 the first clause of verse 35 is parenthetical and the second clause continues verse 34: "This child is set for the falling and rising of many in Israel, that the thoughts of many hearts may be revealed." Through the coming of the Messiah the real nature of men will be made known. Verse 35a is difficult. In the context the simplest explanation is "And thou too shalt undergo a searching test"; an interpretation quite possible in the light of Luke 8:19-21. Or: "Men's resistance to thy son will cause thee intense suffering," a rendition perhaps more in key with the general tone of Luke's first two chapters. For Anna compare Judith 8:6, 16:22-23; like Judith she was a centenarian.

The critical problems are those of the Nativity stories in general, and like them are irrelevant to the expositor.

### THE EPISTLE

Malachi 2:17-3:5 belongs to the distressing period that followed the first return from the Babylonian exile; compare Nehemiah 1:3. Most specialists date the prophecy *ca.* b.c. 475. The faithful were beginning to lose heart: "Every one that doeth evil is good in the Lord's eyes! Where is the God of justice?" The prophet replies that despite everything the Day of the Lord is imminent, and then all wrongs will be set right. In 3:1 various popular expectations of the Advent are combined in terms perhaps intentionally vague. God will send no less than three representatives to do His work, a preparatory "messenger," a ruler called "lord" (not "the Lord") and "the angel of the covenant"; the last will hold the judgment, which is described in conventional language. To be noted is the writer's interest in the cultus (3:3*b*–4). On the Purification this may receive special emphasis; but in this case verse 5 had best be omitted.

## SAINT MATTHIAS

### *February 24*

GOSPEL: Matthew 11:25–30. So the Sarum and the Roman missals.
EPISTLE: Acts 1:15–26. So the Sarum and the Roman missals.
The complete silence of the New Testament regarding Matthias before and after his election is continued in early church tradition; commemoration of him at Rome in a special festival is consequently late (eleventh century?).

### THE GOSPEL

An especially appropriate section in view of Matthias' obscurity, from which he was raised to celebrity because of his faith in Christ.

Luke's context for this passage (11:17–20) explains Jesus' words as an outburst of joy. He had sent out disciples to work in His name, and they returned enthusiastic with success. To Jesus, conscious that His own work was nearing its end, this was the most important moment in the history of the world. Those on whom He had to rely for the future were equal to their task; the leaven would continue to work; the seed to grow. So the opening words voice infinite relief from apprehension. By sad experience the "wise and prudent" had been found deaf: Israel's religious leaders had rejected the message. But this no longer mattered. God had raised up efficient workers, whose existence no one would have suspected.

In the original form of the saying—as attested by textual evidence in the Lukan parallel—the phrase "neither knoweth any man the Father, save the Son" appears to be lacking; it was added later to produce a formal parallelism. *I.e.,* verse 27 ran:

> All things are shown me by the Father:
> Only He knows the nature of Messiahship,
> And he to whom the Messiah teaches it.

The Jews had many exalted ideas about the Messiah—but they never attained the conception that Jesus and the disciples learned from God through experience. Compare the story of the Temptation (Lent 1).

The colouring of verses 28–30 is intensely Jewish. "Yoke" is a recognized term for "the authority of the Law," so that here Jesus' yoke is contrasted with that of the scribes who had made the burden intolerable. "Meek and lowly of heart" is best paraphrased "gentle and knowing the needs of the lowly." As a whole: "The scribes by their rules put salvation out of the reach of ordinary men and women; I bring it wholly within their power to achieve."

Unification of verses 25–27 and verses 28–30 is found in their common theme of "the daily round, the common task"; in Christianity sainthood is not reserved for accomplished virtuosity.

Critically neither of the verse-groups is wholly free from difficulties, although these difficulties are by no means insuperable. In any case both groups, by whomsoever framed, perfectly represent Christ's spirit.

## THE EPISTLE

This section belongs to some special tradition, of unidentifiable origin. Verses 18–19—parenthesized in the Revised Version—are probably an explanatory note of Luke's. No attempt should be made to reconcile this account of Judas' death with that in Matthew 27:3–10; how the traitor actually perished was no part of the church's official "tradition."

In the story of Matthias' election there is a slight confusion. The "Twelve" and "all the apostles" were not identical, the latter being a wider group that included the former (I Corinthians 15:5–7). The function of the "apostles" was to be witnesses of Christ's resurrection (Acts 4:33, etc.), and in this sense Saint Paul could claim to be an apostle in the full sense of the word (I Corinthians 9:1, etc.). The qualifications named in verses 21–22a have to do with a quite different office, that of bearing accurate witness to the historic teaching of Jesus. And this in the earliest church was the specific function of the Twelve; they were the guardians of the "tradition." (It is for this reason that Luke feels justified in picturing the Twelve as Jerusalem's "Sanhedrin," or college of presbyters.) So it was to the ranks of the Twelve that Matthias was really elected; he was already an "apostle."

Subsequent vacancies among the Twelve may have been filled in similar fashion. However, with the death of the last qualified eyewitness of Jesus' work on earth, the Twelve as a body naturally ceased to exist. But by this time the preservation of the "tradition" had been committed to the local presbyters everywhere. Compare II Timothy 2:2, etc.

Lots were "given" by placing the names (on parchment or on counters) in a bowl. This was then shaken until one of them flew out and so actually "fell."

Practical exposition of this section, if attempted, must centre in the pains taken to preserve an accurate "tradition."

# THE ANNUNCIATION

### March 25

GOSPEL: Luke 1:26–28. So (omitting verse 38c) the Sarum and the Roman missals.

EPISTLE: Isaiah 7:10–15. So the Sarum and the Roman missals.

This feast first appeared in the East *ca.* 600 and was adopted in Rome rather more than a century later. Like Circumcision and Purification its date is obtained from Christmas; in this case reckoning nine months earlier. And, like Purification, this mode of reckoning leaves the festival without relation to the surrounding season.

Properly speaking the Annunciation commemorates the first moment of the Incarnation and so, like Purification, is a feast of Christ rather than of Mary. Compare the collect, secret and post-communion in the Roman missal.

## THE GOSPEL

The outlook is wholly Jewish—note the description of the Messiah in verses 32–33—except perhaps in verse 35*b*; here the Jewish Messianic use of "Son of God" is given a sense for which no Jewish precedent is known. In verses 31 and 35 the Greek futures probably represent Aramaic imperfects: "Thou art (already) conceiving"; "The Holy Spirit is come upon thee, and the power of the Most High is overshadowing thee." Compare Isaiah 7:14. In this way the question in verse 34 is logical. But, obviously, to undertake a critical "defence" of the story is ill-advised; its ultimate truth is for faith, not historical science.

## THE EPISTLE

An obscure passage, endlessly debated by specialists, and no interpretation is free from difficulty. But the prophetic intensity that underlies it debars too commonplace an explanation, and the following—which has excellent scholarly support—seems the least unsatisfactory:

Jerusalem was threatened by the invading armies of the "two kings," and King Ahaz was despondent, refusing even to ask Isaiah's proferred "sign." The prophet rebukes him, and continues: "I see in a vision a woman who is now with child. When her son is born he will be fed with cream and honey until his infancy is passed, but before that time the land will be free." Here "cream and honey" would mean to Oriental ears the food on which the gods were nourished, "ambrosia and nectar." Hence the child is a miracle Child, at whose maturity peace will be restored; he is the Messiah. So the passage may be paraphrased: "You, Ahaz, have lost your faith. But God's power is not shortened. The Messiah is already in being and will soon appear; the King of Peace."

Naturally the miracle in verse 14 is the conception of the Messiah, not his virginal conception; the Hebrew word used is simply that for "young woman." Evil in the world seems triumphant, but soon a Stronger One will be born!

## ASH WEDNESDAY

GOSPEL: Matthew 6:16–21. So the Sarum and the Roman missals.
EPISTLE: Joel 2:12–17. So (with the addition of verses 18–19) the Sarum and the Roman missals.

The Epistle gives justification of fasting in time of need; the Gospel teaches how a fast should be observed.

The extension of Lent by prefixing four days to its first Sunday came either under Gregory (died 604) or shortly thereafter. The occasion was a Lombard invasion and the propers in the Roman missals were written as pleas for deliverance from this danger. But, once instituted, observance of these days did not cease with the danger, and the prayers were explained to refer to spiritual foes. Compare on pre-Lent.

In the late patristic and mediæval church baptized sinners who sought restoration were excluded from attendance at the eucharist from the beginning of Lent until Maundy Thursday. During this time they gave themselves to penitential acts based chiefly on the Old Testament, including the Jewish mourning customs of sitting in ashes (Job 2:8, etc.) or sprinkling ashes on the head (II Samuel 13:19, etc.). So the imposition of ashes was made a formal act at the beginning of the period of penance; by the tenth century prayers for blessing these ashes began to come into use. (The Roman pontifical still contains the service for this "exclusion of penitents," but its use has been discontinued since the twelfth century.) With the constant growth of the penitential spirit in Western Christianity it was argued that every believer needs penance, and so in the twelfth century the imposition of ashes was extended to all.

Their meaning was explained by the symbolists as typifying the corruptible mortality of creatures. But originally it was the discomfort and mournful appearance of the ashes that made them seem appropriate in times of fasting. In any case their use by Christians is not too easy to reconcile with Matthew 6:17.

### THE GOSPEL

No exegetical comment seems needful. The expositor's task is to explain in what sense Lenten fasting is profitable.

### THE EPISTLE

Joel 1:1–2:27 is a close-knit unit, written in or near Jerusalem around B.C. 400. An overwhelming plague of locusts was devastating the land; so utter was the destruction that—to the prophet the climax of misery—even materials for the Temple sacrifices were lacking. Man's sole recourse was to call on God, with fasting and penitence. 2:15–17 describes the ceremonies of such a fast, as they were practised at the time. For the summons by trumpet-call compare Leviticus 23:24. The need is so great that all exemptions are disregarded; even the infants are brought to the assembly; even newly married couples are deprived of their privileges (Deuteronomy 24:5). The people prostrate themselves in the Temple's outer court, separated from the Holy Place by a portico ("porch"); beyond this the priests, facing the altar, make their intercessions.

"That the heathen should rule over them" is a mistranslation; the sense is "lest the heathen mock them" as worshippers of a helpless god.

The mistranslation is due to construing Joel's highly graphic pictures of the locusts as descriptions of human invaders; it was for this reason that this section seems originally to have been chosen for Ash Wednesday. With the reinterpretation of the enemies as the hosts of Satan this error ceased to be important, as these were admirably typified by the destroyers, whether human or otherwise. It is this reinterpretation that makes expository use of the section possible on Ash Wednesday.

## SAINT MARK

### April 25

GOSPEL: John 15:1–11. A lengthening of the Sarum Gospel (John 15:1–7), which was one of the "common" Gospels for saints' days. The Roman missal uses it for feasts of martyrs in Eastertide, but for Saint Mark's day provides Luke 10:1–11. This is likewise an older "common," which reappears on Saint Luke's day. So neither the Sarum nor the Roman section was meant to allude specially to Saint Mark.

EPISTLE: Ephesians 4:7–16. A lengthening of the Sarum Epistle (Ephesians 4:7–13), undoubtedly chosen because of the mention of "evangelists" in verse 11. The Roman missal has Ezekiel 1:10–14, an older "common" for feasts of Evangelists.

The facts of Mark's life are familiar. From the human standpoint his recovery after his desertion of Saint Paul is perhaps the most appealing event. But his importance rests in his missionary success, above all of course in the written summary of his message that he has left us.

The feast of Saint Mark is late, not being observed in Rome until Carolingian days. And even in Alexandria, with which tradition invariably connects the Evangelist, there is no certain mention of observance at an earlier time. Non-Roman calendars vary greatly in their dates for the festival.

In the Roman missal April 25 is also kept as the day of the "Greater Litanies," where "greater" is used in the sense of "older." (The contrast is with the "lesser"—*i.e.,* "newer"—litanies of the Rogation Days.) These litanies are a Christianized form of the pagan Robigalia. They have nothing to do with Saint Mark but were used long before his feast was established; certainly in the sixth century and probably much earlier.

## THE GOSPEL

Saint Paul's conception of the mystical Body of Christ, illustrated by a different figure that is preserved throughout the passage: faithful members of Christ through their union with Him receive abundant strength for lives of fruitful and joyous activity. Compare Luke 10:17-20 for the same truth in Synoptic terms.

The section is free from real difficulty, but the expositor should note that in the Evangelist's purpose "ye" addresses all Christians everywhere; it is in no wise restricted to the apostles who make up Christ's audience at the scene. Verse 2 states a commonplace in viticulture; the vinedresser prunes off useless branches and cleanses the others with some soapy compound. Verse 3 is typically Johannine. Christians are already God's children, so that the remnants of sin that remain in them must not be allowed to cause gloomy brooding: God's pardon is full and free. For the doctrine of prayer in verse 7 compare on Easter 5. A true member of Christ will be so filled with Christ's spirit that he will pray only for what Christ will approve: hence his prayers are certain to be answered. Compare Augustine's famous "Love God—and do as you please."

## THE EPISTLE

The Gospel's theme of fruitful activity is further developed, with more accent on life within the church.

Verses 9–10 are a parenthesis, and the passage will be clearer if it is omitted, since verse 11 explains what is meant by "measure" in verse 7. Before this parenthesis Psalm 68:18 is quoted from the Aramaic version, "gave gifts to men," where the Hebrew has "received gifts from men." Verses 9–10 then endeavour to prove that this citation is relevant. If one "ascends," he must have first "descended" into the "lower parts," i.e., "the earth." (The genitive is appositive, not partitive.) But only One has both "ascended" and "descended." Hence Psalm 68:18 refers to Christ. For modern congregations Jewish scholasticism of this sort is hardly helpful.

In verse 11 "pastors and teachers" are one class, not two: by the time Ephesians was written organization was beginning to be stabilized. The King James's "edifying the body" is better translated "building up the body" in the Revised Version; the metaphor is perhaps not consistent but the sense is clear enough. In verse 15 "cherishing the truth" or "dealing truly" is better in the context than "speaking the truth." The precise force of the terms in verse 16 is debated but the meaning is unmistakable; note the intense stress on social relationships.

## SAINT PHILIP AND SAINT JAMES

### May 1

GOSPEL: John 14:1–14. So the Sarum and the Roman missals. A passage indicated of course by the dialogue with Philip.

EPISTLE: James 1:1–12. A Reformation substitute for the Sarum (and Roman) Wisdom 5:1–5, a "common." The Prayer Book selection was also a pre-Reformation "common," which had the double advantage to the Reformers of not being from the Apocrypha and of bearing James's name.

Of Philip the Apostle we know just about nothing at all; in the Gospel for today any one else might equally well have been used to ask his question, and the same applies to the other passages in which he appears in St. John. In later tradition he is confused with Philip the evangelist.

The Saint James commemorated is the Apostle known as "the less" (*i.e.,* "the little"), the son of Alphæus. Of him we know only the name. Later tradition identified him with James "the Lord's brother," an entirely different person.

The Roman Basilica of the Apostles, begun by Pelagius I, was finished some time after 561 by his successor John III and was dedicated on a May 1. For some unknown reason it was put under the special patronage of these two saints, who have nothing in common and were never—as far as we know—conjoined anywhere else. Most non-Roman martyrologies give November 14 as Saint Philip's day, while Saint James's varies widely: December 26–28, October 23, and April 30 are all found.

## THE GOSPEL

The Evangelist's constant theme of the hopeful confidence gained through Christ. The standard English versions render verse 1 correctly; the first "believe" is indicative, the second imperative. "You" in verse 2 addresses Jesus' disciples universally: they have become a multitude no man can number but heaven's "abiding places" are infinitely many. (Is Jewish particularism in mind?) The questions in verses 5 and 8 are not really those of apostles but are such as believers ask everywhere. In verse 6 it is best to translate "the way; even the truth and the life"; "truth" and "life" together make up the "way." In verses 10–11 the unexpected but wholly legitimate conversion of "words" into "works" is most effective: "The words of our Saviour are alive; they have hands and feet" (Luther). For the saying about prayer at the end compare on Easter 5. "In my name" = "in my service," "as my representative."

## THE EPISTLE

It is usually held nowadays that what we call "The Epistle of James" is a Christianized version of an earlier Hellenistic Jewish

"Testament of Jacob"; in Greek "Jacob" and "James" are the same. Originally it consisted of Jacob's exhortations to each of his sons in turn; compare the Testaments of the Twelve Patriarchs. With what "James" the Christian editor wished to connect his revision is wholly uncertain; in any case the writing has nothing to do with any New Testament character.

Unity—perhaps not designed by the writer—in this section can be gained by taking as the theme "trial" ("temptation") with which it begins and ends. How can we profit by trouble? By the character-development it brings when met bravely. No doubt we may often be tormented by perplexity, uncertain how to act (verse 5). But God will show the right way to them who call upon Him in firm faith (verses 5*b*–6). Verses 9–10 are difficult but can be understood as apocalyptic in a time of persecution. Then distinctions between the poor and rich are levelled but both should be thankful; the poor because they are elevated to sainthood, the rich because they escape the fate about to come on the unrighteous mighty ones of the earth. The "burning heat" is the sirocco, which in a single day will blast a countryside.

## ASCENSION DAY

GOSPEL: Luke 24:49–53 (American; first introduced in 1928) and Mark 16:14–20 (English and the earlier American Prayer Books). The latter is in the Sarum and the Roman missals. The former is used in the Greek Church and has various Western precedents, as in the Ambrosian rite; it is far preferable.

EPISTLE: Acts 1:1–11. So in the Sarum and the Roman missals.

All the resurrection appearances of Christ accepted in the Christian tradition occurred within a short interval of time and after that were never renewed. To see the Risen Lord on earth was the passionate desire of every believer, and the claims of individuals that they had actually done so would assuredly not have met with scrupulous criticism. None the less, after a very few weeks, when the missionary preaching was begun, the tradition was unanimous that no more such appearances could be expected until the Parousia. To be sure there were visions of Christ in heaven (Acts 7:56, etc.) but these were felt to be something different. Even Saint Paul, despite his insistence that he had seen Jesus just as truly as any of the others, was perfectly aware that it was not in the same way.

The only explanation of these facts is that the final vision contained something to convince the beholders that it was a definite farewell.

Theologically, this farewell was only to earthly limitations; not to believers' souls. On the contrary. It was the Ascension that made possible the true presence of Christ with His people; it is only as lifted up that He can draw all men to Him.

Liturgically the festival is not mentioned by Tertullian, Origen or Cyprian, but Augustine speaks of it as observed "by the whole world." At Rome a vigil was added in the seventh century and an octave in the twelfth.

### THE GOSPEL

(American.) Luke 24:44–53 is a compressed summary of resurrection traditions, made in precisely the same manner as earlier compressed summaries of Jesus' teachings; none of the Evangelists treat the resurrection story differently from the other events of the ministry.

In the earliest days Galilean and Jerusalem Christians were in rivalry about the importance of the appearances on their own soil; Matthew (with Mark?) uses a Galilean source, Luke one from southern Palestine. Verse 50b is a mere transition phrase, exactly like many others in the Gospels. Its purpose is solely to link over from Jerusalem (verse 33) to Bethany, and no attempt should be made to visualize what it describes.

"And was carried up into heaven" and "worshipped him and" are later additions to the text.

## THE GOSPEL

(English.) There is no longer any doubt that the last twelve verses from Mark are of second-century composition. Of recent years, also, it has become increasingly probable that more was in this addition than is contained in most of the manuscripts that give it; between verses 14 and 15 certain codices add the equivalent of several more verses. (For their content recent commentaries must be consulted.) It was the omission of this extra matter that produced the brusque transition from Christ's rebuke to His command to preach.

In the passage as it stands note the overemphasis on the evidential value of physical miracles in verses 17–18 and 20b, and the semi-creedal formulations in verses 16 and 19.

Homiletic exposition is not to be recommended.

## THE EPISTLE

The extraordinary phrasing of the opening paragraph is most curious in a writer of Luke's ability; contrast the beautiful precision of Luke 1:1–4. So later editorial retouching is really conceivable although its extent cannot be determined. But it may include the "forty days," on which the other sources are silent.

In verse 4 "being assembled with them" should be "eating with them"; compare Luke 24:43. Punctuate: "Speaking of the things pertaining to the kingdom of God, and eating with them, he commanded." Verse 7 may be a softened variant of Mark 13:33, but verses 7–8 together state ideally the proper Christian attitude toward apocalyptic. Verse 11 is a perfect climax.

# SAINT BARNABAS

## June 11

GOSPEL: John 15:12–16. So the Sarum missal; the "common" for a vigil of an Apostle. The Roman missal has Matthew 10:16–22.

EPISTLE: Acts 11:22–30. A Reformation substitute for the Sarum Ephesians 2:19–22, also a "common." The Roman missal has the discontinuous passage Acts 11:21*b*–26, 13:1–3.

Barnabas first appears in Acts in the familiar passage 4:36–37; his title "son of exhortation" (not "of consolation") means that he was an extraordinarily powerful preacher. But his great claim to commemoration is that he was the first prominent member of the Jerusalem church to engage definitely in Gentile work; to this he committed himself so thoroughly as to seek the co-operation of Saint Paul (Acts 11:25–26). The two worked together zealously in Antioch, Cyprus and Asia Minor (Acts 13–14), although in Luke's account Barnabas is so overshadowed by his great companion as scarcely to appear individually. In the reasons Luke gives for their final separation (Acts 15:36–41) Barnabas was in the right, as Saint Paul himself came eventually to admit (Colossians 4:10–11). But Galatians 2:13 may hint that Luke does not tell the whole story.

The ecclesiastical commemoration of Barnabas as an "Apostle" is due to Acts 14:4, 14; compare on St. Matthias. At Rome the festival was instituted in the eleventh century or later.

### THE GOSPEL

The elements are all characteristically Johannine, but the boldness of verse 14 should receive full attention, emphasizing the fact that not exalted apostles but Christians in general are really addressed. The ideal of Judaism is obedience to a Law, whether or not it is understood: a precept may seem arbitrary or meaningless, but to question its obligation is rebellion against God. Christian authority is totally other; in effect, nothing else than the law of love, something that any one can understand. In this way God deals with us not as servants but as friends, taken—so to speak—fully into His confidence. Here the terminology of the Fourth Evangelist goes even beyond that of Saint Paul, for the latter was still content to speak of Christians as God's "servants." John, however, failed to impress later Christianity, which reverted rapidly to Old Testament language and even went beyond it; devotional writers gravely set forth that confidence in one's relations to the Father is spiritual pride, and vie with one another in coining phrases to express abjectness. This is one very real reason why traditional Christianity has lost its hold.

### THE EPISTLE

The venture of faith that led a Jew to commit himself to Gentile work can hardly be overemphasized. And Barnabas' courage is seen to be still greater if—as is very probable—verse 22 is an overstatement; Luke's intense sense of discipline may have led him to exaggerate the formal character of the appointment.

The inclusion of verses 27–30 was a mistake, since the mention of Barnabas at the end of verse 30 does not associate him with the contents of the paragraph.

## SAINT JOHN BAPTIST

### *June 24*

GOSPEL: Luke 1:57–80. A Reformation lengthening of Luke 1:57–68 in the Sarum and the Roman missals.

EPISTLE: Isaiah 40:1–11. The Sarum and the Roman missals have Isaiah 49:1–7, a much less desirable choice.

For the historic significance of the Baptist compare on Advent 3 and 4.

The prominent place John occupies in the Gospels made him familiar to Christians everywhere, and commemoration began at least in the fifth century, although the date of its introduction in Rome is obscure. The day of his death was fixed—for some wholly unknown reason—on August 29, but the Gospel account of his birth is so elaborate that his nativity became the chief festival. In Rome this was computed mechanically according to Luke 1:36 as six months before Christmas (noting that while viii.Kal.Jan. is December 25, viii.Kal.Jul. is June 24). But this computation was an afterthought, for the Visitation is observed—evidently from an older tradition—on July 2; this presupposes October 2 as the day of John's birth.

### THE GOSPEL

The story comes presumably from the followers of John. There is no trace of Christian influence; throughout the Baptist is viewed as God's prophet in his own right. The miracles in verses 57–66 show his importance, while the song of Zacharias describes his work in terms of the purest Jewish Messianism. For the name "John" compare 1:13; it means "the Lord is gracious." The "fear" in verse 65 comes from a sense of contact with the supernatural. When Zacharias uttered the Benedictus is not told. "Horn of salvation" in verse 69 symbolizes victorious onslaught; the figure is taken from battling cattle or deer. Verse 70 is parenthetical and "salvation" in verse 71 resumes the same word in verse 69. In verse 72 God's "memory" of His covenant is the "mercy" He shows to the fathers. The ideal in verses 74–75 is quietistic, Palestine, freed from the defilement of the Gentiles, will be devoted to the pure worship of God. To Luke and all Christians "the Lord" in verse 76 was of course Christ, but the original meaning was "God" (Malachi 3:1). The remission of sins given through John's baptism was knowledge of salvation (verse 77). Verse 78b: "Because of this (mercy) the Messianic dawn—beginning at the zenith—will soon be here."

The section is much too long for satisfactory exposition. If the earlier portion (practically the pre-Reformation Gospel) is chosen the treatment will be somewhat difficult, as these miracles at the Baptist's birth have far from the significance of those in the Nativity stories. Exposition of verses 68–79, however, should be undertaken from time to time, at least in churches where the Benedictus is in liturgical use, as congregations generally do not understand it. The homiletic transformation of the pietistic legalism into Christian values is distinctly worth effort.

## THE EPISTLE

To the Jews of the captivity any thought of a return at first seemed hopeless: not only were the physical difficulties of the journey overwhelming but the way was blocked by powerful enemies. So this prophecy of Deutero-Isaiah (*ca.* B.C. 540) is the cry of faith confronted by the humanly impossible—and triumphing over it. "Talk not of deserts and mountains—God will cleave a highway through them" (verses 3–5). "Talk not of invincible foes—to God they are but as grass" (verses 7–8). "Talk not of weakness and fainting—God will protect even the most feeble" (verses 9–11).

Verses 1–2 are the summary of all Deutero-Isaiah. The prophets of old predicted punishment, which has come to pass. Now a new prophet is called with a new message, of hope. The opening of verse 6 can be more clearly translated:

> God's voice commands: "Cry!"
> I said: "What shall I cry?"
> God replied: "All flesh is grass," etc.

The application of the passage to the Baptist is obvious. He, too, was confronted by the humanly impossible and was not intimidated by it. No doubt he may have been disappointed at the first results of his work. Just so the prophet may well have been disappointed by the first fulfilment of his prediction: in place of all Israel marching back in triumph over a miraculous causeway, only a handful of rather ineffectual adventurers actually returned. But from the efforts of these few the way was really prepared for all later Judaism. And from the efforts of John the way was opened for Jesus Christ.

## SAINT PETER

### *June 29*

GOSPEL: Matthew 16:13–19. So the Sarum and the Roman missals.
EPISTLE: Acts 12:1–11. So the Sarum and the Roman missals.

The observance of June 29 as the festival of Saint Peter (and Saint Paul) can be traced back with certainty to the year 336. But it is doubtless of considerably earlier origin, and appears to be eventually the day of the removal of the Apostles' relics to the catacombs during the Valerian persecution of 258. In non-Roman tradition other days were sometimes kept.

The Leonine and Gelasian sacramentaries use June 29 also for the commemoration of all the Apostles.

### THE GOSPEL

In Mark 8:27–33 Peter acknowledges Jesus' Messiahship in the name of the Twelve; he, however, shows immediately that his understanding of what Messiahship involves is unworthy, so much so that Jesus rebukes him scathingly. This is in accord with a primary purpose of the Second Gospel: to prove that the Twelve and even —or especially—their leader were never able to rise to Christ's own conception of His work. While He transcended early limitations, they remained enmeshed in nationalism. (Compare on the Transfiguration.) Hence—this is Mark's implicit conclusion—full Christianity is to be sought in the universalism of Saint Paul, not in the Jewish restrictions of Peter and the rest.

Against this contention the leaders of Jewish Christianity protested, and Matthew 16:17–19 embodies their reply. The highest form of Christianity is that whose chiefest exponent was the great Apostle of the circumcision. It is untrue that his conception of Christ savours not of God but of men; on the contrary "Flesh and blood hath not revealed it unto thee, but my Father who is in heaven." And this group made great play with the undoubted fact that the name "Cephas," "Peter," "Rock," was given Simon by Jesus in person: surely this can only mean that this Rock is the foundation-stone of the church. So Peter must be its chief-steward, the master-servant, who is entrusted with all the keys of the house. (The picture of the key-bearer as the door-keeper is wrong.) So what he "binds"—*i.e.,* prohibits—or "looses"—*i.e.,* allows—should be obligatory on all. Compare Isaiah 22:22.

This tradition appealed entirely to the First Evangelist, who incorporated it into his revision of Mark; as, however, he did not feel justified in omitting Mark's contrary polemic (Matthew 16:22-23) the result is a certain incoherence. Another incoherence is found in verse 18*b.* "The gates of hell" are not, as generally understood, "the armies of Satan" but are simply a paraphrase for "death." That "my Church shall never die" is perhaps conceivable language but it is very unnatural. And there is reason—supported by real testimony in patristic quotations—to think the words are textually corrupt.

As a whole Matthew 16:13-19 is late. In verses 13 and 16 "Son of Man" and "Son of God" in a Messianic context are contrasted in a sense foreign to the language of Jewish apocalyptic. The appearance of "church" in verse 18 is paralleled for the Synoptic tradition only in Matthew 18:17, where it is more defensible ("the local community"), although even this latter verse is certainly not a saying of Jesus. The conception of the Christian church as a new institution founded by Jesus does not appear until the separation between Judaism and Christianity was well advanced. In the Synoptists the pointblank identification of the (visible) church with the kingdom is peculiar to late passages in the First Gospel (13:41, 13:49, etc.). And no fact is more firmly fixed in the Synoptic sources than that Jesus rigidly refused to name the greatest in the kingdom (Mark 9:34, Matthew 18:1, Luke 22:24, etc.; compare on Saint James and Saint Bartholomew).

What this passage gives, therefore, is a specimen of heated church controversy in the first century. So to render it helpful to a modern congregation is difficult in the extreme, for historically it is only one more example of the perversions of history that invariably grow out of passion. At best it witnesses to the devotion that Saint Peter inspired among those who loved him—but this devotion is by no means unmixed with the desire to defend legalistic observances that have been called in question. And, above all, if Christianity had accepted this picture of Saint Peter as the key-bearer, it would have remained a Jewish sect.

That, however, Jesus did really call Simon "the Rock" rests on wholly independent authority (Mark 3:16, etc.). Despite all his thoughtless impetuousness he was a man on whom Jesus could thoroughly rely. No doubt he never rose to intellectual heights. Our Gospel section makes clear that to the end of his life he remained what Saint Paul calls him in Galatians 2:7, a faithful son of the Law, bound to feel that Gentile converts lacked something as long as they remained outside the Jewish pale. (Compare Matthew 23:2-3, 5:19, etc.) None the less he not only gave Saint Paul the right hand of fellowship; he himself made Gentile converts and ministered to them, realizing that the truth could be wider than his personal sympathies and understanding. And in this way he remained a "Rock" to the end.

## THE EPISTLE

Compare Acts 4:1-21, 5:17-26. It is quite possible that the account in Acts 4 is the source of the stories in Acts 5 and 12. In any case legendary elements in the present section are evident: the exorbitant pains (sixteen soldiers!) taken to guard one man, the stupor cast on every one in the prison and—particularly—the unjust fate of the soldiers in verse 19. But use can be made of God's care to preserve Peter, who still had work to do, as contrasted with the fate of James, whose work was done.

# SAINT JAMES

*July 25*

GOSPEL: Matthew 20:20–28. A Reformation lengthening of Matthew 20:20–23 in the Sarum and the Roman missals.

EPISTLE: Acts 11:27–12:3*a*. A Reformation substitute for Ephesians 2:19–22 (a "common") in the Sarum missal. The Roman missal has I Corinthians 4:9–15.

The early martyrdom of James naturally prevented associating his name with any local church outside Palestine. So while some attempt was made to honour him with Saint John on December 27 (compare on the Post-Christmas Days), the institution of a special feast seems not to have taken place in Rome until the eighth century. Possibly July 25 was then already dedicated to some later saint of the same name, who was displaced in favour of the Apostle.

The Spanish cult of Saint James did not begin until the ninth century.

## THE GOSPEL

This Matthæan version of Mark 10:35–45 is very little changed from the more primitive form, but the substitution of "the mother" for "James and John" avoids suggesting apostolic egotism.

This passage looks back to the martyrdom of James—and probably of (this) John also—as an accomplished fact. Christ's cup had truly been drunk, Christ's baptism had indeed been accepted. But even martyrdom is not an achievement so supreme as to raise the sufferer to the highest rank in God's eyes. Spiritual authority comes only from spiritual character, not from any act; and the degree of such character can be known to God alone. One thing, however, is certain. Christian authority is displayed only in Christ-likeness, where nothing ministers to pride, where everything is bent on the task of perfect service.

**THE EPISTLE**

The Reformers felt that Acts 12:1-3a, with its description of the martyrdom, was more appropriate than the generalities of the older section. Unfortunately, however, to gain better liturgical length they prefixed the last four verses of Acts 11, which are wholly irrelevant to the theme of the day.

# THE TRANSFIGURATION

## *August 6*

Not in the English Prayer Books. Restored to the American Prayer Book in 1892.

GOSPEL: Luke 9:28-36. The Sarum and the Roman missals have the parallel Matthew 17:1-9. The Markan section would have been preferable to either.

EPISTLE: II Peter 1:13-18. The Sarum and the Roman missals have II Peter 1:16-19.

This feast was known in the East at the beginning of the sixth century. Its spread in the West was slow; it was not formally adopted in Rome until 1457.

**THE GOSPEL**

In Mark 9:2-8, which reappears in Luke without important variations, the Transfiguration is a repetition of the scene of Saint Peter's confession, although transposed—so to speak—into a higher key. Peter acknowledges that Jesus is Messiah—he is permitted to behold something of the glory that was hidden from the world. But his conception of Messiahship is so nationalistically limited that he rebels when the way of the cross is made known to him—he wishes to confine the heavenly figures in earthly tabernacles. Christ rebukes him for failing to see how utterly God's plan transcends national prosperity—God rebukes him for failing to see that an earthly dwelling is utterly unworthy of God's "Son." The theme is consequently the contrast between pure religion and its lower forms. "Neither in this mountain nor in Jerusalem! God is a Spirit!" The third chapter of II Corinthians is an admirable commentary.

In Luke's account certain details not found in Mark suggest that he has access to some independent tradition, but not enough is recoverable for reconstruction. And what ultimately lies behind all the versions is even less capable of critical analysis. From Luke 9:32a it might be argued that everything goes back to a dream Peter had soon after Jesus had formally accepted the Messianic title. This would be quite comprehensible; the disciples' minds were at that time filled with apocalyptic visions, while Luke 9:36a (= Mark 9:8) would then describe the awakened return to reality. All this, however, is merely speculation, and the insistence on silence preserved until later (Luke 9:36b = Mark 9:9) may have important significance. But the purpose and message of the section are independent of all such considerations.

## THE EPISTLE

II Peter—in the main an expansion of Jude—was written to combat the antinomian principles of certain Gnostics. 1:5-11 states the thesis: Christianity is a religion of righteousness. Then 1:12-21 asserts: This thesis was the constant theme of the Apostles, something that Christians must never forget. And (verses 16-18) the Apostles knew the truth, for they saw Christ's glory face to face. In this way the Transfiguration serves an apologetic purpose in supporting apostolic authority against Gnostic vagaries.

The choice of this particular miracle for such a demonstration seems scarcely ideal, but the underlying assumption is sound. They know most about Jesus who are in closest contact with Him, and the testimony of such is unvarying. The religion that he taught is no nexus of arbitrary rules and observances; in the faith He gave us righteousness is all-in-all.

# SAINT BARTHOLOMEW

*August 24*

GOSPEL: Luke 22:24–30. So the Sarum missal; it is a "common." The Roman missal has Luke 6:12–19.

EPISTLE: Acts 5:12–16. In the Sarum missal this is a "common," although for Saint Bartholomew's Day itself is provided the alternative "common" Ephesians 2:19–22. The Roman missal has I Corinthians 12:27–31.

Of the historic Bartholomew we know only the name; there is no justification for identifying him with the Nathaniel of the Fourth Gospel. In later tradition he appears as one of the five Apostles of the East (compare on Saint Thomas), and an Oriental cult is attested in the early sixth century. At Rome a feast was instituted in the ninth century, or perhaps a little earlier.

## THE GOSPEL

For verses 24–27 compare on Saint James; for verses 28–30 compare on Conversion of Saint Paul. The two paragraphs together contrast the humility of Christian service with the value God places on this service.

## THE EPISTLE

A description of apostolic power, in which the expositor need only translate physical healing into spiritual healing.

Exegetically the antecedents of the pronouns in verses 12*b*–14 are confusing; so confusing, in fact, that the accuracy of the text is questioned. But the problem is important only to professional exegetes.

# SAINT MATTHEW

*September 21*

GOSPEL: Matthew 9:9–13. So the Sarum and the Roman missals.
EPISTLE: II Corinthians 4:1–6. A Reformation substitute for the

Sarum (and Roman) "common of an Evangelist," Ezekiel 1:10–14.

Of the Matthew who was one of the Twelve our historic knowledge is scanty. In the Gospel for this day the First Evangelist identifies him with the "Levi" of Mark 2:14, but the identification is questionable; could the same individual bear two *Jewish* names, neither of which has Christian significance? But that Matthew was really a publican may be safely assumed; this would help explain the confusion (if such exists). What is vastly more important, however, is the high probability that the name attached to the First Gospel is that of the writer of its great source, the Sayings document. The historic Matthew drew up a selection of Jesus' teachings, which is altogether the most reliable that we have; its objectivity shows that to its compiler the need of men to know Jesus was everything, and his own preferences nothing.

On the other hand, of "Matthew" the otherwise obscure editor of the present First Gospel we can tell more. Chiefly, of course, that he produced what is without question the most influential book in the world; something that is glory enough for any man. Otherwise nearly all that was said of Saint Peter (on Saint Peter's Day) applies equally well to him, except that his personal missionary labours were presumably not so fruitful. He was, like Peter, a Jewish-Christian convinced of the superiority of his own type of faith, but none the less passionately committed to spreading the message universally, and to accepting Gentile converts as true brothers in Christ. It is this aspect of his work that may be most fruitful to the expositor. But no less characteristic is his insistence that faith must justify itself by its fruits (7:15–23, etc.), so that for Gnostic antinomianism he has only intense horror (24:11–12). Noteworthy also is a strange combination of concepts. His belief in the corporate nature of Christianity is so intense that he identifies the present kingdom pointblank with the visible church (13:41, etc.). And yet he is impatient of ecclesiastical organization; all Christians are equal, and to only God or Christ belong such titles as "Teacher," "Father," "Master" (23:8–10; compare 18:15–20).

As one of the "Apostles of the East" his commemoration in the West was delayed; it reached Rome in the ninth century. Curiously enough, despite the infinite importance of his Gospel, Matthew was never a popular saint; churches dedicated in his honour, *e.g.,* are extraordinarily few.

## THE GOSPEL

Verse 9 may represent a dramatization of the fact that Jesus enrolled a publican among the Twelve; compare on Saint Andrew. This class was ostracized by all the moralists of the ancient world, Jewish or Gentile, because of the dishonesty practically inseparable from their profession; but they were not economically submerged; on the contrary some of them were very rich. (It is also well to remember that the publicans of Galilee were not hated because they served Rome, for they did not do so; they were employed by the Jewish municipalities or by Herod Antipas.) The "sinners" were Hebrews who notoriously disregarded the Mosaic Law and were consequently treated as apostates from Judaism. To the Pharisees both publicans and "sinners" seemed so outside the pale of possible salvation that attempts to reach them were regarded as a waste of time. It was precisely because their spiritual state was so degraded that Jesus sought them out—and found in them unsuspected possibilities of good. One publican, in fact, He was even able to raise to the apostolate.

## THE EPISTLE

The passage is so close-knit and the allusions to the situation in Corinth so numerous that a paraphrase may be helpful. For the moment verse 5 is omitted.

"Since work done for Christ has the splendour just described, we who through God's mercy have been called to it do not let ourselves become careless. Nor do we dare undertake it with any but the purest motives. The Jews speak of my 'clever insincerity'; they say my interpretations of the Bible 'falsify God's Word.' Utterly wrong! My sole endeavour is to keep rigidly to the truth. So rigidly as to satisfy the strictest demands the most exacting consciences can conceive; nay more, to remember always that God's continual presence make absolute truthfulness essential. The Jews say, too, that my preaching is 'incomprehensible.' No doubt it is to them! But that is because worldliness has blinded them. And how great is that blindness that cannot see the radiance in the Christian message! We who believe see in Christ nothing less than God's very Image. This vision is God's gift to us. The same God who at creation said 'Let there be light!' has sent His light into our hearts, to enable us to recognize His glory in the face of Jesus Christ."

There are, of course, possibilities of slightly varying interpretation in matters of detail; for these the commentaries must be consulted.

In verse 4 "the god of this world" as a title for Satan is derived not from dualism but from apocalyptic; the world has fallen so far under his rule that he has become its god. Christ is called here "the Image of God" in the sense explained in verse 6, to know Christ is to know God. (But in Pauline thinking it is the exalted Christ, not the earthly Jesus, that is meant.) The mystical intensity of the language may well reflect some experience of the Apostle's (his conversion?).

In verse 4 "lest they should see the light" is better than "lest the light should shine upon them," especially since "upon them" is not in the true text of the passage.

Verse 5 is half-parenthetical and is best treated separately: "The Jews say I use my ministry to gain personal power. On the contrary! I not only serve Christ but for His sake I regard myself as the servant of my converts."

Faithful exposition of this section will involve some effort. But the preacher who has mastered the exegesis will find that the present-day application is immediate.

## SAINT MICHAEL AND ALL ANGELS

*September 29*

GOSPEL: Matthew 18:1–10. So the Sarum and the Roman missals.
EPISTLE: Revelation 12:7–12. A Reformation substitute for the
Sarum (and Roman) Revelation 1:1–5.

The first church in Italy to be erected in honour of Saint Michael
was a little basilica north of Rome. September 29 was the day of
its (fifth century) dedication.

Expository application on this day will depend largely on the
preacher's personal viewpoint.

### THE GOSPEL

A revision of the older form in Mark 9:33–47, with results that
are somewhat confusing. In Mark 9:33–37 the child is the object
not the subject of the virtue commended; *i.e.,* it is the willingness
to minister even to children, not the child-like character, that is in
point. So there is a natural transition to verses 38–41, which treat
of willingness to minister to those whose faith is imperfect, and
it is these, not children, who are the "little ones" of verse 42.
To rebuff such because of their lack of development is one of the
gravest sins that man can commit. So grave is it, in fact, that anything bitter or arrogant in the missionaries' character must be dealt
with remorselessly (verses 43–47).

This orderly development in Mark was not appreciated by the
First Evangelist. At the beginning the mention of the child has
caused him to introduce his verse 3 (from Mark 10:15), which is
incongruous. Verse 4 endeavours—not too smoothly—to connect
this addition with Mark's version. As a result, verses 3–5 mean as
they stand: "Become like little children (verse 3), by humbling
yourselves as little children (verse 4), displaying your humility in
willingness to minister to little children (verse 5)."

Then for some reason Matthew omitted Mark's verses 38-41 and went on immediately to his verse 42 (Matthew's verse 6). This makes the "little ones" there mean not "imperfect believers" but "children" once more, and the verse asserts that one of the most grievous of sins is to pervert the mind of a child, a lesson reinforced by verses 7-9 (Mark's verses 43-47, retouched). Verse 10 is then a climax: "Men may despise children, but not so God. On the contrary He commits them to the especial care of the mightiest of all the angelic host"; angels "who always behold the face of the Father" are "Throne Angels."

For an expository sermon on childhood the passage may then serve very well. The only question is whether the Evangelist intended the meaning that strict exegesis is bound to find here. It does not accord with what follows in verses 12-14, which deal with seeking out the "lost"; can this be applied to little children? Hence it may very well be that Matthew really had the Markan conceptions in mind and did not realize the confusing results of his own editing. If this is true, exposition had best not be attempted.

For Saint Michael's Day, of course, verse 10 is the important sentence. But the language is merely pictorial. Taken literally it would amount to saying that when the "little ones" grow more mature their guardianship is transferred to angels of lesser dignity, since so much care is no longer required. The most that can be made of it is that it enunciates a vital truth—God's care for the weak—in very "popular" terminology.

As an authentic saying of Jesus its support as an isolated sentence in the First Gospel is not all that can be desired, while, moreover, Jesus' sense of the Father's immediate presence was so vivid as to leave no room for significant intermediaries.

## THE EPISTLE

An interlude in chapter 12's allegorical description of the Jewish-Christian church. In apocalyptic Satan was normally thought of as the ruler of this world, who had set his throne in the sky. The Seer, however, tells us that at the Ascension of Christ (verse 5) the devil was thrust out of the place he had seized and was cast down to the earth; thus clearing the way for the divine victory about to come to pass (verses 10–12a). But the consequences for terrestial creation are fearful. Satan, in the agony of despair, is wrecking everything he can reach (verse 12b); this helps explain the sufferings of the "last woes" that all men must undergo.

Every advance on the road of righteousness is followed by an onslaught from thwarted evil. This is a fair rendition of the thought underlying the apocalyptic imagery. But no attempt should be made to evaluate the details—including the angelology.

# SAINT LUKE

## October 18

GOSPEL: Luke 10:1–7. So in the Sarum and the Roman missals; an older "common" in both.

EPISTLE: II Timothy 4:5–15. A Reformation substitute for the Sarum "common" Ezekiel 1:10–14. The Roman missal has II Corinthians 8:16–24.

Debate about the authorship of the Third Gospel and Acts goes on endlessly and with little prospect of reaching a generally accepted conclusion. But no compelling arguments have been adduced which prevent holding that both works were actually written by Luke, the companion of Paul, who is included in the first person plural used in the familiar "We" sections of Acts. Traditional views as to his outlook, however, may need correction. He was by no means a thorough Paulinist. That he was an enthusiastic supporter of the Gentile mission Acts, of course, declares at length. Yet to him the final Christian authority remained in Palestine; Gentile converts occupied a subordinate status and were subject to the rules that Jerusalem imposed (Acts 15, 21:25). In accord with this Saint Paul himself is given a deference to the Twelve and (afterward) to James which differs markedly from the attitude taken in the Epistles, and his every Jewish characteristic is accented to the uttermost (Acts 21:24 is the extreme instance). In other words, to Luke the Christian church is not only a living organism but a formal organization as well. In it nothing takes place haphazard, but all is done under proper rule and government. Luke's greatest significance, consequently, is as an advocate of a recognized and universal church polity; Acts makes explicit the "catholic" conception of the church.

In the Third Gospel the personality of the writer is more in the background, for the source material with which he worked was less susceptible to rearrangement for special purposes. And Luke, of all four Evangelists, was the most careful about not introducing his own point of view in the received evangelic tradition; it is probably for this reason that—contrary to superficial opinion—his Gospel has the least to say about the Gentile mission.

The Third Gospel has, with good reason, been called "the most beautiful book in the world." Still, current research tends increasingly to the conclusion that the loveliest passages in it come from an earlier source rather than from Luke's own hand. But he deserves full credit for recognizing their beauty and for preserving them to the world.

Commemoration of Saint Luke began in Constantinople in the fourth century, but he was the last of the Evangelists to be honoured in Rome (tenth century). Both in the East and the West his day is regularly given as October 18.

## THE GOSPEL

Why this passage was selected as a "common" for Evangelists is anything but clear from its contents, but it may have been chosen because of some (not very early) tradition that Mark and Luke were members of the Seventy. It is quite unadapted to its purpose, although it has a very real interest of its own.

Critically the relation of the "Charge to the Twelve" and the "Charge to the Seventy" is as follows. Instead of one or two missions of large groups, Jesus sent out disciples whenever He judged their preparation sufficient (Luke 9:60). On such occasions He naturally instructed them in more or less the same terms, and collections of the instructions were made and preserved for the use of later missionaries. Some of these rules Mark included in his Gospel (6:8–11), dramatizing them as given at a single mission of the entire Twelve. Luke in his own work duly reproduced this passage from Mark (Luke 9:1–6), but in a different source (the Sayings) found a fuller list of these special teachings, which he assigned to a second mission (the "Seventy").

The charge presupposes the historic conditions of Jesus' ministry; short journeys in wholly Jewish territory, where hospitality might normally be expected as a matter of course (contrast Luke 22:35–36). It presupposes also that His work had gone on some time. Every one in Palestine knew who He was and what His disciples represented, so that refusal of hospitality was a deliberate affront to Jesus' message. Indeed (verse 3) "wolves" were numerous, ready to hamper the messengers and to do them all the damage they could (although as yet there was no danger of actual martyrdom); more harm than good might be done by attempting to preach under such conditions (compare Matthew 7:6). The most immediate test of friendly hearing was the response to the conventional Jewish greeting "Peace be unto you!" If this was rejected—a savage insult among Semites—it was futile to attempt anything more. Still, at least the messenger profited by his kindly attempt! (verse 6b).

Verse 2 accords badly with verse 1, since in so small a country seventy missionaries were not "few." The purpose of the self-denial imposed in verse 4a is self-evident, but under the circumstances it also ensured discrimination in picking an audience. Verse 4b likewise guards against recklessness, for the formal greeting of a casual wayfarer meant nothing. Verse 7: "Do not be afraid of abusing your host's welcome; you give more than you can receive."

Perfect advice to well-meaning modern "evangelists"; when it is not heeded the results are often woeful.

### THE EPISTLE

A passage chosen by the Reformers because of the mention of Luke in verse 11 and perhaps also because of "evangelist" (in an entirely different sense) in verse 5. It is a pity that they did not end the selection with verse 11a, for what follows has no expository value.

The exegesis is free from difficulty. Critically, it may be well to remember that the Pastorals as a whole are deutero-Pauline; this relieves the slightly egotistic tone of verses 7–8. Verses 9 ff., however, may well be a fragment of a genuine letter of the Apostle's. What underlies the allusions in verses 12–15 we do not know.

## SAINT SIMON AND SAINT JUDE

### October 28

GOSPEL: John 15:17–27. So (without verses 26–27) the Sarum and the Roman missals, as a "common."

EPISTLE: Ephesians 2:19–22 (American; first introduced in 1928) and Jude 1–8 (English and the earlier American Prayer Books). The Sarum missal has Romans 8:28–39; the Roman Ephesians 4:7–13.

In all four of the New Testament lists of the Twelve Simon is given the title "Cananæan" (Aramaic) or "Zealot" (Greek). Around the year A.D. 60 the Zealots appear as the party of extreme and militant nationalism, to whom war against Rome was the divinely appointed way of deliverance; according to Josephus they were chiefly responsible for the final catastrophe. He does not mention them as existing a generation earlier, possibly because the party was then too small to be of importance. Or it may be that in the New Testament "Cananæan" has some other (unrecoverable) meaning. If the word is to be taken in Josephus' sense, Simon had allied himself with an extremist group before he came under Jesus' influence, and the title clung to him to distinguish him from others of the same name. But we know nothing about him; in the New Testament he never appears personally.

In the lists in Luke-Acts "Simon" is followed immediately by "Jude"; hence the association of the two. Jude is also said to be "son of James," but this James is unidentifiable. In Mark instead of "Jude" we have (before "Simon") "Thaddeus," who reappears in Matthew also, although with "Lebbæus" as a well-attested variant. (That one name is the Aramaic form, the other the Hebrew, is not convincing.) Harmonizing devices are not very satisfactory (compare on St. Matthew), and it is possible that when the Gospels were written Christians were no longer certain about the name of at least one member of the Twelve. Yet, if Jude and Thaddeus were really distinct, both must have had real prominence in the early church; perhaps Lebbæus also.

Jude speaks in John 14:22, although really only as an (impersonal) interlocutor.

The Epistle bearing Jude's name belongs late in the first century, when antinomian Gnosticism was manifesting itself as a deadly peril. This letter, however, does not seem to be pseudonymous, for it frankly treats the Apostolic age as past (verses 17–18); it may have been written by some otherwise unknown Jude, for the name was very common. But if "Jude" is used as a recognized literary convention, the Apostle seems less likely to have been meant than the brother of the "James" in Mark 6:3, for this James was really distinguished. Yet, naturally, the writer may have confused the two. "James," "Simon" and "Jude" appear both in the apostolic lists and among the "brethren" of Jesus, but in view of Mark 6:4 and (especially) Acts 1:14 there can be no identity.

In later tradition the Luke-Acts association of Simon and Jude is maintained. Both are said to have been "Apostles of the East," with Persia as their field, and to have been martyred on the same day. Early Oriental commemoration appears to have been on July 1; why Rome (in the ninth century or slightly earlier) selected October 28 is unknown. The Eastern churches commemorate them separately on varying dates and with no little confusion between "Jude" and "Thaddeus."

### THE GOSPEL

For full realization of the implications here it must be remembered, as always in John, that around A.D. 100 a Christian community was a small, intensely intimate group, rigidly isolated from the hostile "world." Unless mutual love prevailed such a group was bound to perish. Nor must the hatred of those without dismay believers, for their manner of life was a perpetual rebuke to the corrupt civilization surrounding them. It was Christ's perfect righteousness that stirred the Jews to enmity! So it was inevitable that His disciples should receive the same treatment; they must not expect to fare better than He did.

Whenever unrepentant evil is confronted with good it grows furious (verse 21). Of course if Christ had not sent out His missionaries, the "world" would not have been stirred to persecute them —but it is the "world," not Christ, that is to blame. Some persecutors claim to act for religious motives, particularly the Jews who denounce Christians to the governors. But if a religion worships a deity lacking the righteousness revealed in Christ, then that religion is false (verse 23). Verse 24 resumes both verses 22 and 23; here Jesus' "works" are His words (14:10). For a first-century audience the proof from prophecy (Psalm 69:4) in verse 25 gave special corroboration. Note in this verse "their law"; Johannine Christianity regards Judaism as an alien religion.

For verses 26–27 compare on Ascension 1.

**THE EPISTLE**

(American.) Compare on St. Thomas.

**THE EPISTLE**

(English.) While certain forms of antinomian Gnosticism masked their nature with a pretentious philosophy and some ascetic practices, other types made no such pretext but were frankly filthy. They quite literally turned "God's grace" (the free pardon promised sinners) "into lasciviousness," and by every act and teaching "denied the Master" whom they professed to serve. Jude has to deal not with intellectual doubts but with brazen shamelessness. Compare on Epiphany 6 and Trinity 1 for treatment of a less flagrant type of allied teaching.

In the context "the faith once and for all delivered" in verse 3 is the Christian moral standard, with doctrinal implications only in the background. In verse 6 the reference is to Genesis 6:1-4. This passage was popular in Jewish literature, and the aberrations of these angels were often treated as more disastrous to the world than Adam's fall. The citation of Sodom and Gomorrah in verse 7 is not exaggerated invective but describes only too specifically the conduct of the libertines denounced. Their "dreams" (verse 8) are their theories, propounded as divine revelations given in trance. "Despise dominion and speak evil of dignities" should be "Reject the Lord and blaspheme the angels of glory." Gnosticism very commonly treated the God of the Old Testament as hostile to the God of the New Testament. From this these extremists argued that the former should be flouted on all occasions; disdain of this God and His angels (through whom the Law was given; Acts 7:53, etc.) was to be shown by actions exactly opposite to those the Decalogue commands.

At the Reformation it was natural enough to take the Epistle for this day from a letter ascribed to the saint commemorated. But this letter deals with a situation so lurid that expository treatment is scarcely profitable. Even today there are groups in which the vilest perversities are practised in the name of religion, but these are so self-condemned that denunciation is a waste of time. About all that can be usefully made of the passage is to point out what depths of human depravity there can exist. In these the most that they who have to deal with them can hope is that they may "on some have mercy with fear, hating even the garment spotted by the flesh" (verse 23).

# ALL SAINTS' DAY

## *November 1*

GOSPEL: Matthew 5:1-12. So (omitting verse 12*b*) the Sarum and the Roman missals.

EPISTLE: Revelation 7:2-4, 9-17 (American; first introduced in 1928) and Revelation 7:2-12 (English and the earlier American Prayer Books). The latter is in the Sarum and the Roman missals.

A Syrian festival of "All Martyrs" was instituted *ca.* 360. This was adopted in Rome in 609 or 610 as the feast of the rededication of the Pantheon, which took place on May 13, perhaps also the day observed in Syria. Under Gregory III (died 741) commemoration of confessors was added, making the festival genuinely "All Saints," and the day became popular for pilgrims. But those coming from a distance found the season inconvenient, and so in 835 Gregory IV changed the date to November 1. An octave was added *ca.* 1480.

Observation of November 2 as "All Souls," when the faithful who had not achieved canonization were remembered, began at Cluny in 998, and was given Roman acceptance in the fourteenth century. But in Anglican tradition "All Saints" is "All Souls" as well; this accords better with the New Testament doctrine of "sainthood."

### THE GOSPEL

Verses 3–10 have a conscious poetic structure. All the second clauses are synonyms: "they shall be comforted," "they shall inherit the Land (of promise)," "they shall be filled (with righteousness)," "they shall obtain mercy," "they shall be called the children of God" —all these phrases are identical with "theirs is the kingdom of heaven" with which the series begins and closes. Similarly "they that mourn," "they which do hunger and thirst after righteousness," "the pure in heart" form one synonym series, and "the gentle" (*not* "meek"), "the merciful," "the peacemakers" a second, both illustrating "the poor in spirit," which in turn is a synonym for "they which are persecuted for righteousness' sake."

In more detail, "the poor" is a technical term in Judaism for "the pious in Israel who suffer unrighteous oppression"; the Evangelist's addition of "in spirit" is meant to indicate this. These men "mourn" over the evil condition of the world because they "hunger and thirst after righteousness," or—what is the same thing—because they are "pure in heart," uncompromising in their love of good. And in their relation to others they are "gentle," "merciful," and "peacemakers." Yet in a society exalting force and selfishness they are bound to be "persecuted."

It is therefore a grave mistake to disassociate the Beatitudes from each other, as if each treated a distinct virtue. The expositor must explain them as a unit. But it is well to remember that the type of character that they describe is not quite Jesus' complete ideal of sainthood; they lack in particular emphasis on the positive activity demanded in, *e.g.*, Matthew 5:45.

The impersonal form of these verses indicates that they were used by Jesus in His public preaching to the people. But verses 11–12 are addressed exclusively to disciples. For the situation compare on St. Luke; this saying belongs late in the ministry, although within Jesus' lifetime. The form in Luke 6:20–23, however, has been remodelled to address the early Palestinian church.

**THE EPISTLE**

In the American Prayer Book verses 5–8 have been omitted from the traditional section and verses 13–17 added.

The glory of this passage will only be harmed by homiletic attempts at detailed analysis, and the best pulpit use is to reserve it to close a sermon on blessedness; anything added afterward would be hopeless anticlimax.

Critically it is worth knowing—although emphatically not for pulpit mention—that verses 1–8 are from some earlier Jewish apocalypse. In this, after the sealing of the tribes was completed, the angels of verse 1 released the winds to wreck the earth. As it stood it could serve Saint John admirably as a description of God's care for the Jewish Christians, and he so used it (compare on Innocents). Then he looked beyond the limits of Israel and added his vision; its ecstasy so carried him away that the introduction (verses 1–3) was completely forgotten.

The "elders" and the "living creatures" in verse 11 are not to be identified; to ask their precise spiritual significance is to display incapacity for understanding the Apocalypse. A possible alternative translation of the close of verse 14 is: "Who, through the blood of the Lamb, have washed their robes and made them clean."

PART FOUR

APPENDIX

# THE IMPORTANT BOOKS

Beissel, Stephen. *Entstehung der Perikopen des römischen Messbuches.* Freiburg, 1907.

Frere, Walter Howard. *Studies in Early Roman Liturgy.* I. *The Kalendar* (1930). II. *The Roman Gospel-Lectionary* (1934). III. *The Roman Epistle-Lectionary* (1935). Oxford.

Grisar, Hartmann. *Das Missale im Lichte römischer Stadtgeschichte.* Freiburg, 1925.

Klauser, Theodor. *Das römische Capitulare Evangeliorum.* I. Typen. Münster, 1935.

Eisenhofer, Ludwig. *Handbuch der katholischen Liturgik.* Freiburg, 1932–1933.

Fendt, Leonhard. *Die alten Perikopen.* Tübingen, 1931.

# COMPARATIVE TABLE

Column 1: American Prayer Book of 1928.
Column 2: English Prayer Book of 1661.
Column 3: English Prayer Book of 1549.
Column 4: The Sarum missal.
Column 5: The Roman missal.
Column 6: The seventh-century Roman lists.

Parts of a verse are usually disregarded.

The (rare) variations in the English Prayer Books between 1549 and 1661 are noted when they occur.

—— = "as in first column"; "Same" = "like first preceding passage."

In the Epistle lists "E" = Frere's "Early" series, the pre-Carolingian Roman use, largely seventh century. "C" = the "Comes," Frere's "Standard" list.

In the Gospel lists the symbols P, L, S and D are taken from Klauser. He describes P as "purely Roman, *ca.* 645"; L as "purely Roman, *ca.* 740" (this corresponds closely, with a few variants noted in Klauser's apparatus, to Frere's "Earlier" list); S as "purely Roman *ca.* 755" (this corresponds to Frere's "Standard" list, except for a slightly different numeration and the addition in Frere of a Gospel for Thursday after Ash Wednesday); D as "Roman-Frankish, after 750" (practically Frere's "Vitus-4 type").

Fc is the ninth-century French list from Centula (Paris BN 93) printed in Klauser's appendix; compare Frere's "Developed Martina" type.

Fg is the ninth-century French list from Saint-Germain-des-Près (Paris BN 13171), whose textual variants from Fc are printed in Klauser's appendix ("13174" in Frere, p. 101, is a misprint).

NOTE. When Frere and Klauser differ in their reproduction of a manuscript, Klauser is usually to be preferred. In case of doubt for E and P Dom G. Morin's lists in the *Révue Bénédictine* for 1910–1911 should be consulted.

# COMPARATIVE TABLE

## ADVENT 1

| 1928 | 1661 | 1549 | SARUM MISSAL | ROMAN MISSAL | 7TH CENT. ROMAN LISTS |
|---|---|---|---|---|---|
| Rom 13:8–14 | —— | —— | Rom 13:11–14 | Same | Jer 23:5–8 |
| Mt 21:1–13 | | | Mt 21:1–9 | Lk 21:25–33 | Mt 21:1–9 |

In E the Epistles for Next Advent and Advent are interchanged; C has Rom 13:11–14.

In the present Roman missal the introduction of a new Gospel for Advent 4 has moved the former Gospels for Advent 2–4 back one Sunday and has caused the loss of Mt 21:1–9.

## ADVENT 2

| | | | | | |
|---|---|---|---|---|---|
| Rom 15:4–13 | —— | —— | —— | | —— |
| Lk 21:25–33 | | | | Mt 11:2–10 | |

## ADVENT 3

| | | | | | |
|---|---|---|---|---|---|
| I Cor 4:1–5 | —— | —— | —— | Ph 4:4–7 | —— |
| Mt 11:2–10 | | | | Jn 1:19–28 | |

In the present Roman missal the Epistles for Advent 3 and Advent 4 have been interchanged to make Advent parallel Lent ("gaudete" = "laetare" as mid-season Sundays).

## ADVENT 4

| | | | | | |
|---|---|---|---|---|---|
| Phil 4:4–7 | —— | —— | —— | I Cor. 4:1–5 | —— |
| Jn 1:19–28 | | | | Lk 3:1–6 | |

The Gospel in the present Roman missal has been taken from Ember Saturday, to which Lk 3:1–6 is assigned in P and subsequent Roman use (including the present missal). The change, however, was made too late to have been due to "vacant" Sunday usage. Probably an additional pre-Christmas Gospel dealing with the Baptist was desired, while Mt. 21:1–9 may have been thought inappropriate to Advent.

## CHRISTMAS

| | | | | | |
|---|---|---|---|---|---|
| Tt 2:11–15 | —— | —— | —— | —— | —— |
| Lk 2:1–14 | | | | | |
| | | | Tt 3:4–7 | Same | Same |
| | | | Lk 2:15–20 | Same | Same |
| Hb 1:1–12 | —— | —— | —— | —— | —— |
| Jn 1:1–14 | | | | | |

When Christmas (Epiphany) was adopted from the East, the Eastern custom of several masses, each with its own lections, was adopted with it. At first, however, the second mass was that of St. Anastasia, with no reference to Christmas.

## ST. STEPHEN

| | | | | | |
|---|---|---|---|---|---|
| Acts 7:55–60 | —— | —— | Acts 6:8–10+ 7:54–60 | Same | Same |
| Mt 23:34–39 | —— | —— | —— | —— | —— |

In the Leonine Sacramentary this feast is given on August 2 (3), the death day of Pope Stephanus I.

## ST. JOHN

| | | | | | |
|---|---|---|---|---|---|
| I Jn 1:1–10 | —— | —— | Sir 15:1–6 | Same | Same |
| Jn 21:19–25 | —— | —— | Jn 21:19–24 | Same | Same |

## INNOCENTS

| 1928 | 1661 | 1549 | SARUM MISSAL | ROMAN MISSAL | 7TH CENT. ROMAN LISTS |
|---|---|---|---|---|---|
| Rev 14 : 1–5 | — | | | | |
| Mt 2 : 13–18 | — | — | — | — | |
| | | | | | Mt 2 : 13–23 |

The shorter form of the Gospel appears in Fg.

## CHRISTMAS 1

| 1928 | 1661 | 1549 | SARUM MISSAL | ROMAN MISSAL | 7TH CENT. ROMAN LISTS |
|---|---|---|---|---|---|
| Gal 4 : 1–7 | — | | | — | Col 1 : 25–28 |
| Mt 1 : 18–25 | — | Mt 1 : 1–25 | | Lk 2 : 33–40 | |

Special provision for Christmas 1 is comparatively late; in the Sarum missal lections as in the Roman missal are for "the sixth day after Christmas, whether Sunday or not." The Prayer Book Epistle is that for Christmas 2 in E; for Christmas 1 in C. The Gospel in the Roman missal first appears in D and as a (Carolingian) gloss in P and L. The Prayer Book Gospel is a lengthening of the Gospel for the Christmas vigil in R and most later western lists (Mt 1 : 18–21).

## CIRCUMCISION

| 1928 | 1661 | 1549 | SARUM MISSAL | ROMAN MISSAL | 7TH CENT. ROMAN LISTS |
|---|---|---|---|---|---|
| Phil 2 : 9–13 | Rom 4 : 8–14 | Same | Tt 2 : 11–15 | Same | |
| Lk 2 : 15–21 | | | Lk 2 : 21 | Same | Lk 2 : 21–32 |

Christmas was observed with an octave certainly before 700 and probably much earlier; the Epistle in the Sarum and Roman missals is that of the first mass for Christmas, while the Gospel in P (repeated in L, S, D, F, etc.) continues that for the second mass of Christmas. While this Gospel was undoubtedly selected because of the mention of the "eighth day" in v. 21, no further liturgical attention was paid to the fact of the circumcision. Observance of this began in Gaul in the sixth century but did not reach Rome until a much later date. Then vv. 22–32 were dropped; they were already used for the Purification.
The English Prayer Book Epistle was adopted in 1549; the American Epistle in 1928.

## CHRISTMAS 2

| 1928 | 1661 | 1549 | SARUM MISSAL | ROMAN MISSAL | 7TH CENT. ROMAN LISTS |
|---|---|---|---|---|---|
| Isa 61 : 1–3 | | | | | Gal 4 : 1–7 |
| Mt 2 : 19–23 | | | | | |

First introduced in 1928. A gloss in C provides Isa 61 : 1–3˙+ 21 : 11–12 as an alternative for the second mass of Christmas. The Gospel has no precedent.
For Christmas 3 and 4 E provides I Tim 1 : 15–17 and Heb 3 : 1–6. How these Sundays were reckoned is obscure.

## EPIPHANY

| 1928 | 1661 | 1549 | SARUM MISSAL | ROMAN MISSAL | 7TH CENT. ROMAN LISTS |
|---|---|---|---|---|---|
| Eph 3 : 1–12 | — | — | Isa 60 : 1–6 | Same | Same˥ |
| Mt 2 : 1–12 | — | — | — | — | — |

The Prayer Book Epistle was adopted in 1549.

## EPIPHANY 1

| 1928 | 1661 | 1549 | SARUM MISSAL | ROMAN MISSAL | 7TH CENT. ROMAN LISTS |
|---|---|---|---|---|---|
| Rom 12 : 1–5 | — | — | Isa 60 : 1–6 | — | — |
| Lk 2 : 41–52 | — | — | Jn 1 : 29–34 | Lk 2 : 42–52 | Same |

The Sarum use provides for a full liturgical Epiphany octave; the services on Epiphany and Epiphany 1 are identical except for the Gospel and the sequence. As a result the Sarum Epistles and Gospels for the following Sundays have all been moved back.

## EPIPHANY 2

| 1928 | 1661 | 1549 | SARUM MISSAL | ROMAN MISSAL | 7TH CENT. ROMAN LISTS |
|---|---|---|---|---|---|
| Rom 12 : 6–16a | — | — | Rom 12 : 1–5 | — | — |
| Mk 1 : 1–11 | Jn 2 : 1–11 | Same | Lk 2 : 42–52 | Jn 2 : 1–11 | Same |

The American Gospel was adopted in 1928. Mk 1 : 4–11 appears in L and elsewhere for January 7th.

## EPIPHANY 3

| 1928 | 1661 | 1549 | SARUM MISSAL | ROMAN MISSAL | 7TH CENT. ROMAN LISTS |
|------|------|------|--------------|--------------|------------------------|
| Rom 12:16b-21 | —— | —— | Rom 12:6-16a | —— | —— |
| Jn 2:1-11 | Mt 8:1-13 | Same | —— | Mt 8:1-13 | Same |

## EPIPHANY 4

| Rom 13:1-7 | —— | —— | Rom 12:16b-21 | Rom 13:8-10 | Same |
|------------|------|------|---------------|-------------|------|
| Mt 8:1-13 | Mt 8:23-34 | Same | —— | Mt 8:23-27 | Same |

The Epistle adopted in 1549 preserves the continuity of Romans; this section is not used in the early lists.

## EPIPHANY 5

| Col 3:12-17 | —— | —— | Rom 13:8-10 | —— | |
|-------------|------|------|-------------|------|---|
| Mt 13:24-30 | | | Mt 8:23-27 | —— | —— |

E and C provide for only four Sundays after Epiphany; the second supplement to C, however, provides I Tim 1:15-17 (for Christmas 3 in E) for the "Sunday before Septuagesima, if necessary." The Epistle in the Roman missal and the Prayer Book is "unappropriated" in E, and is used for this Sunday in the tenth century.

## EPIPHANY 6

| I Jn 3:1-8 | —— | Col 3:12-17 | I Th 1:1-10 | |
|------------|------|-------------|-------------|---|
| Mt 24:23-31 | —— | Mt 13:24-30 | Mt 13:31-35 | Mk 6:47-56 |

The lections in the Roman missal are both late. Until 1661 the Prayer Book directed the repetition of the lections for Epiphany 5.

For Epiphany 7-9 P, etc., provide Mt 12:9-15, Lk 9:1-6, Mt 22:2-14; to these L adds for Epiphany 10 Mt 15:21-28. Conceivably this list looks back to the time before the introduction of Quinquagesima and Lent 1-3.

## SEPTUAGESIMA

| I Cor 9:24-27 | —— | —— | I Cor 9:24-10:4 | Same | Same |
|---------------|------|------|-----------------|------|------|
| Mt 20:1-16 | —— | —— | | | |

The Gospel is apparently originally that of the New Year (spring agriculture) moved back through the insertion of Quinquagesima-Lent 3. The Epistle is probably also for the New Year.

## SEXAGESIMA

| II Cor 11:19-31 | —— | —— | II Cor 11:19-12:9 | Same | Same |
|-----------------|------|------|-------------------|------|------|
| Lk 8:4-15 | —— | —— | | | |

The Epistle is in honour of the Station at St. Paul's-Without-the-Walls.

## QUINQUAGESIMA

| I Cor 13 | —— | —— | —— | —— | —— |
|----------|------|------|------|------|------|
| Lk 18:31-43 | —— | —— | —— | —— | —— |

Purely pre-Lent.

## ASH WEDNESDAY

| Joel 2:12-17 | —— | —— | Joel 2:12-19 | Same | Same |
|--------------|------|------|--------------|------|------|
| Mt 6:16-21 | | | | | |

Instituted either by Gregory (d. 604) or shortly afterward for fasting and prayer against the Lombard invaders. Hence the military Epistle.

### LENT 1

| 1928 | 1661 | 1549 | SARUM MISSAL | ROMAN MISSAL | 7TH CENT. ROMAN LISTS |
|---|---|---|---|---|---|
| II Cor 6 : 1–10 | —— | —— | —— | —— | —— |
| Mt 4 : 1–11 | —— | —— | —— | —— | —— |

The opening of Lent from ca. 500 to the institution of Ash Wednesday.

### LENT 2

| | | | | | |
|---|---|---|---|---|---|
| I Th 4 : 1–8 | —— | —— | I Th 4 : 1–7 | Same | |
| Mt 15 : 21–28 | —— | —— | —— | Mt 17 : 1–9 | |

Marked "vacant" in E and P because of the vigil of the preceding Ember Saturday. The Epistle in the Roman missal is a variant Epistle for that Saturday; the Gospel is the Gospel for that Saturday. The Sarum Gospel is the Gospel for the preceding Thursday in S.

### LENT 3

| | | | | | |
|---|---|---|---|---|---|
| Eph 5 : 1–14 | —— | —— | Eph 5 : 1–9 | Same | Same |
| Lk 11 : 14–28 | —— | —— | | | |

In the sixth century the baptismal scrutiny was set for the Wednesday following this Sunday and both lections look forward to this rite.

### LENT 4

| | | | | | |
|---|---|---|---|---|---|
| Gal 4 : 21–31 | —— | —— | Gal 4 :22–5 : 1a | Same | Same |
| Jn 6 : 1–14 | —— | —— | | | |

Epistle for the Station at Holy-Cross-in-Jersualem. Gospel for distribution of bread and and the "agape" at the Lateran, instituted (apparently) when Lent began on the following day (ca. 400).

### LENT 5

| | | | | | |
|---|---|---|---|---|---|
| Heb 9 : 11–15 | —— | —— | —— | —— | —— |
| Jn 8 : 46–59 | —— | —— | —— | —— | —— |

### LENT 6

| | | | | | |
|---|---|---|---|---|---|
| Ph 2 : 5–11 | —— | —— | —— | —— | —— |
| Mt 27 : 1–54 | —— | Mt 26–27 : 56 | Mt 26–27 | Same | Same |

In 1661 Mt 26 was transferred to Morning Prayer.

### MONDAY

| | | | | | |
|---|---|---|---|---|---|
| Isa 63 : 1–19 | —— | —— | Isa 50 : 5–10 | Same | Same |
| Mk 14 | —— | —— | Jn 12 : 1–36 | Jn 12 : 1–9 | Jn 12 : 1–36 |

The Prayer Book Epistle was obtained by dividing the combined Sarum Epistle for Wednesday; the Gospel by dividing Mark's Passion used on Tuesday.

### TUESDAY

| | | | | | |
|---|---|---|---|---|---|
| Isa 50 : 5–11 | —— | —— | Jer 11 : 18–20 | Same | Same |
| Mk 15 : 1–39 | —— | Mk 15 | Mk 14 : 1–15 : 46 | Same | Jn 13 : 1–32 |

The use of Mark's Passion for this day is comparatively late. The Prayer Book Epistle is taken from Monday in the Sarum missal.

### WEDNESDAY

| | | | | | |
|---|---|---|---|---|---|
| Heb 9 : 16–28 | —— | —— | Isa 63 : 1, 53 | Same | Isa 62 : 11+ 63 : 1, 5, 7, 53 |
| Lk 22 | —— | —— | Lk 22–23 : 53 | Same | Same |

The Prayer Book Epistle has no early precedent. Luke's Passion is divided between Wednesday and Thursday.

## THURSDAY

| 1928 | 1661 | 1549 | SARUM MISSAL | ROMAN MISSAL | 7TH CENT. ROMAN LISTS |
|---|---|---|---|---|---|
| I Cor 11 : 23–26 | I Cor 11 : 17–34 | Same | I Cor 11 : 20–32 | Same | |
| Lk 23 : 1–49 or | ——— | Lk 23 | Jn 13 : 1–15 | Same | |
| Jn 13 :1–15 | | | | | |

Mass not said on Maundy Thursday until the eighth century. The Roman Epistle appears in C, and the Gospel in L.

## · FRIDAY

| | | | | | |
|---|---|---|---|---|---|
| Heb 10 : 1–25 | ——— | ——— | Ex 12 : 1–11 | Same | Same |
| Jn 19 : 1–37 | ——— | Jn 18–19 | Same | Same | Same |

In C and E Ex 12 : 1–11 is given in conjunction with Hos 6 : 1–6, apparently as alternatives; in later Roman use both are employed. In 1661 Jn 18 was transferred to Morning Prayer.

## SATURDAY

| | | |
|---|---|---|
| I Pet 3 : 17–22 | ——— | ——— |
| Mt 27 : 57–66 | ——— | ——— |

No equivalent in pre-Reformation usage.

## EASTER VIGIL

| | | | | | |
|---|---|---|---|---|---|
| | | | Col 3 : 1–4 | Same | Same |
| | | | Mt 28 : 1–7 | Same | Same |

The original Easter mass, celebrated toward or at dawn. Removed to Saturday morning ca. 400, leaving Easter "vacant"; the gap was then filled by the present Roman mass (below), formed out of Easter week services.

## EASTER

| | | | | | |
|---|---|---|---|---|---|
| I Cor 5 : 6–8 | | | I Cor 5 : 7–8 | Same | Same |
| Mk 16 : 1–8 | | | Mk 16 : 1–7 | Same | Same |
| Col 3 : 1–4 | Col 3 : 1–7 | Same | | | |
| Jn 20 : 1–10 | ——— | ——— | | | |

The service for the first celebration in the American Prayer Book (introduced in 1892) is that for the second service in the 1549 Prayer Book; the later English Books have no equivalent. The American reshortening of the second Epistle to its original length was made in 1928.

The use of John for the Easter Gospel has a Mozarabic parallel but was probably made at the Reformation without thought of precedent.

## MONDAY

| | | | | | |
|---|---|---|---|---|---|
| Acts 10 : 34–42 | ——— | ——— | Acts 10 : 34, 37–43 | Same | Same |
| Lk 24 : 13–35 | ——— | ——— | ——— | ——— | ——— |

The old Easter week services were held primarily for those who had just been baptized; hence the Epistle.

## TUESDAY

| | | | | | |
|---|---|---|---|---|---|
| Acts 13 : 26–41 | ——— | ——— | Acts 13 : 16, 26–33 | Same | Same |
| Lk 24 : 36–48 | ——— | ——— | Lk 24 : 36–47 | Same | Same |

The Epistle is for the newly baptized.

# COMPARATIVE TABLE

## EASTER 1

| 1928 | 1661 | 1549 | SARUM MISSAL | ROMAN MISSAL | 7TH CENT. ROMAN LISTS |
|---|---|---|---|---|---|
| I Jn 5:4–12 | —— | —— | I Jn 5:4–10a | Same | Same |
| Jn 20:19–23 | | | Jn 20:19–31 | Same | Jn 20:24–31 |

The Epistle is for the newly baptized.

In the older Roman lectionaries (P, etc.) Jn 20:19–23 is appointed for Saturday of Easter week; prefixing this section to that for Sunday is comparatively late.

## EASTER 2

| | | | | | |
|---|---|---|---|---|---|
| I Pet 2:19–25 | —— | —— | I Pet 2:21–25 | Same | Same |
| Jn 10:11–16 | | | | | |

## EASTER 3

| | | | | | |
|---|---|---|---|---|---|
| I Pet 2:11–17 | —— | —— | I Pet 2:11–19 | Same | Same |
| Jn 16:16–22 | | | | | |

## EASTER 4

| | | | | | |
|---|---|---|---|---|---|
| Jas 1:17–21 | —— | —— | —— | —— | —— |
| Jn 16:5–15 | | | | | |

## EASTER 5

| | | | | | |
|---|---|---|---|---|---|
| Jas 1:22–27 | —— | —— | | | |
| Jn 16:23–33 | | | Jn 16:23–30 | Same | Same |

## ASCENSION

| | | | | | |
|---|---|---|---|---|---|
| Acts 1:1–11 | —— | | | | |
| Lk 24:49–53 | Mk 16:14–20 | Same | Same | Same | Same |

The Lukan section—often used for the day after Ascension Day—was introduced in the American Prayer Book in 1928 to replace the (unauthentic) Markan account.

## ASCENSION 1

| | | | | | |
|---|---|---|---|---|---|
| I Pet 4:7–11 | —— | —— | —— | —— | —— |
| Jn 15:26–16:4a | | | | | |

## WHITSUNDAY

I Cor. 12:4–14
Lk 11:9–13

A 1928 service, with no precedent.

| | | | | | |
|---|---|---|---|---|---|
| Acts 2:1–11 | —— | —— | | | |
| Jn 14:15–31b | | Jn 14:15–21 | Jn 14:23–31 | Same | Same |

The 1549 shortening of the Gospel was discontinued in 1552.

## MONDAY

| | | | | |
|---|---|---|---|---|
| Acts 10:34–48 | —— | —— | Acts 10:34, 42–48 | Same | Same |
| Jn 3:16–21 | —— | —— | —— | —— | —— |

The Epistle is for the newly baptized.

The Gospel has nothing to do with Whitsunday. On this day the Station was at St. Peter-ad-Vincula, the Prefecture church; hence the "judgment" theme.

## TUESDAY

| 1928 | 1661 | 1549 | SARUM MISSAL | ROMAN MISSAL | 7TH CENT. ROMAN LISTS |
|---|---|---|---|---|---|
| Acts 8 : 14–17 | —— | —— | —— | —— | —— |
| Jn 10 : 1–10 | —— | —— | —— | —— | —— |

The Epistle (certainly) and the Gospel (probably) are for the newly baptized.

## TRINITY

| | | | | |
|---|---|---|---|---|
| Rev. 4 : 1–11 | —— | —— | Rev. 4 : 1–10a | Rom 11 : 33–36 |
| Jn 3 : 1–15 | —— | —— | | Mt 28 : 18–20 |

The Sarum lections are those for the octave of Whitsunday, which were equally adapted to Trinity Sunday after its institution in England (eleventh century?). No provision for this Sunday, however, is made either in the E Epistle list or the P and L Gospel lists; it first appears in C and S, indicating that full liturgical observance of the octave came late. The Epistle is derived from that of the older All Saints Sunday, which had (in E) Rev 4 : 1+7 : 9–12, with Rev 7 : 13–17 as an alternative. At a later date the summer Ember Days were set in Whitweek, causing Whitsunday to lose its octave in Roman use. For Pentecost 1 were then provided I Jn 4 : 8–21 and Lk 6 : 36–42, the latter an alternative Gospel for Ember Saturday in P. Trinity Sunday was not made official in Rome until 1334; hence the independent lections. In pre-Reformation England (not Rome) the feast received an octave, thus advancing the following Sunday lections by a week.

### THE POST-TRINITY LECTIONS

The development of the Gospel and Epistle lectionaries for summer and autumn was almost entirely independent. The only exceptions are the two Sundays (Trinity 4 and 18) which were originally "vacant" after the summer and autumn Embertides. In the first of these both Epistle and Gospel are alternatives provided in E and P for Ember Saturday; in the second both lections seem to have been chosen with reference to the ministry.

Otherwise the development of the Epistles proceeded as follows. In E provision is made for ten Sundays after Easter in a list drawn entirely from the Catholic Epistles. How this list is to be reconciled with the fact that Easter 7 = Whitsunday is not explained. Conceivably the Epistle appointed for this day (I Jn 4 : 8–21) might have been used on Whitsunday, for it contains a lovely saying about the Spirit; conceivably "except Whitsunday" may have been tacitly understood. In any case the Epistles in E for Easter 7–9 appear in the Prayer Book for Trinity 1–3 and that for Easter 10 is used at Trinity 5. (For Trinity 4 see above.)

For the remainder of the summer and autumn E provides a list of forty-two sections taken from the Pauline canon (including Hebrews). This list follows, together with the Prayer Book Sundays at which these sections have been utilized.

| | | | |
|---|---|---|---|
| 1. | Rom | 5 : 6–11. | |
| 2. | | 5 : 18–21. | |
| 3. | | 6 : 3–11. | Trinity 6. |
| 4. | | 6 : 19–23. | Trinity 7. |
| 5. | | 8 : 1–6. | |
| 6. | | 8 : 12–17. | Trinity 8. |
| 7 | I C | 10 : 6–13. | Trinity 9 (lengthened). |
| 8. | | 12 : 2–11. | Trinity 10. |
| 9. | | 15 : 39–46. | |
| 10. | II C | 3 : 4–7. | Trinity 12 (lengthened). |
| 11. | | 4 : 5–10. | |
| 12. | | 5 : 1–11. | |
| 13. | | 6 : 14–7 : 1. | |
| 14. | Gal | 3 : 16–22. | Trinity 13. |
| 15. | | 5 : 16–24. | Trinity 14. |
| 16. | | 5 : 25–6 : 10. | |
| 17. | Eph | 3 : 13–21. | Trinity 16. |
| 18. | | 4 : 1–6. | Trinity 17. |
| 19. | | 4 : 23–28. | Trinity 19 (readjusted). |
| 20. | | 5 : 15–21. | Trinity 20. |
| 21. | | 6 : 10–17. | Trinity 21 (lengthened). |
| 22. | Ph | 1 : 6–11. | Trinity 22 (lengthened). |
| 23. | | 3 : 17–21. | Trinity 23. |

| 24. | Col | 1 : 9–14. | Trinity 24 (readjusted). |
|---|---|---|---|
| 25. |  | 1 : 12–18. | |
| 26. |  | 2 : 8–13. | |
| 27. |  | 3 : 5–11. | |
| 28. |  | 3 : 12–17. | |
| 29. | I Th | 2 : 9–13. | |
| 30. | II Th | 2 : 15–3 : 5. | |
| 31. |  | 3 : 6–13. | |
| 32. | I Tm | 1 : 3–14. | |
| 33. |  | 2 : 1–7. | |
| 34. |  | 6 : 7–14. | |
| 35. | II Tm | 1 : 8–13. | |
| 36. |  | 2 : 22–3 : 15. | |
| 37. | Heb | 1 : 13–2 : 3. | |
| 38. |  | 10 : 32–38. | |
| 39. |  | 4 : 11–16. | |
| 40. |  | 12 : 3–9. | |
| 41. |  | 12 : 12–23. | |
| 42. |  | 13 : 17–21. | |

As is evident, the sections in this series were utilized in order in the later Roman tradition on which the Prayer Book rests, although the reason for the adoption of the sections chosen and the rejection of the others is wholly unknown.

At Trinity 11 the substitution of I Cor 15 : 1–11 for No. 9 was already made in C; this is the only section not in the above list that was adopted in Roman use for the post-Pentecostal Sundays. At Trinity 15 No. 16 was still used in the Sarum missal for the same Sunday and is still used in the Roman missal for the preceding Sunday; the substitution of Gal 6 : 11–18 for this section was a Reformation change.

The earliest recoverable scheme of the summer and autumn Gospels—that of P—follows an entirely different plan. The sequence is determined by the three feasts, the Apostles (= SS. Peter and Paul, June 29), St. Lawrence (August 10) and St. Cyprian (September 14). The list, beginning with the Sunday before the Apostles and containing no lection for the first Sunday following, with the Prayer Book Gospels that correspond, is:

| 1. Apostles | –1. | Lk 5 : 1–11. | Trinity 5. |
|---|---|---|---|
| 2. Apostles | 2. | Mt 5 : 20–24. | Trinity 6. |
| 3. Apostles | 3. | Mk 8 : 1–9. | Trinity 7. |
| 4. Apostles | 4. | Mt 7 : 15–21. | Trinity 8. |
| 5. Apostles | 5. | Lk 16 : 1–9. | Trinity 9 (English). |
| 6. Apostles | 6. | Lk 10 : 25–37. | |
| 7. Apostles | 7. | Lk 18 : 10–14. | Trinity 11. |
| | | | |
| 8. Lawrence | 1. | Mk 7 : 31–37. | Trinity 12. |
| 9. Lawrence | 2. | Lk 10 : 23–37. | Trinity 13. |
| 10. Lawrence | 3. | Lk 17 : 11–19. | Trinity 14. |
| 11. Lawrence | 4. | Mt 6 : 24–33. | Trinity 15. |
| 12. Lawrence | 5. | Lk 7 : 11–16. | Trinity 16. |
| | | | |
| 13. Cyprian | 1. | Lk 14 : 1–11. | Trinity 17. |
| 14. Cyprian | 2. | Mt 22 : 23–23 : 12. | Trinity 18 (shortened). |
| 15. Cyprian | 3. | Mt 9 : 1–8. | Trinity 19. |
| 16. Cyprian | 4. | Mt 18 : 23–35. | Trinity 22. |
| 17. Cyprian | 5. | Mt 22 : 15–21. | Trinity 23. |
| 18. Cyprian | 6. | Mt 9 : 18–22. | Trinity 24. |
| 19. Cyprian | 7. | Jn 6 : 5–14. | Next Advent. |

The relation to the Prayer Book scheme is obvious. The only Gospel that does not reappear is No. 6, which is a virtual duplicate of No. 9, a duplication that was corrected at Rome a century later (in D).

No. 14 is the one originally chosen for the Sunday after the autumn Embertide; hence its disproportionate length.

This list provides for the maximum number of Sundays possible between August 10 and September 14 (34 days), but too few are allowed for between September 10 and Advent (a maximum of 79 days), while no provision is made for the Sundays between Whitsunday and Apostles—1. Of these latter a maximum of six is possible, although one of them would be taken care of as occurring after the summer Embertide, while very soon another was appropriated as the octave of Whitsunday.

In the manuscripts of P No. 1 is curiously designated. In many it is called the Gospel for "the first Sunday after Pentecost before the Apostles"—a concurrence that is impossible—while in others "second" is substituted for "first," but still marking a concurrence that could rarely take place. The explanation is that "Apostles—1" is the original designation, but the Gospel was detached from this position and used for Pentecost 1 or 2 at a later time.

The lists in L and S add nothing noteworthy, except that most manuscripts of L use Lk 6 : 36–42 for Pentecost 1 and No. 1 in P is definitely placed at Pentecost 2, some manuscripts of S supply Lk 14 : 16–24 for Pentecost 3, while both lists move Nos. 2–7 back one Sunday, contenting themselves with six Sundays after Apostles.

D, however, undertakes to fill the Pentecostal gap. For Pentecost 2 it gives Lk 15 : 1–10 (for Trinity 3 in the Prayer Book), for Pentecost 3 Lk 16 : 19–31 (for Trinity 1), for Pentecost 4 Lk 14 : 16–24 (for Trinity 2) and uses No. 1 in P for Pentecost 5. As in P no Gospel is given for Apostles 1 and Nos. 2–4 have their original place. But for Apostles 5 a new Gospel is given, Lk 19 : 41–47 (for Trinity 10) and Nos. 5–7 are assigned to Apostles 6–8. Nos. 8–12 correspond in both lists, but Nos. 13 and 14 are numbered as Lawrence 6 and 7, and those from No. 15 on are counted after Michaelmas. Michaelmas 1 = No. 15, Michaelmas 2 = No. 18, Michaelmas 3 has a new Gospel, Mt 22 : 2–14 (used for Trinity 20 in the Prayer Book), Michaelmas 4–6 = Nos. 16–18, Michaelmas 7 has a new Gospel, Mk 12 : 28–34 (not in the Prayer Book), and Christmas—5 (called "Advent") has No. 19. Although the Gospels for Michaelmas 2 and 6 are duplicates, D thus provides fairly adequately for the long season.

The only Trinity Prayer Book Gospels not in the above list are those for Trinity 10 and 21. These first appear in Fg, which follows the Gallican custom of numbering consecutively after Pentecost. The scheme is identical with the Prayer Book list, with but two exceptions: for Pentecost 10 it has the Gospel for Trinity 10 (omitting No. 5) and for Pentecost 11 it has the (duplicate) No. 6. All that was needed was to remove the duplicate by moving Fg's Gospel for Pentecost 10 forward a Sunday and to fill the gap by restoring No. 5; the result is the English Prayer Book list—and for the same Sundays, since Fg's Gospel for Pentecost 2 is the Prayer Book's Gospel for Trinity 1, and so on.

### TRINITY 1

| 1928 | 1661 | 1549 | SARUM MISSAL | ROMAN MISSAL | 7TH CENT. ROMAN LISTS |
|---|---|---|---|---|---|
| I Jn 4 : 7–21 | —— | —— | I Jn 4 : 8–21 | I Jn 3 : 13–18 | |
| Lk 16 : 19–31 | —— | —— | | | Lk 14 : 16–24 |

E's Epistle (v. 16–21 only) for Easter 7. By using this Epistle for Pentecost 1 the Roman missal has its sections all one Sunday earlier.

D's Gospel for Pentecost 3; Fg's for Pentecost 2. By using the Embertide Gospel for Pentecost 1 the Roman missal has its sections for this and the next Sunday each one Sunday earlier.

### TRINITY 2

| I Jn 3 : 13–24 | —— | —— | I Jn 3 : 13–18 | I Pet 5 : 6–11 | |
|---|---|---|---|---|---|
| Lk 14 : 16–24 | —— | —— | | Lk 15 : 1–10 | |

E's Epistle for Easter 8; D's Gospel for Pentecost 4, Fg's for Pentecost 3.

### TRINITY 3

| I Pet 5 : 5–11 | —— | —— | I Pet 5 : 6–11 | Rom 8 : 18–23 | |
|---|---|---|---|---|---|
| Lk 15 : 1–10 | —— | —— | | Lk 5 : 1–11 | |

E's Epistle for Easter 9; D's Gospel for Pentecost 2. Fg's for Pentecost 4. The anticipation of the Embertide Gospel (next in sequence) in the Roman missal now brings its Gospels each two Sundays earlier.

### TRINITY 4

| Rom 8 : 18–23 | —— | —— | | I Pet 3 : 8–15 | |
|---|---|---|---|---|---|
| Lk 6 : 36–42 | —— | —— | | Mt 5 : 20–24 | |

In both E and P these lections are alternatives for Ember Saturday. L's Gospel for Pentecost 1, Fg's for Pentecost 5. In the Roman missal these lections have became disassociated.

### TRINITY 5

| I Pet 3 : 8–15a | —— | —— | | Rom 6 : 3–11 | |
|---|---|---|---|---|---|
| Lk 5 : 1–11 | —— | —— | | Mk 8 : 1–9 | |

E's Epistle for Easter 10. The Gospel was originally (appropriately) appointed for the Sunday before St. Peter's day (so in some mss. of P); Fg assigns it to Pentecost 6.

## TRINITY 6

| 1928 | 1661 | 1549 | SARUM MISSAL | ROMAN MISSAL | 7TH CENT. ROMAN LISTS |
|---|---|---|---|---|---|
| Rom 6 : 3–11 | —— | —— | —— | Rom 6 : 19–23 | |
| Mt 5 : 20–26 | —— | —— | Mt 5 : 20–24 | Mt 7 : 15–21 | |

Epistle is No. 3 in E's "unappropriated" list. P's Gospel for Apostles 2, Fg's for Pentecost 7.

## TRINITY 7

| | | | | | |
|---|---|---|---|---|---|
| Rom 6 : 19–23 | —— | —— | —— | Rom 8 : 12–17 | |
| Mk 8 : 1–9 | —— | —— | —— | Lk 16 : 1–9 | |

Epistle is No. 4 in E's list. P's Gospel for Apostles 3, Fg's for Pentecost 8.

## TRINITY 8

| | | | | | |
|---|---|---|---|---|---|
| Rom 8 : 12–17 | —— | —— | —— | I Cor 10 : 6–13 | |
| Mt 7 : 15–21 | —— | —— | —— | Lk 19 : 41–47a | |

Epistle is No. 6 in E's list. P's Gospel for Apostles 4, Fg's for Pentecost 9.

## TRINITY 9

| | | | | | |
|---|---|---|---|---|---|
| I Cor 10 : 1–13 | —— | —— | I Cor 10 : 6–13 | I Cor 12 : 2–11 | |
| Lk 15 : 11–32 | Lk 16 : 1–9 | Same | Same | Lk 18 : 9–14 | |

Epistle is No. 7 in E's list, lengthened at the Reformation. The English Gospel is that of P for Apostles 5; it does not appear in Fg, which for Pentecost 10 has Lk 19 : 41–43. The American Gospel was introduced in 1928.

## TRINITY 10

| | | | | | |
|---|---|---|---|---|---|
| I Cor 12 : 1–11 | —— | —— | | I Cor 12 : 2–11 | I Cor 15 : 1–10a |
| Lk 19 : 41–47a | —— | —— | | | Mk 7 : 31–37 |

Epistle is No. 8 in E's list. The Gospel is used in D for Apostles 5 and is used (shortened) for Pentecost 10 in Fg. For Pentecost 11 Fg uses P's for Apostles 6; this is the only Trinity-tide Gospel in Fg that does not reappear in the Prayer Book.

## TRINITY 11

| | | | | | |
|---|---|---|---|---|---|
| I Cor 15 : 1–11 | —— | —— | | I Cor 15 : 1–10a | II Cor 3 : 4–11 |
| Lk 18 : 9–14 | —— | —— | | | Lk 10 : 23–27 |

One of the three Epistles in the period Trinity 6–24 that is not taken from E's list; it appears in C for Pentecost 12. P's Gospel for Apostles 7, Fg's for Pentecost 12.

## TRINITY 12

| | | | | | |
|---|---|---|---|---|---|
| II Cor 3 : 4–11 | —— | —— | —— | Gal 3 : 16–22 | |
| Mk 7 : 31–37 | —— | —— | —— | Lk 17 : 11–19 | |

Epistle is No. 10 in E's list (lengthened). P's Gospel for Lawrence 1, Fg's for Pentecost 13.

## TRINITY 13

| | | | | | |
|---|---|---|---|---|---|
| Gal 3 : 16–22 | —— | —— | —— | Gal 5 : 16–24 | |
| Lk 10 : 23–37 | —— | —— | —— | Mt 6 : 24–33 | |

Epistle is No. 14 in E's list. P's Gospel for Lawrence 2, Fg's for Pentecost 14.

## TRINITY 14

| | | | | | |
|---|---|---|---|---|---|
| Gal 5 : 16–24 | —— | —— | —— | Gal 5 : 25–6 : 10 | |
| Lk 17 : 11–19 | —— | —— | —— | Lk 7 : 11–16 | |

Epistle is No. 15 in E's list. P's Gospel for Lawrence 3, Fg's for Pentecost 15.

### TRINITY 15

| 1928 | 1661 | 1549 | SARUM MISSAL | ROMAN MISSAL | 7TH CENT. ROMAN LISTS |
|---|---|---|---|---|---|
| Gal 6 : 11–18 | ——— | ——— | Gal 5 : 25–6 : 10 | Eph 3 : 13–21 | |
| Mt 6 : 24–34 | ——— | ——— | Mt 6 : 24–33 | Lk 14 : 1–11 | |

Epistle a Reformation substitute for the Sarum selection, which is No. 16 in E's list. P's Gospel for Lawrence 4, Fg's for Pentecost 16.

### TRINITY 16

| | | | | | |
|---|---|---|---|---|---|
| Eph 3 : 13–21 | ——— | ——— | | Eph 4 : 1–6 | |
| Lk 7 : 11–17 | ——— | ——— | Lk 7 : 11–16 | Mt 22 : 34–46 | |

Epistle is No. 17 in E's list. P's Gospel for Lawrence 5, Fg's for Pentecost 17

### TRINITY 17

| | | | | | |
|---|---|---|---|---|---|
| Eph 4 : 1–6 | ——— | ——— | ——— | I Cor 1 : 4–8 | |
| Lk 14 : 1–11 | ——— | ——— | ——— | Mt 9 : 1–8 | |

Epistle is No. 18 in E's list. P's Gospel for Cyprian 1, Fg's for Pentecost 18.

### TRINITY 18

| | | | | | |
|---|---|---|---|---|---|
| I Cor 1 : 4–8 | ——— | ——— | ——— | Eph 4 : 23–28 | |
| Mt 22 : 34–46 | ——— | ——— | ——— | Mt 22 : 1–14 | |

Post-Embertide lections, disassociated in the Roman missal. Epistle in C for Pentecost 19. P's Gospel (shortened) for Cyprian 2, Fg's for Pentecost 19.

### TRINITY 19

| | | | | | |
|---|---|---|---|---|---|
| Eph 4 : 17–32 | ——— | ——— | Eph 4 : 23–28 | Eph 5 : 15–21 | |
| Mt 9 : 1–8 | ——— | ——— | | Jn 4 : 46–53 | |

Epistle (lengthened at the Reformation) is No. 19 in E's list. P's Gospel for Cyprian 3, Fg's for Pentecost 20.

### TRINITY 20

| | | | | | |
|---|---|---|---|---|---|
| Eph 5 : 15–21 | ——— | ——— | ——— | Eph 6 : 10–17 | |
| Mt 22 : 1–14 | ——— | ——— | ——— | Mt 18 : 23–35 | |

Epistle is No. 20 in E's list. The Gospel is used for Michaelmas 3 in D and for Pentecost 21 in Fg.

### TRINITY 21

| | | | | | |
|---|---|---|---|---|---|
| Eph 6 : 10–20 | ——— | ——— | Eph 6 : 10–17 | Phil 1 : 6–11 | |
| Jn 4 : 46–54 | ——— | ——— | Jn 4 : 46–53 | Mt 22 : 15–21 | |

Epistle (lengthened at the Reformation) is No. 21 in E's list. The Gospel is used for Pentecost 22 in Fg; in P and later lists it is used for the Friday after Low Sunday.

### TRINITY 22

| | | | | | |
|---|---|---|---|---|---|
| Phil 1 : 3–11 | ——— | ——— | Phil 1 : 6–11 | Phil 3 : 17—4 : 3 | |
| Mt 18 : 21–35 | ——— | ——— | Mt 18 : 23–35 | Mt 9 : 18–26 | |

Epistle (lengthened at the Reformation) is No. 22 in E's list. P's Gospel for Cyprian 4, Fg's for Pentecost 23.

### TRINITY 23

| | | | | | |
|---|---|---|---|---|---|
| Phil 3 : 17–21 | ——— | ——— | ——— | Col 1 : 9–14 | |
| Mt 22 : 15–22 | ——— | ——— | Mt 22 : 15–21 | Mt 24 : 15–35 | |

Epistle is No. 23 in E's list. P's Gospel for Cyprian 5, Fg's for Pentecost 24. The lections in the Roman missal are really for Next Advent and are always so used; when needed, services are supplied from the Epiphany sequence. The Roman Gospel is not ancient.

## TRINITY 24

| 1928 | 1661 | 1549 | SARUM MISSAL | ROMAN MISSAL | 7TH CENT. ROMAN LISTS |
|---|---|---|---|---|---|
| Col 1 : 3–12 | —— | —— | Col 1 : 9–11 | | |
| Mt 9 : 18–26 | —— | —— | Mt 9 : 18–22 | | |

In E's list No. 24 is Col 1 : 9–14, as in the Roman sequence, above. P's Gospel for Cyprian 6, Fg's for Pentecost 25.

## NEXT ADVENT

| | | | | | |
|---|---|---|---|---|---|
| Jer 23 : 5–8 | —— | —— | —— | | Rom 13 : 8–14 |
| Jn 6 : 5–14 | | | | | |

The Epistle for Christmas—5 in C, for Christmas—4 in E; really an Advent selection. P's Gospel for Cyprian 7, Fg's for Pentecost 26.

## ST. ANDREW

| | | | | | |
|---|---|---|---|---|---|
| Rom 10 : 9–21 | —— | —— | Rom 10 : 10–18 | Same | Same |
| Mt 4 : 18–22 | | | | | |

November 30 as date of martyrdom was perhaps held in the third century. The feast sixth century in Rome; earlier in the East.

## ST. THOMAS

| | | | | | |
|---|---|---|---|---|---|
| Heb 10 : 35–11 : 1 | Eph 2 : 19–22 | Same | Same | Same | |
| Jn 20 : 24–31 | —— | —— | Jn 20 : 24–29 | Same | |

The first tradition (Origen) makes Thomas's field Parthia; later this becomes India. Commemorated at Edessa in the fifth century; at Rome not until the ninth (probably), but D assigns Jn 15 : 12–16 for the feast.

The American Epistle was introduced in 1928; the older Epistle was a "common."

## CONVERSION OF ST. PAUL

| | | | | | |
|---|---|---|---|---|---|
| Acts 9 : 1–22 | —— | —— | —— | | |
| Mt 19 : 27–30 | —— | —— | Mt 19 : 27–29 | Same | |

The lections are those in E and P for the feast of St. Paul on June 30. The special feast in honour of his conversion originated in Gaul in the eighth century and was not adopted in Rome until much later.

## PURIFICATION

| | | | | | |
|---|---|---|---|---|---|
| Mal 3 : 1–5 | —— | | Mal 3 : 1–4 | Same | |
| Lk 2 : 22–40 | —— | Lk 2 : 22–27a | Lk 2 : 22–32 | Same | |

Originated in Palestine in the fifth (?) century; adopted in Rome ca. 600. But no provision for lections in either C or P. L has the present Roman Gospel.

Before 1661 the Prayer Books directed use of the Epistle for the preceding Sunday.

## ST. MATTHIAS

| | | | | | |
|---|---|---|---|---|---|
| Acts 1 : 15–26 | —— | —— | —— | —— | |
| Mt 11 : 25–30 | —— | | | | |

Eleventh (?) century in Rome.

## ANNUNCIATION

| | | | | | |
|---|---|---|---|---|---|
| Isa 7 : 10–15 | —— | —— | —— | —— | |
| Lk 1 : 26–38 | —— | | | | |

Observance of the day began ca. 600 in the east and was adopted in Rome in the eighth century. L provides the present Gospel.

## ST. MARK

| 1928 | 1661 | 1549 | SARUM MISSAL | ROMAN MISSAL | 7TH CENT. ROMAN LISTS |
|------|------|------|--------------|--------------|------------------------|
| Eph 4 : 7–16 | ——— | ——— | Eph 4 : 7–13 | Ezk 1 : 10–14 | |
| Jn 15 : 1–11 | | | | Lk 10 : 1–11 | |

A ninth-century festival; the lections are all "commons."

Since the sixth century (at least) April 25 was observed in Rome for "Greater Litanies" (= Rogations). The lections in E and P are Jas 5 : 16–20, Lk 11 :.5–13; this Gospel is assigned for the Rogation Days in the American Prayer Book (since 1928).

## ST. PHILIP AND ST. JAMES

| Jas 1 : 1–12 | ——— | ——— | Wisd 5 : 1–5 | Same | Same |
|------|------|------|--------------|------|------|
| Jn 14 : 1–14 | | | | | |

The observance of these saints was combined through the dedication of a Roman basilica to their honour in the sixth century. E places the feast immediately after that of St. Peter and St. Paul, but C puts it on May 1.

## ST. BARNABAS

| Acts 11 : 22–30 | ——— | ——— | Eph 2 : 19–22 | Acts 11 : 21b–26 13 : 1–3 | |
|------|------|------|--------------|------|------|
| Jn 15 : 12–16 | ——— | ——— | ——— | Mt 10 : 16–22 | |

Eleventh (?) century in Rome. The Sarum lections are both "commons."

## ST. JOHN BAPTIST

| Isa 40 : 1–11 | ——— | ——— | Isa 49 : 1–3, 5–7 | Same | Same |
|------|------|------|--------------|------|------|
| Lk 1 : 57–80 | ——— | ——— | Lk 1 : 57–68 | Same | Same |

The Roman origin of this feast is obscure.

## ST. PETER

| Acts 12 : 1–11 | ——— | ——— | ——— | ——— | ——— |
|------|------|------|------|------|------|
| Mt 16 : 13–19 | ——— | ——— | ——— | ——— | ——— |

Certainly observed in Rome in the fourth century, possibly in the third (as the feast of St. Peter and St. Paul together).

## ST. JAMES

| Acts 11 : 27– 12 : 3a | ——— | ——— | Eph 2 : 19–22 | I Cor 4 : 9–15 | |
|------|------|------|--------------|------|------|
| Mt 20 : 20–28 | ——— | ——— | Mt 20 : 20–23 | Same | |

Eighth century at Rome. Added to C, with Epistle Sir 39 : 6–13. Gospel in D is Lk 12 : 2–8.

## TRANSFIGURATION

| II Pet 1 : 13–18 | | | | II Pet 1 : 16–19 | Same |
|------|------|------|------|------|------|
| Lk 9 : 28–36 | | | | Mt 17 : 1–9 | Same |

Observed ca. 500 in East but not adopted at Rome until 1457. Dropped at the Reformation but restored to the American Prayer Book in 1892.

## ST. BARTHOLOMEW

| Acts 5 : 12–16 | ——— | ——— | Eph 2 : 19–22 | I Cor 12 : 27–31 | |
|------|------|------|--------------|------|------|
| Lk 22 : 24–30 | ——— | ——— | | Lk 6 : 12–19 | |

Ninth century or a little earlier in Rome. C's Epistle is Eph 2 : 19–22, D's Gospel Lk 22 : 24–30. The lections are all "commons."

### ST. MATTHEW

| 1928 | 1661 | 1549 | SARUM MISSAL | ROMAN MISSAL | 7TH CENT. ROMAN LISTS |
|------|------|------|--------------|--------------|------------------------|
| II Cor 4 : 1–6 | ——— | ——— | Ezk 1 : 10–14 | Same | |
| Mt 9 : 9–13 | ——— | ——— | | | |

Ninth century or a little earlier in Rome. C's Epistle is Eph 4 : 7, D's Gospel Mt 9 : 9–13.

### ST. MICHAEL

| | | | | | |
|------|------|------|------|------|------|
| Rev 12 : 7–12 | ——— | ——— | Rev 1 : 1–5 | Same | Same |
| Mt 18 : 1–10 | ——— | ——— | | | |

The dedication day of a church outside of Rome (fifth century).

### ST. LUKE

| | | | | | |
|------|------|------|------|------|------|
| II Tim 4 : 5–15 | ——— | ——— | Ezk 1 : 10–14 | II Cor 8 : 16–24 | |
| Lk 10 : 1–7 | ——— | ——— | | | |

Fourth century in Constantinople; tenth century in Rome. The Roman Epistle identifies "the brother whose praise is in the gospel" (v. 18) with Luke. The older lections are "commons."

### ST. SIMON AND ST. JUDE

| | | | | | |
|------|------|------|------|------|------|
| Eph 2 : 19–22 | Jude 1–8 | Same | Rom 8 : 28–39 | Eph 4 : 7–13 | |
| Jn 15 : 17–27 | | | Jn 15 : 17–25 | Same | |

Ninth century or a little earlier in Rome. C's Epistle is Rom 8 : 28–39, as in the Sarum missal, D's Gospel Jn 15 : 1–11. D describes the feast as "Simonis Cananaei et Simonis Zelotis" (!). The American Prayer Book substituted an ancient "common" for the section adopted at the Reformation (1928).

### ALL SAINTS

| | | | | | |
|------|------|------|------|------|------|
| Rev 7 : 2–4, 9–17 | Rev 7 : 2–12 | Same | Same | Same | |
| Mt 5 : 1–12 | | | | | |

A festival of "All Martyrs" began in Syria in the fourth century and was adopted in Rome in the seventh. E provides as its Epistle Rev 4 : 1, 7 : 9–12, with Rev 7 : 13–17 as an alternative, and sets it on Pentecost 1, as in the Greek church. But no corresponding entry appears in C, nor is a Gospel provided in the early lists. In the eighth century the feast was made "All Saints," and it was transferred to November 1 in 835.

The American Epistle was altered in 1928.

# INDEX OF SCRIPTURE PASSAGES